THE POCKET BOOKS

JOHN VERNEY

By HORACE ANNESLEY VACHELL

Author of

"The Hill," "The Other Side," etc.

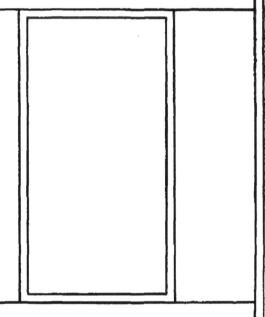

GEORGE H. DORAN COMPANY

NEW YORK

CONTENTS

CHAPTER		PAGE
I.	JOHN'S CHIEF	3
II.	WE MEET SHEILA	13
III.	SCAIFE	29
IV.	SHEILA TAKES AN INTEREST IN POLITICS	45
V.	JOHN MAKES UP HIS MIND	56
VI.	PARTNERS	65
VII.	STRATH ARMYN	76
VIII.	A GLIMPSE OF THE DEMON	92
IX.	THE UNEXPECTED	112
X.	CONTAINS TRIUMPH AND DEFEAT	129
XI.	A FREE-TRADE LEAFLET	144
XII.	BLUDGEONINGS	164
XIII.	THE PLAIN TRUTH	177
XIV.	THE LIONS OF SAMARKAND	188
XV.	DESMOND SENDS FOR JOHN	201
XVI.	A CARD UP THE SLEEVE	222
XVII.	THE FAILING HEALTH OF MR. LITTLEDALE	236
XVIII.	WHICH INTRODUCES MR. BOTT	249
XIX.	THE FREE-TRADE LEAFLET	260
XX.	ANOTHER LEAFLET	286
XXI.	CORNERED	296
XXII.	LORD SAMARKAND	316

JOHN VERNEY

CHAPTER I

JOHN'S CHIEF

JOHN VERNEY happened to be particularly busy when Lady Wrexham and her daughter, Penelope Bargus, came into the library of Charles Desmond's house in Eaton Square. The dowager was a stout, red-faced old woman with prominent blue eyes, which she blinked short-sightedly, as if she didn't quite see everything that was going on. John, however, knew that the august lady missed nothing of importance, although sometimes she was incapable of recognizing nobodies. She wore slightly old-fashioned clothes, and suffered from the heat. She disliked John, partly because he had a sense of humour, and partly because he happened to be the nephew of a foolish explorer who had lost a handsome fortune by the collapse of some business in which, with criminal negligence, he had been outrageously swindled by a friend and partner. Her daughter, Penelope, who kept house so admirably for Charles Desmond, had better reason for concealing dislike of her brother-in-law's secretary; but John knew well enough that this tall, slim, graceful creature, with her expression of

3

suavity and guilelessness, was jealous of him because
he enjoyed, perhaps indiscreetly, the confidence of his
Chief.

" Where is Mr. Desmond, John?"

Penelope spoke with precision, as if she had studied
(not in vain) the gentle art of phrase-making. The
dear lady — many persons thus addressed her — exhibited a too nice serenity. Sensitive souls, not able
to possess themselves in patience, confessed to a feeling of exasperation when they beheld her standing,
let us say, at the head of Charles Desmond's staircase,
and receiving Greeks and Trojans alike with the same
sweetly complacent smile. There was an air about
her of "God, after all, has been good to me." She
subtly diffused the Bargus sense of righteousness.
which endures for ever in that remarkable family,
A certain languid melancholy grace prepared the
stranger for the information that her "story" had been
a sad one. Upon the eve of marriage, sudden illness
and death had taken from her a rising young Under-
Secretary, to whom she was absolutely devoted.

John answered Miss Bargus:

"He went out a few minutes ago. He is very busy."

"You know my mother, I think?"

John smiled.

"I have had the honour of being presented to Lady
Wrexham five times. How do you do?"

Lady Wrexham, without shaking hands, answered
with asperity:

"I am far from well. Heavens! what a room!"

The room, nevertheless, was charming, not too full of fine Hepplewhite furniture, and lined with good old books upon whose mellow bindings the fresh light of spring fell caressingly. The general note suggested, indeed entreated, a surrender of twentieth-century activities, and yet in the middle of this agreeable sanctuary, justifying the exclamation of Lady Wrexham, stood a Cabinet Minister's desk, the bench of a workman, strewn with the tools of his craft, the papers, the pamphlets, the books of a fighting politician. The contrast between this desk and the quiet room in which it seemed so oddly out of place had always aroused John Verney's interest, because he recognized in himself conflicting activities and passivities. Leisure beckoned, promising sweet silences and privacies, but hitherto he had turned resolutely from her lure. He was glad that he had to work hard, and he did work very hard, as hard as any paid secretary in London.

Miss Bargus advanced upon the desk, but John raised a prohibitive finger.

"Please don't touch those papers."

Penelope answered suavely: "Really, I can't permit such disgraceful untidiness. Did you say Mr. Desmond was out? Surely he has not forgotten that Sheila will be here directly?"

"The Chief thought that you had gone to Victoria to meet her."

Penelope dilated her delicate nostrils, as if scenting rebuke. "My mother arrived unexpectedly, so I sent Pragson."

John glanced at Lady Wrexham, who had sunk into the most comfortable arm-chair. Penelope attacked the disorder of the desk for the second time. When John protested she murmured smilingly: "My good, faithful John, I believe your solicitude for Mr. Desmond is even greater than my own; but you forget that I acted as his secretary when you were a boy at school. Mamma!"

"Yes, dear."

"Poor Charles has had a trying morning, evidently." She turned to John. "Who has been here?"

John replied curtly:

"Deputation from Whitechapel."

Lady Wrexham sniffed.

"Ah," she remarked, "that accounts for this extraordinary smell of fried fish. Why does Charles let such people bother him?"

She looked at her daughter, but John answered:

"He doesn't. He lets 'em bother me. I dare say Mr. Desmond is smoking a cigar outside. I'll go and see."

"Thank you," said Lady Wrexham stiffly. She thought that she had detected an impertinent twinkle in John's left eye.

As John went out, Penelope said in her smooth, even tones: "A dear fellow, but rather too officious sometimes. Now, mamma, let's surprise Charles. You must help me."

Penelope removed two volumes of an encyclopædia from a chair.

"My dear! Charles might not like it."

"Not like it? He's preaching order from morning till night. Please arrange those newspapers."

Lady Wrexham obeyed. She detested untidiness, but she disliked even more being ordered about.

"You always have your own way, Penelope."

At this Penelope expressed guileless surprise:

"My own way? Hardly ever. I spend my life pleasing others. Do you think I enjoy doing house-maid's work?"

"Charles speaks of you, my dear, as the Pink of Perfection. Dear me! how hot it is! Can't you open the window?"

Penelope moved to the window, opened it, and ex-claimed:

"Good gracious!"

"What is it?" demanded Lady Wrexham.

Through the opened window penetrated a sound of voices raised in excitement.

"A dog-fight. And Charles is in the thick of it. John Verney is looking on."

Both ladies stood at the window. An expression of disgust formed itself upon Penelope's face. Her mother, on the contrary, belonging to a robuster gen-eration, betrayed excitement and approval.

"Bravo, Charles!" she exclaimed. "He's separated them."

"Foolish fellow," murmured Penelope.

As she spoke there was a hoarse cry from the small crowd that had collected, and a moment later Charles

Desmond entered the library carrying a terrier in his arms, and followed by John. Penelope. said promptly:

"Dear Charles, of course you can never resist taking the part of the under-dog in any fight."

"Is this your own dog, Charles?" said Lady Wrexham, with slight asperity. She resented being overlooked. Her illustrious son-in-law apparently had not seen her. Her face softened when Desmond said, with the utmost geniality:

"Ah! is that you, Lady Wrexham? I was walking up and down when a gigantic collie tackled this poor little beast and tried to eat him up."

"I ask again — is it your own dog?"

"Never saw it before. Nice little tyke — eh, Pen?"

"You run such extraordinary risks," murmured Penelope.

Outside a small crowd had collected. A boy, peering through the iron railings of the area, was singing shrilly: "For 'e's a jolly good feller."

"Better speak to them," suggested John. Desmond nodded and went to the window. Holding up his hand to quell the disturbance, he said in his pleasant musical voice:

"The little dog and I are more frightened than hurt." As cheers broke out again, he added, laughing: "Thank you very much."

He shut the window, still laughing, for it pleased him to be reminded that he was as popular as ever. Penelope said anxiously:

"You are sure the collie didn't bite you?"

"Quite." He kissed the cheek which Lady Wrexham turned to him, and exclaimed:

"By Jove, Pen, why aren't you at Victoria?"

"Mamma came up from Dullingham, so I sent Pragson!"

"Pragson? Sheila will be disappointed at seeing Pragson." He added grumblingly: "She's so sinfully ugly, poor woman!"

"Mamma wants to talk to you," said Penelope. "I'll look after this little waif. He belongs to the people next door."

She took the terrier and left the room. John glanced interrogatively at his Chief, who said: "Return in five minutes, my dear fellow."

As John went out, Lady Wrexham said sharply:

"I come to see you, Charles, on a matter of importance, and you give me five minutes!"

Desmond rang the bell before he sat down at his desk.

"Bless you," he said cheerfully. "In Downing Street I transact business of national importance in five minutes."

"Which explains quite adequately why you are likely to be turned out of Downing Street."

"Capital! What a debater you would have made! Well, well, I see you mean to shoot me sitting. Pepper away!"

Lady Wrexham looked down a nose which was well shaped, but a thought too pointed at the tip. Everybody near Dullingham — where she lived — knew that she spoke her mind to the great man, who had always appeared to her something of a trifler.

"Really, Charles, your choice of language ——"

"You see I was self-educated — not my own that!.— at Harrow. Oh, damn!"

"Charles!"

"I beg your pardon. Somebody has been disarranging the papers on my desk."

"Penelope and I tried to evolve order out of chaos, as a little surprise."

"I'm much obliged to you."

"You are such an advocate of order and method."

"Yes, yes; without order and method where are we? Lost, lost! But I must have things within reach."

Smiling genially, he began to throw some papers on the floor. Lady Wrexham said austerely:

"When you are quite ready to attend to me —— "

"Forgive me. What's wrong?"

"Ever since dear Alicia's death —— "

The butler entered as Desmond frowned. Allusions to his dear Alicia exasperated him, because the fact that he had made a muddle of his marriage was well known to Alicia's mother, who had brought about the match. But Alicia, as mistress of his house and mother of four sons and a delightful daughter, shone impeccable. He had owed much to his wife's tact and intelligence, and yet he was conscious that Alicia had never loved him, and that he had never loved her. Always this rankled, because having so much — high

health, a wide popularity, fame, and a moderate fortune — the supreme thing was withheld.

The butler coughed discreetly. Desmond looked
up.

"Ah, Trinder! Tell the cook to give us *méringues*
for luncheon."

"Very good, sir.'

Lady Wrexham, annoyed at the interruption, exclaimed tartly:

"You are not ordering *méringues* for me?"

"That little puss Sheila loves them.˙ Plenty of
méringues, Trinder."

"Very good, sir."

Trinder was going out, when Desmond stopped him.

"How about the flowers for the table?"

"I ordered lilies-of-the-valley, sir."

"You remembered that lilies-of-the-valley are Miss
Desmond's favourite flower? Wonderful man you are,
Trinder!"

Trinder disappeared with a demure smile. All
Desmond's servants adored him, because he praised
them so judiciously. Nevertheless, being an Irish-
man, and of an impulsive temperament, he had been
known to throw his boots at Trinder's head. Lady
Wrexham assumed her most austere air, as Desmond
remarked:

"Touch of the poet about Trinder. I dare say
you've noticed it."

"I never notice idiosyncrasies in servants. It ruins
them. I was speaking just now of Alicia. Ever since

your wife's death, nine years ago, I have wondered
what would happen when Sheila grew up."

"Happen? What should happen?"

"I take it that she will marry."

"Of course she will marry."

"Then, is it not time to think of getting rid of your
secretary?"

"Get rid of John? Why?"

"Do you mean to hand Sheila over to a pauper?"
Desmond laughed.

"To put your mind at rest," he said pleasantly, "I'll
confess that I've found a husband for little Sheila,
although I hope she won't marry for some years yet.
She and John are like brother and sister."

"Um! that sounds very — familiar. Is it indiscreet
to ask whom you have found?"

"Not at all. Esmé Kinloch."

"She might do better — and worse."

"He is a charming fellow. The world's his oyster,
and Sheila the pearl in it. He told me so. And she
likes him. See you again at luncheon. As regards
Sheila, you can trust me."

"I hope I can," said the august lady.

CHAPTER II

WE MEET SHEILA

CHARLES DESMOND had a very high regard for John Verney. At Harrow, John had been the closest friend of his favourite son, who was killed during the Boer War. The famous Minister's other sons had chosen to serve the State, respectively as soldier, diplomat, and barrister. Each had done well, but each, in a sense, had drifted apart from a father who was necessarily engrossed with his own and the nation's affairs. For many years Desmond's party had been in power. Now they were confronted with a General Election and a possible defeat. Desmond, the most sanguine of politicians, told John that he had enjoyed a long innings, and that the country, in his opinion, wanted to see what the other fellows would do. The Socialists, of course, had something up their sleeves: a tremendous appeal to the Industrials: largesse to be filched from the few and flung to the many. Also without doubt, the Liberals had organized a big campaign, whereas the Conservatives had exhibited a disposition to sit smilingly upon fences. Desmond himself could not accept Tariff Reform in its entirety. For many years a Free Trader, he had been constrained to consider a modified form of Protection,

13

but exactly how this was to be brought about with justice to all industries, and without commercial stagnation and dislocation, he avowed himself unable to say.

John entered the library and went to his desk, piled high with letters and papers awaiting Desmond's signature. Picking these up, he advanced towards his Chief, who frowned and waved a fretful hand.

"I want to talk to you," he said.

As he spoke he looked keenly at his secretary, taking stock of him, appraising him, for the first time, as a possible suitor of his daughter. Part of his success as a statesman had been due to a habit of dealing quickly with matters of pressing but secondary importance. He had already decided that Lady Wrexham was justified in giving him a hint, and, in any case, considering the matter from John's point of view, it was time that the dear fellow should fight for his own hand, including, of course, the hand of another man's daughter. He decided instantly that for the moment there was no danger, but John, although no "thruster," had a quiet way with him. He might become dangerous.

John, half smiling, dropped the letters. One of Desmond's endearing weaknesses — and he had many — was the evasion of work which might be postponed without calculable injury.

"Sit down, Jonathan."

When his Chief called him "Jonathan," John knew that the father was thinking of his gallant son "Cæsar," whose body lay in the graveyard near Ladysmith. He sat down, with a glance at the massive clock upon the chimney-piece. Within a very few minutes, Sheila Desmond would rush into the room — Sheila, whom he had not seen for nearly eight months. He made certain that Desmond wished to talk about her. To his astonishment, his Chief said abruptly:

"John, you must go to Parliament."

John shrugged his shoulders.

"Anything else?" he asked.

"Yes; we'll talk of the other things afterward."

As he spoke, John smiled with an ironic sense of the limitations imposed upon him by fate. After taking his degree at Oxford, the hope of a Fellowship and ambitions involving physical activities had been rolled in the dust of a bad fall in the hunting-field. For some weeks life was threatened. In any case it seemed likely that John would rise from his bed an incurable cripple. Thanks to his mother's devotion and the skill of a great surgeon, he did not actually limp, but he fared forth upon the world's highway with a slightly stumbling gait. The death of his uncle, and the discovery that he was crippled in fortune as severely as in health, exercised, perhaps, a tonic effect. He was compelled to readjust values. When a fairer measure of health came back to him, his mother urged him to accept Charles Desmond's offer of a secretaryship, and to turn his academic ambitions into a political channel. And then, within a year of his appointment, Mrs. Verney died suddenly.

Nobody had ever guessed how much his mother had been to John. Their intercourse was absolutely free from that friction which so often wears away the goodly bond between parent and child. She had been his companion and closest friend. Although a woman of her own generation, with the graciousness, the dignity, the self-restraint, of that generation, she had displayed surprising aptitudes in adapting herself to modern conditions and modern thought. To John she never appeared either old or old-fashioned. The dreadful possibility of losing her never obtruded itself till the morning of her death. And afterward, reading her diaries, he learned with poignant astonishment that during many years she must have suffered intermittent pain borne with serenest fortitude and patience.

Since that grievous blow he had been sensible of a loss of keenness. He did his work admirably, but he had come to regard himself, not as a looker-on, but as playing "back" in the game of life. Verney-Boscobel had been deeply mortgaged to pay in full his uncle's obligations. In time, perhaps, with a fair increase in land-values, that mortgage would be lifted. Then — say in twenty years — John might become member for his own division in the New Forest.

Desmond continued:

"What are you going to do, if the Radicals knock us out? And mind you, just between ourselves, they may. Within six months I should be out of office. Suppose I wanted you, would it pay you to stick to me? And can't you serve me and the country more

efficiently in the House? I see a big chance for you,
Jonathan. I do indeed. And I think I can steer
you to something worth while. You are six-and-twenty.
Lord! how I wish I were your age!"

"You know I can't afford it, Chief."

"I have been talking to Reginald Scaife about you."

Reginald Scaife — "the Demon" of Harrow days —
had been another of his dead son's intimate friends.
Desmond, indeed, had sought out Cæsar's friends
and made of them a small body-guard, which en-
circled and preserved some very dear memories.
Egerton, "the Caterpillar," Duff, still known as "the
Duffer," Esmé Kinloch, the graceful "Fluff," were
the principal members of this compact little society.

"You have been talking to Scaife about me?" said
John.

"He feels very friendly toward you."

"I am rather surprised to hear that."

Desmond stared at John's face, and laughed
pleasantly.

"You admit that Scaife is a remarkable young
man?"

"I never doubted it."

"He knows you disliked him at Harrow, but that's
done with. He sincerely wishes to serve you."

"How?"

Desmond did not answer immediately. He believed
that he knew John; and he believed also that he knew
Scaife, now looming large upon the political horizon.
Scaife, as a dashing squadron leader in "Scaife's

Horse," had covered himself with glory during the
Boer War. After the war, he entered his father's
business, and since that time had been hand in glove
with two of the big newspaper men. It was whispered
that the inflation of Scaife's Limited was due to the
power of the Press. The Scaifes sold out at the top
of the boom, and the son then invested a million in
Scaife's Weekly and a couple of dailies. Later, he
entered Parliament as a Liberal Unionist, and jumped
to the front as a debater of extraordinary ability and
force. Hitherto, he had fought on the side of the
angels, although many old school-fellows remembered
that he was called "Demon" at Harrow. He became
a leader in philanthropic and municipal enterprise,
avoiding any expression of fiscal views. His intimate
friends were not quite sure how he stood. None
questioned the ultimate fact that Reginald Scaife
was making a tremendous appeal to the masses. He
presented a public park to Samarkand, a town in the
Midlands, which the elder Scaife had built and owned;
he endowed a library and a school of Arts and Crafts;
he built a magnificent swimming bath. Afterward,
his particular papers supported all schemes for the
amelioration of suffering and poverty. Scaife's Open-
Air Fund, Scaife's Homes for Children, Scaife's Lodg-
ing Houses, Scaife's Baths, became, so to speak, a
vast floating capital with which — so it was presumed
by the worldly and cynical — the famous contractor's
son would make in due time a supreme appeal to the
multitude. Nevertheless, upon such questions as the

Drink problem and Protection, the young man said modestly that he had not yet dared to form an opinion.

"How can Scaife help me?" asked John, half ashamed because he could not give his old enemy due credit, and sensible that his Chief was disappointed.

He remembered Charles Desmond's first meeting with Scaife, the luncheon at the Tudor Creameries, and Scaife's silence during a memorable meal. And then afterward Scaife's scornful remark: "I played 'possum. Put that into your little pipe and smoke it."

Charles Desmond replied slowly:

"Scaife is prepared to offer you a fancy price for Verney-Boscobel."

"Is he?" John spoke harshly. "Verney-Boscobel is not for sale."

"I feared you would take the sentimental view — for it is sentimental. You can't live there. You need money for your career. You haven't a moment to lose. However, that's your affair. There is an alternative. Scaife sees opportunities for development in the land bordering the estuary. If you won't sell the manor, will you take him into partnership with a view of trebling the value of the lower half of the estate?"

"That, of course, is different. But why does he make such an offer?"

"He put it to me on business grounds, but I can't help thinking —— "

"Yes?"

"That he really has your welfare at heart."

"Oh!"

"He spoke of Cæsar, and Cæsar's affection for you. He said some handsome things about you, Jonathan. He is coming to us in Surrey for this week-end, but he asked me to pave the way, to sound you. It would mean a sum of money down, large enough to admit of your standing for Parliament, and it might mean a fortune in the not too distant future. Now, I'll sign those letters."

"Sheila will be here directly."

"So she will. Jonathan, we said good-bye to a child eight months ago, but a young woman is coming home to-day. I fear we shan't keep her long."

"I suppose not."

Desmond saw that John had flushed. He continued suavely:

"Esmé Kinloch is head over ears in love with the little witch."

"So he tells me."

"What do you think of Esmé?"

John in reply slightly altered a quotation:

> "If his heart at high floods
> Swamps his brain now and then,
> He's the richer for that
> When the tide ebbs again."

"Yes, yes; a good fellow. By the way, why don't you look out for a nice little heiress — eh?"

"I haven't the cheek to ask an heiress, big or little, to marry me."

"Pooh! Cheek, my dear Jonathan, is a young politician's most valuable asset, provided he has brains to use it discreetly. Well, well, choose a wife whose virtues do not throw your own weaknesses into too glaring relief. Avoid perfection or an iceberg."

"I promise that," said John, as a gay laugh rang out in the hall outside.

"She is here," said Desmond, jumping up.

The door was burst open, and a young lady came pelting in, tempestuously eager to embrace her daddy. She was followed by Penelope Bargus.

"By Jove!" exclaimed the delighted father.

He kissed Sheila, and held her at arm's length, carefully noting the changes.

John's eyes grew soft as he gazed at father and daughter. Each adored the other. Sheila believed Charles Desmond to be the Bayard of politicians, a patriot incapable of considering or serving any interest alien to that of his country. John, let us admit, did not share this "vision splendid." He held his Chief in reasonable esteem and sincere affection; but he knew, none better, that a personality charming rather than strong had been turned by Party and Poverty into a highly accomplished actor. If Desmond posed as Patriot — as more than one enemy affirmed — John decided that the pose was unconscious. But the question bit deep. What would happen when Sheila laid aside her rose-coloured spectacles? It was an insult to the girl's intelligence to suggest that she would wear them all her life.

The exact nature of Desmond's understanding of his daughter was not so easily apprehended. He treated her as a child. More than once he confessed to John that he hated to see her petticoats being lengthened, and at the time John had wondered whether instinct had inspired this hatred. Did his Chief smell trouble? By rather an odd coincidence Sheila had been despatched to France at a time when the Cabinet Minister had been persuaded to entertain and conciliate some rather undesirable visitors from the Colonies. During the visitation John rejoiced because Sheila was in a convent where English newspapers happened to be taboo.

As soon as Desmond released his daughter, she rushed at John, greeting him fervently:

"Oh, Jonathan! How delightful it is seeing you again. How nice you look! So different from the nuns at Passy."

"She's come on tremendously, hasn't she, Pen?" asked Desmond.

"She is your daughter," said Penelope.

John was thinking that this radiant creature looked like a Dryad escaped from confining woods, and re-joicing in the sunlight. An adorable hide-and-seek smile played about the corners of her mouth — the loveliest feature in her face, not too primly small (like Aunt Pen's) nor too large, but the rare right thing, a delicious compromise between a firm chin and the softest eyes in the world. The eyes, a golden brown, the colour of wet kelp, might find it easy to say "yes"; the chin was delicately designed to say "no," but the curved mouth suggested the enticing word "perhaps."

She danced about the room.

John could remember her as a child of nine upon the occasion of his first visit to Cæsar's people. When he took leave of her, she had held up a dimpled face to be kissed, and had said in the presence of Cæsar and the nurse: "I like John Verney; he's a nice boy. Some day, perhaps, I shall marry him." And ever since John had thought of her as a bright particular star that might one day fall to earth for him.

Then Penelope said sweetly:

"Your dear father is very busy, my darling."

"Busy? Not a bit of it! Sit you down, Sheila. Did you have a decent crossing?"

Penelope glided from the room, as Sheila perched herself upon her father's knee; she glanced at John, who was about to follow Penelope.

"Don't go, John," said Desmond.

John, much gratified, sat down as the bland Trinder came in to announce that the First Lord of the Admiralty was in the drawing-room.

"Bother!" said Sheila. "Must you see him? He's such a messy old man."

"First Lords must be heard even if they're not fit to be seen."

"We're so cosey."

"So we are; so we are. John, you shall see him."

"He won't like that, Chief."

"Pooh! Be civil."

John marched not too willingly to the door. He was going out, when Desmond's genial voice called him back.

"Smile, my dear boy! Always smile when you interview either a superior or an inferior."

"And which is the First Lord?" demanded Sheila.

"That is not for me to say," answered John.

As the door closed, Desmond said warmly:

"There goes the best secretary in England. I don't know how I shall rub on without him."

"Good gracious! Is he leaving us?"

"He ought to be in Parliament. Have you any influence with John?"

"I think so." She smiled demurely.

"My dear, you must use it. Yes, yes — a happy thought! I'll take you into my confidence. You remember Reginald Scaife, Cæsar's friend?"

"Yes, but I never met him. I should like to."

"He wants to develop a part of Boscobel Manor. It means everything to John, but he never liked Scaife. Can I count on you for the right word?"

"If I get the chance, of course."

"John is sure to tell you about it."

"But it will be dreadful losing him — dear Jonathan!"

"He may go far, although —— "

He paused, half smiling. Sheila repeated softly: "Although —— "

"Well, my child, to be perfectly frank, John is almost too good for the job."

"Too good for a job that is good enough for my Daddy?"

Desmond pinched her cheek and then kissed it, but his voice was serious as he replied: "I am a party man. It was licked into me early that our salvation depended upon standing shoulder to shoulder, and seeing things eye to eye, or pretending to."

"Pretending to? I can't see you — pretending."

He met her candid glance with slight nervousness.

"Sheila, from now on I shall talk more plainly to you. We've got a big fight ahead, and I like a fight. I shall fight till I drop, but — dash it! — I may have to do things I detest."

He paused again, stroking her hand, which was singularly like his own. Of all his children, the only two who strongly resembled him both in feature and character had been Cæsar and Sheila. The others in temperament and face belonged to the stolid, stodgy, plodding, self-complacent family of Bargus. Bargus represents beer, bullion, and beatitudes. The Desmonds, on the other hand, are notoriously gay, and, judged by the Bargus foot-rule, frivolous.

"What things?" demanded Sheila.

Desmond laughed, not too easily.

"Suffering gladly fools and liars. That tears me. We have to use fools and liars. Personally I detest compromise, but compromise is the glue which keeps a party together. Nasty stuff, glue! John loathes glue."

"I'm so glad."

"Meanwhile he is poor, which is a handicap, and proud. Also he hides his remarkable ability instead of advertising it. He wrote some brilliant letters for the Press and allowed me to get the credit."

"How nice of him!"

"But how foolish!"

At this moment John came back.

"Well?"

"He insists on seeing you. It's about that article."

"Did you tell him you wrote it?"

"Hardly."

"I shall tell him. If he wants second-hand information from me, when you can give him the other thing, so be it."

He hurried from the room, leaving John staring rather awkwardly at the smiling, dimpled face of the girl. She said slyly:

"So we don't advertise ourselves. How silly!"

John crossed to his desk. The young lady pouted. John might be, and probably was, inordinately preoccupied with political matters, but he must be made to understand that Miss Desmond had returned to England.

"John dear."

"Yes?"

"I've grown two inches in eight months."

John allowed his eyes to linger for an instant upon her arched instep. Then, very slowly, they travelled from the hem of her trim travelling-skirt to the crown of her hat.

"Three, I should say."

"Only two."

"Three, at least. I measured you in this room, against that door."

"Did you? Measure me now."

She walked to the door and removed her hat, looking up at John from beneath long lashes, but without a touch of coquetry. John was thinking how like she had grown to his friend. When she laughed, he could hear Cæsar: when she spoke, certain inflections seemed to raise Cæsar from the dead. She was laughing now, because John really enjoyed being teased.

"Is my head quite level?"

"Your head never will be quite level."

He put a book upon it, and fetched a pencil. His face was close to hers, almost touching it, when she said:

"Last time, I took my slippers off."

"You threw one at me."

"What a memory you have — for trifles!"

"Trifles? It nearly knocked a tooth out. There. Five feet seven. I knew I was right. Just three inches difference."

"Two. My heels are an inch higher. You never allowed for that, Jonathan, did you? Now, come over here, and tell me about yourself. You look rather stiff and starchy. Is there any Bargus blood in you?"

"Not a drop!"

"Good! You know that grandmamma is here?"

"I do."

"She is so bossy. She bosses Daddy. I'm awfully glad that I'm all Desmond."

"But you're not."

"From Bargus pride may the Lord deliver me."

"There's a lot of Bargus in you."

"How dare you say that!"

"You try to boss me. At this moment I have half a dozen things which must be polished off before luncheon."

"Trinder says there are *méringues* for luncheon. The dear old man's pronunciation of the word tasted as sweet as the thing itself."

John rose, and went to his desk.

"Don't mind me! Do exactly what you like!"

The mockery in her voice made him exclaim hoarsely:

"That's it. Fellows in my position can't do exactly what they like."

"Now I wonder what you mean by that?"

He stood still, thrusting his hands into his pockets. Then he saw the mischief in her eyes.

"I shall leave you in Wonderland."

With that he turned a slightly heated face from the pretty rogue, and tackled his work.

CHAPTER III

SCAIFE

THE Corner—Charles Desmond's small domain in Surrey — stood high upon a heathery, pine-clad hill between Weybridge and Woking. House and garden possessed an intimate charm. Hither, during thirty years of active life, had come scores of interesting men and women. Beneath the tall elms which flanked each side of the lawn, Disraeli and Gladstone had talked together. The former had planted a *picea nobilis:* the latter a *pinsapo.* Both trees had flourished, and were known familiarly as Roland and Oliver. Between them might be seen a placid, pastoral landscape — England at her best, the mother country so zealously tended by her sons. Charles Desmond liked to boast that from his garden nothing could offend the hypercritical eye. Some ugly cottages had been hidden behind a gracious wall of yew, lilac, and laburnum; a clump of tall firs blotted out a distant asylum. Desmond's guests understood that this was a paradise for hard workers, a recreation-ground, from which the mean and sordid side of life was to be excluded. The talk rang in tune with the smiling woods and fields. In the library none had smelled the penetrating odour of fried fish.

Here, during the Whitsuntide recess, were gathered together some old friends. Esmé Kinloch, now a budding diplomat, brought his mother, the beautiful Duchess of Trent. Because Esmé had been at Harrow with John, both members of the ancient Manor, Desmond had persuaded Duff to join them. "The Duffer" was now a parson, a curate in Stepney, but still a boy, with a boy's optimism and enthusiasm damped not yet by contact with the submerged tenth.

"This is ripping," he said to John.

With a sweep of his arm he embraced everything and everybody. A dozen yards away a huge umbrella shaded a large table, at which Miss Bargus was putting sugar into the tea and the talk. Around it were wicker chairs, made comfortable and attractive with apple-green and white cushions.

"Isn't it?" John replied.

"And it goes on all the time?"

"More or less."

"What a change after Whitechapel! Miss Bargus tells me the Demon is coming down."

"Yes."

"I'm glad to hear that. He's turned out a trump. Sent me a thumping cheque the other day. Wonderful chap! Amazing!"

"Quite," said John.

"How you hated him!"

"That's all over."

"It warms the cockles of one's heart to see the Ethiopian turning white. Good old Demon!"

"He doesn't like to be called 'Demon.'"

"Thanks for the hint."

"Listen! That's his motor."

A purr was to be heard, increasing in volume of sound. The Duffer glanced at John with a shadow upon his freckled face, quite clean-shaven and surmounted, as of yore, by a crop of bristly red hair.

"That fierce purr suggests a wild beast."

"Machinery is merciless," said John.

A minute later Scaife was walking across the lawn. He strode on masterfully, sure of himself.

"What a fellow!" murmured the Duffer.

As he spoke they heard again the angry purr of the motor, and then the wailing cry of the tri-horn — three notes, oddly dissonant but not discordant.

"Scaife looks older than you, Jonathan."

The same thought passed through Desmond's mind when the young men shook hands. John was tall, thin, a thought pale, with a pair of noticeable gray eyes extraordinarily steady. He displayed a suggestion of the scholar's stoop, and he wore shabby tweeds with distinction. Upon his face lay a whimsical expression, as if he were comically aware of his disabilities.

Scaife, in striking contrast, appeared a magnificent specimen. Rodin would have made a masterpiece of him as "Success." One could not picture him in shabby clothes, or with a stoop, or with any expression upon his handsome, clean-shaven face save that of conscious power.

He had the great chest of him who breathes deep of life, the clear, glowing skin of the athlete, the keen eyes of the fighter — hazel eyes, set wide apart, and overhung by thick, dark brows. The Duchess said afterward that he was too spick and span, but his manners were admirable. He held John's hand, looked him squarely in the eyes, and laughed genially.

"It is jolly seeing you fellows," he exclaimed.

"I don't think you've met my girl," said Charles Desmond.

John was watching Scaife closely as he turned to take Sheila's outstretched hand. His keen eyes brightened; the pupils seemed to dilate. At that moment Sheila's likeness to Cæsar was extraordinary, and John saw that Scaife was affected. He shook hands, and bowed with slightly exaggerated deference. The bow from a foreigner would have been perfect. Curiously enough, when Scaife greeted the Duchess he did not bow. John wondered whether this subtle flattery had been wasted upon a girl of eighteen. Then he felt Fluff's arm being slipped within his own, and Fluff's voice, so little changed, saying: "Let's have a stroll together."

Fluff had grown into a tall, slim young man, who, properly be-wigged and dressed up, might have been mistaken in the dusk for his exquisite mother. Since the death of Alastair Kinloch he had become a personage in the eyes of match-making mammas, inasmuch as he would inherit his mother's fortune, which was considerable.

As soon as they were out of earshot, Fluff said irritably:

"What is the wreathed-in-smiles Demon doing in Paradise?"

"He smiles because he has passed the golden gate."

"What's the game? Politics, I suppose. They tell me Scaife *père* is watering at the mouth for a peerage."

"Why not?"

"Pah! A peerage for the Butcher of Badavarchy! He won't be able to buy that from us."

"What do you mean by Butcher of Badavarchy?"

"Ask any Highlander. It's history in Ross-shire. Old Scaife paid cash for a ten years' lease of an immense deer-forest. He fenced a large part of it, and used to have disgusting drives. Never asked any one to shoot with him. Blazed away at everything — unshootable stags, hinds, even calves. Any amount of beasts were wounded. There was an awful row about it. The whole thing was beastly, brutal, horrible, an unspeakable slaughter. And the Demon was there."

"Perhaps against his will?"

"And now he's here. Why?"

John replied evasively: "I see no earthly reason why he shouldn't be here. As for being his father's son, well, his record shows that a stream may rise higher than its source."

"If he comes here after — Sheila!"

"He never met her till to-day."

"He's tremendously ambitious. It's just struck

me that the one thing likely to advance his ambitions
would be a marriage with a girl like Sheila. Only, of
course, she wouldn't look at such a bounder."

"She *is* looking at him," said John, with a short
laugh. "And he's worth looking at. As for calling
men bounders —— "

. He stopped, squeezing Fluff's arm affectionately.

"Go on!"

"Nothing. Only it sounds rather caddish, coming
from you."

"I don't care."

"Look here, Fluff. I'm trying to purge my mind
of the Demon as he was. And, by Jove! you must do
the same."

"I can't — that's flat. In your heart of hearts you
think as I do."

"Does it matter a hang what we think?" asked John.

"You might warn Sheila."

"I don't know much about women," John admitted,
"but I believe you know even less."

"I've told you how it is with me, Jonathan?"
When John nodded, Fluff added: "My mother thinks
her a perfect darling. I wonder if I have a dog's
chance?"

"Not an unborn puppy's chance if you run down
a guest in her father's house. You won't score
that way."

During that afternoon and evening, however, Scaife
scored, as even Fluff was obliged to admit. John
noticed that he spoke of things and persons with

detachment, suppressing his own opinions. He seemed
to have acquired a power of eliciting confidence from
others. In easy talk with the Duchess, and Sheila,
and Desmond, he established intimacy and freedom.
The cleverness of his method astounded John and confounded Fluff. Scaife, without a toot from his own
horn, pulled down walls. The Duffer listened to the
People's Friend, simmering with enthusiasm. Obviously, Scaife was God's chosen instrument, the Divine
scourge, wherewith poverty and misery and ignorance
would be lashed from the slums of great cities.

At dinner, Penelope persuaded the young man to
relate the story of how he carried despatches through
the Boer lines into Ladysmith.

"It's such a chestnut," protested Scaife. He happened to catch the eye of the Duchess, who said, rather
coldly, so John thought:

"We should like your own version of it, Mr. Scaife."

"Do tell us everything!" entreated Sheila.

Accordingly the story, too familiar to be repeated at
length, was told. Scaife began fluently:

"I was with another fellow —— "

"Ormsby," said Fluff.

"Yes, Ormsby."

"A particular pal of mine," added Fluff.

This statement seemed to disconcert Scaife slightly,
but he went on till he came to the dramatic moment
of meeting a Boer sentry, who challenged him. Scaife
paused. He had suddenly realized that this part was
not quite fit for a dinner-table.

"What did you do?" asked Sheila, leaning forward, her eyes sparkling with excitement. John thought of Desdemona and the Moor, for Scaife's complexion was almost dark enough to justify the comparison. Across the table, Fluff, crumbling his bread with white delicate fingers, appeared like a bit of fine porcelain. Scaife suggested bronze.

"I had to put him to sleep," said Scaife quietly.

"Oh! You mean that you —— "

"Exactly," said Charles Desmond. "Go on, Scaife!"

But Sheila refused to be silenced. "He was armed and you were unarmed. How did you put him to sleep?"

Scaife hesitated.

"With his strong hands," said the Duchess. From the tone of her voice Scaife understood that details were to be skipped.

He finished his story, well aware that he had captured Sheila's interest, and in doing so had once more slipped through lines which many men might fail to pass. When the talk became general he remained silent. Sheila, who sat next to Scaife, remained silent also, but presently she said softly:

"I wanted to meet you so much, Mr. Scaife."

He met her glance boldly, but to her surprise said nothing. She continued with slight hesitation:

"It seems odd that you have not been here before?"

"Odd?" He laughed. "Oh no, not at all. It's odd that I should be here now."

Her eyebrows went up.

"What do you mean?"

"A great many delightful houses are closed to me and mine."

"Oh!"

"I have always faced disagreeable facts, Miss Desmond."

She sank her voice to a whisper, but her eyes remained fixed upon his.

"You have a right to be here. You were my brother's friend."

Scaife glanced about him. Everybody was chattering gaily. Under cover of the prattle he said gravely:

"I might have come here before, but to be absolutely frank, I rather funked it."

"Why?"

"Perhaps instinctively. Your brother, Miss Desmond, was very dear to me; so dear that I was almost afraid of meeting you, and when I did meet you — this afternoon — " he paused, frowning. Then in a different voice he went on: "I beg your pardon: I've — I've let my tongue run away with my discretion, but your likeness to Cæsar moved me profoundly. Tell me, are you interested in the coming General Election?"

She assented, with a faint blush upon her cheeks, and Scaife, gazing at her, told himself that she was adorable.

After dinner, when the ladies had left the dining-room, Desmond spoke of the political situation. Every man present knew that Scaife had been elected by his father's townsmen of Samarkand as an independent candidate, standing triumphant at the head of the poll. While Scaife sipped his port, his host said demurely:

"Next time, the Samarkanders will demand a confession of faith."

Scaife laughed.

"I shall paddle my own canoe, sir, up-stream if necessary."

"Hear, hear!" exclaimed the Duffer.

"Um!" said Charles Desmond, who had always paddled with the current.

For an instant, there was a pause. Fluff opened his lips and closed them. John kept his eyes upon Scaife. Of the five men present Scaife alone appeared at his ease. He sipped his port, and murmured: "A very fine wine, a big wine."

Desmond said tentatively: "Are you quite sure of your seat?"

"Cock-sure. We own the place."

This curt confidence raised a smile; and the entrance of servants with coffee and cigars diverted the talk into easier channels. Desmond began to talk of the famous victory at Lord's, and the Duffer's drives to the boundary, and Scaife's "throw in" at the last moment.

The five men became boys again.

Later, in the smoking-room, after the others had gone to bed, Scaife and John talked together for nearly

an hour. Scaife's vigour of speech and action — he
walked up and down the room as he talked — was
overwhelming. He became, too, the Scaife of old — a
youth wise beyond his years. John could almost believe that they were back again at the Manor, and that
presently Cæsar would burst in with his jolly laugh,
and — if the Demon continued jawing — hurl a book
at his head. And now, as then, Scaife was showing that
he understood another's business as thoroughly as he
had mastered his own.

"I want to help you if you will allow me. I believe
that we can coin money at Verney-Boscobel without
laying a desecrating finger upon the Manor. Sell
me a half interest in that land on each side of the estuary,
and I'll find more money to develop it. We'll build
small, pretty houses by the dozen, and turn Boscobel
into a thriving town. You have a gold-mine in sight,
tons of undeveloped ore. Let me put up the necessary
machinery!"

"Why do you make this offer?"

"There's money in it, and something, perhaps, which
I value more. You used to hate me, Jonathan."
He continued swiftly: "How that worried me, because
— I hardly expect you to believe me — I wanted your
friendship. It was the one thing at Harrow I wanted
which I didn't get. You made me see that I was inferior clay. Well, so I am."

"I behaved like a prig."

"Cæsar and you rolled me in the dust, and I gnashed
my teeth. But, on my honour, I admired and

respected you even when I lay awake at night planning how best I could annoy you."

"Let's bury what is unpleasant in the past to-night. It's done with," said John, eager to respond to the cordial candour of his ancient enemy.

"It's done with," added Scaife quickly.   "Provided the past doesn't discolour the present.   Desmond says you are keen to go into Parliament."

"Yes."

"Anything else up your sleeve?"

"What do you mean?"

"Well, I have a score of ambitions outside the House of Commons."

"When I'm in the House I'll think of them," said John. He would have liked to reply boldly: "Ambitions — yes, I want to marry Sheila Desmond; I want to knock the mortgage off Verney-Boscobel.   I want to get office."

Under his present circumstances it was audacious to entertain such vaulting ambitions, unthinkable to present them to a man hitherto regarded as an enemy. He heard Scaife saying:

"My dear fellow, you are as ambitious as I am.   I know what you've been up to — and so do others. Don't imagine for a moment that you've been hiding your light under Charles Desmond's bushel. You're a marked man.   All the same —— "

"Yes?"

"If you mean to crawl along the old grooves——!"

"Only sons of millionaires can be independent."

"I'm not independent. Of course you will take your seat under the wing of Desmond, but the country is beginning to wonder what he'll do."

He looked sharply at John, with a certain interrogation. "I'm not trying to pump you. I shall have a talk with Desmond to-morrow. This is his opportunity."

Then, with a genial laugh, he clapped John upon the shoulder, and said: "I want you as a working partner."

"Me?"

"Yes — why not? We can work together in and about Boscobel, and in and about the House of Commons."

"Socialism does not appeal to me," said John.

"You think I'm making a cheap bid for popularity? A great many people share your rather hasty judgment on that. I don't blame them. All the same I'll say to you, and you can take it for what it's worth, that I am sincere in my desire to better the condition of the people to whom I belong. My grandfather was a navvy, and navvies made us rich. I am the People's Friend — and they know it. Also they are going to have their innings, and nothing you fellows can do or say will prevent it. The old order is played out."

"Not yet."

"You will die hard, I dare say, but already a lot of you are talking of running away. The Duchess told me this afternoon that her brother-in-law was making large investments in Canada and America, sending square chunks of capital out of a country that can use to the best advantage every penny it can come by. Is that patriotism? Is that playing the game, as you Verneys played it when Cromwell was the People's Friend?"

John held his peace.

"I don't want to rub it in, but, mark me, the country, as a whole, is as sick of one party as the other, sick of misrepresentation, sick of incapacity in high places, sick to death of being humbugged."

John nodded.

He was wondering whether Scaife had read his thoughts. Why did Scaife put into words these thoughts? Impulse stirred him to reply with enthusiasm, to reveal what he had kept hidden, but he could only blurt out, with evident shyness:

"I'm awfully obliged to you." In a warm voice he continued: "I must think over the Boscobel scheme. It would be an immense thing for me."

"That is a cold-blooded business proposition. The other — my wish to work with you in Parliament — is nearer my heart. What a charming girl Miss Desmond is!"

"Yes."

"She reminds me so strongly of dear old Cæsar. By Heaven! when she looked at me this afternoon I had to bend my head, for I felt the tears coming into my eyes."

"Good night," said John.

He lit his candle and went to bed. Scaife lit a
fresh cigar, and when John had left the room a laugh
escaped from his lips. He had scored — and he could
measure the score to the last notch. Early in life,
when his school-fellows called him the Demon, he had
obeyed the ancient injunction to know himself, and
that self-knowledge was his most valuable asset.

Still smiling, he threw himself upon a comfortable
sofa, and half closed his eyes. Then he laughed again,
as if intoxicated with the sense of his ability to pass
through almost impregnable lines. For years he had
tried to enter the charmed circle which held every friend
of Cæsar Desmond except himself. The expressed
wish to do an old enemy a service had let him in.

"I can hold the fort now," he muttered.

Rapidly he reviewed the incidents of the past few
hours, and the actors upon a stage hitherto inaccessible
to his father's son. He would tell that father exactly
what had happened, and the old man would stick out
his great jaw, and chuckle grimly. He had said again
and again: "Why don't you make yourself solid with
Charles Desmond?" Always the son replied: "Give
me time and I shall."

His nimble mind dwelt lightly upon Kinloch and
Duff, as pawns in the game to be played. John,
he had reason to take more seriously as a knight of
unexpected moves. John had excellent brains, but
a body none too good. And the poor fellow was
cursed with an inherited quixotic instinct which constrained him to consider the welfare of others before

his own. It would be good fun heaping coals of fire upon John's head.

Then he thought of Sheila, and immediately his face softened. He had challenged her interest with his reference to Cæsar, and he was clever enough to know that with Sheila the simple truth had availed him more than any artifice. The likeness to her brother had, indeed, moved him profoundly. His father had trained him to recognize what he wanted, and to concentrate undivided energies upon obtaining it. Before he went to bed he told himself that he wanted Sheila with an intensity which thrilled him to the core. And he wondered, with ever-increasing curiosity, whether she had inspired a similar passion in John Verney. Most probably, he decided. Then, smiling cynically, he remembered that John had nothing to offer Charles Desmond's daughter except a future which he, Scaife, had just made possible. Lastly, he recalled an odd expression in Sheila's eyes, at the moment when he so boldly stared into them. Fear, stronger than fascination, had betrayed itself.

"I must go very slow with her," he reflected.

CHAPTER IV

UNDER the chestnut tree upon the lawn sat Penelope Bargus and Sheila. Penelope was industriously knitting. All the women belonging to the house of Bargus are workers. Proudly they boast of working with hands and heads. Sheila, however, dared to admit that at times she liked doing nothing. She watched her aunt's slim, restless fingers with curiosity, and then scrutinized her placid face. From the moment when Penelope came to rule over Charles Desmond's house, Sheila had accepted her aunt at that lady's own valuation. Penelope inspired in her niece respect and affection, although from the first she had divined possibility of trouble. Once, long ago, Sheila refused to say grace after bread-and-butter tainted by onion. Penelope, omnipotent in salon and nursery, exacted obedience. She never forgot the defiant sparkle in the child's eyes, as she folded her hands, and said in a loud clear voice: "For a nasty, horrid tea, may the Lord make me truly thankful — but He won't!" An indiscreet nursemaid giggled, and shortly afterward was obliged to find another situation.

Sheila stared at Penelope, wondering why perfection was not more adorable. Since her return from France,

45

and the soporific companionship of the good nuns, she had found herself in a state of continuous wonder. Of course Aunt Pen could answer questions. It was so exasperating to reflect that she wouldn't.

Sheila said mischievously:

"Another pair of stockings for Daddy?"

"Yes, dear. This dog-tooth edging is pretty, isn't it?"

"Very."

"Your father is delighted with you, Sheila."

"He told me so for the third time last night. Somehow the nice things a father may say don't have quite the value they ought."

"I'm afraid I'm rather dense."

"Well, when parents praise their children, I suppose they are really praising themselves. Grandmamma always gives me that idea when she talks about you. She takes the credit for what you've done."

Penelope smiled, but her eyes rested more keenly upon the intelligent face upturned to hers. She said in her even sugary tones:

"Dear child, what ideas you have!"

"I'm glad I have ideas. Do men think it is part of the game to pay compliments to women?"

"Some men. Has anybody in particular been paying you compliments? John Verney, I dare say —— "

"Jonathan? Not he."

"Esmé Kinloch, perhaps?"

"Oh, I don't feel a bit bucked when Fluff lays it on."

"Sheila! Where do you get your dreadful slang from?"

"From darling Daddy. He says that slang is to ordinary speech what salt is to porridge."

"We mustn't construe your dear father too literally. Being a public man he has acquired the habit of saying many things which he doesn't quite mean."

"Oh, Aunt Pen! You accuse Daddy of being a humbug."

"An optimist."

"The blessed sort that will go for a long walk in April without an umbrella."

"He sees everything and everybody *en rosé.*"

"The angel!" exclaimed Sheila. "I love optimists. I like Mr. Scaife because he thinks so well of people, and tries to find out what is best in them."

Penelope touched the girl's hair. All her movements were graceful and gracious. She spoke in a soft, modulated tone, which became even softer when others, who possibly had not enjoyed her advantages, raised their voices in the heat of argument. She smiled tenderly as she murmured:

"So Mr. Scaife has been practising on my little girl."

"Practising?"

Penelope considered, pausing in her knitting. She was aware of Charles Desmond's wish to bring about a match between Esmé Kinloch and his daughter, and perhaps she realized that the friendship between the two young people was never likely to develop into a warmer sentiment on Sheila's part. Also, it had occurred to her that this pretty, inquisitive niece might turn out a "handful." Lady Wrexham had said at parting, in her sharp didactic way: "By the way, Pen, if you wish to remain mistress here, marry Sheila off to Esmé Kinloch as soon as reasonably may be." For many years Penelope had told herself that never, never could she return to Dullingham.

"Why do you say 'practising,' Aunt Pen?"

"The word may have been ill chosen. Mr. Scaife is an accomplished public speaker, and in private ——"

"Yes? This is awfully interesting."

"He impressed me — I may be mistaken — as being anxious to extract information without giving much in return. He was very clever to find out that the Duchess's brother-in-law had invested largely in America."

"But what on earth could he get out of me?"

Again Penelope paused, in a quest for the right word.

"There is something to be got out of everybody."

"You don't hint that he has come down here to pump us?"

"No, no, certainly not."

"He talked to me about Jonathan and Daddy, and then about his grandfather, the navvy. He's tremendously proud of his father. Asked me if I thought the worse of a man who belonged to the working classes."

"But Mr. Scaife doesn't."

"He works harder than any man in his employment. That's something to be proud of, as I told Fluff."

"So the pot called the kettle black."

"Aunt Pen" — the girl spoke with an engaging seriousness — "I hate knitting, and practising scales, and reading dull books, but I could work hard at work I liked."

"And what work do you like?"

"I'm mad keen about politics. Of course I get it from Daddy. I'm going to mug up —— "

"Sheila, please —— "

"I shall tackle both sides. Mr. Scaife has given me a list of books. I should like, when Jonathan goes, to become father's secretary. I mean to play the type-writer instead of the piano; and I shall learn shorthand. I spent an hour with Mill last night."

"With whom?"

"John Stuart Mill. I ought to have brought him out here. I think I'll put in another hour before luncheon."

She jumped up and ran lightly away. Penelope frowned, and as the frown passed, she murmured: "Poor Esmé!"

The needles clicked rapidly, and her thoughts kept time with them. If Sheila did not marry, if — as was possible — she showed a desire and the ability to become mistress of her father's house, why, then Penelope's occupation and interest in life would be gone. She would have to return to her mother, or — worse! — retire to some flat in South Kensington.

Presently Desmond and Scaife were to be seen ascending the winding path which led from the meadows at the foot of the hill. The men, so Penelope noted, had been absent for more than an hour; Scaife strolled into the house, Desmond approached his sister-in-law.

"Well?" she said quietly.

Desmond, with a glance about him, sat down beside her. He was slightly warm, not altogether from the gentle exercise he had taken, and he removed his straw hat, as he answered:

"That young fellow is astounding."

Penelope waited. Seldom indeed did she interrupt anybody, and never a man cleverer than herself.

"He has a grasp of things and an audacity —— "

"Was he bold with you or against you?"

"On my honour I should like to answer that question, and I can't. I don't call him slippery, but elusive. He began by saying that he hoped to serve under me as Prime Minister."

"You would make an admirable Prime Minister."

"There has always been the possibility. And in the event of a general shake-up —— "

"Dear Charles, I am so stupid. You must dot your 'i's' with me."

She glanced at him affectionately. Only a very short-sighted person would have mistaken the placid expression upon her face for stupidity.

"Scaife predicts a shake-up."

"Yes?"

Desmond hesitated, speaking in a low voice.

"There will be a great opportunity for somebody. What astonishes me is that a boy of seven-and twenty should see so plainly what my old eyes have seen — and more."

"More?"

"He has planned and plotted an astounding campaign. He is to be reckoned with. Make no mistake there!"

"I haven't," said Pen.

"He will be enormously rich, and he pulls strings. Also, he's a good fellow. He can't speak of Cæsar without emotion. And he wants to put John Verney on his feet."

"Why?"

The monosyllable fell coldly, with a tinkle of ice striking glass.

"Because he was Cæsar's friend."

"Oh!"

"In short, he's warmed the cockles of my heart, and I'm glad I had him down here. He has promised to come again. Where is little Sheila?"

"Flirting with John ——"

"What?"

"John Stuart Mill."

"Bless her heart! I'd sooner she flirted with Esmé Kinloch."

Penelope said nothing, but her needles clicked.

"Have you ever spoken to her?" continued Desmond.

"About what, Charles?"

"About marriage, and all that?"

"Not yet."

He sighed, and then laughed genially. "It's exasperating to know all I do know, and at the same time to realize the difficulty of imparting that knowledge to one's own flesh and blood. Sheila will make the right man a delightful little wife."

Penelope's needles stopped clicking. Her soft, even voice fell quietly upon a pause.

"Would you consider Reginald Scaife the right man?"

"Scaife? She hardly knows him."

"He seems to know and understand her."

"Scaife?" Desmond frowned, pursing up his lips, staring at Penelope's expressionless face. "What do you mean by hurling his name at my head?"

"A wise man never ignores possibilities."

"Scaife! Frankly, you have rather upset me. I'm not a snob, I hope, but Scaife has blood I don't like in his veins. His father is an unscrupulous old ruffian. And his mother — I must think this over. I ought to have foreseen this — this possibility."

"I like Mr. Scaife," said Penelope tranquilly.

"Then —— " Desmond stared at her, but her pale, slightly prominent eyes rested upon the half-finished stocking in her hand. As he waited for enlightenment, she added:

"I, too, am glad he is coming again."

Desmond strolled into the house. Passing through the hall, he found Sheila wrestling valiantly with the Dismal Science. When she saw her father, she said with a grimace: "I know now why men tie wet towels round their heads."

She looked such a child that Desmond felt a queer pang at his heart. He glanced at his watch.

"I've half an hour before luncheon. Come into my room and have a treat."

The word had a special meaning. Before Sheila put her hair up, and ever since the death of her mother, she had been in the habit of coming to her father every Sunday between six and seven. Then she would sit on his knee and talk. It was understood that they were pals during this hour. Each insisted on this. Very often Sheila would speak of her father as distinct from her pal, demanding from the pal advice which was always given as a pal's counsel, not a parent's. For instance, she might say: "My father was not quite pleased with me this morning."

"Really," the pal would reply, "I've an excellent opinion of your worthy father. What had you done?"

"I cheeked the governess."

"Dear, dear! Of course you begged her pardon afterward?"

"I'm afraid I didn't. That's what annoyed Daddy."

"Naturally he was rather ashamed at being the father of a pert young Miss. It wouldn't surprise me to learn that he apologized for you."

"He didn't?"

"From my knowledge of him, it's more than likely."

Since Sheila's return from France, there had been no treats. At the mention of the word, her eyes

sparkled, and she said instantly: "How splendid!"
Desmond walked to the library with Sheila hanging
upon his arm. He sat down, and she jumped upon
his knee. Then they kissed each other — a sort of
grace before meat.

"I want to talk to you of your father, who is a bit
of a moral coward."

"He isn't."

"He funks saying and doing disagreeable things."

"I wish there were more funks of that kind about."

Desmond smiled faintly.

"I suppose you think, child, that I'm a successful
man?"

She answered wonderingly: "And aren't you?"

"I failed in the greatest thing."

"The greatest thing?"

"I did not make your mother happy: she did not
make me happy. Our marriage was disastrous."

She said nothing, but he felt a cheek softly cool
against his; her grasp of his hand tightened.

"There were faults on both sides, Sheila, which we
needn't discuss; but it would break my heart to see
you floundering in the sort of domestic quagmire
which engulfed my happiness and hers, poor creature!
If I could teach you to know the right man when you
meet him."

She murmured with slight confusion:

"But I'm not going to marry for years and years.
I want to stay with you. Are you in an awful hurry
to get rid of me?"

"No, no, but if a gallant fellow should turn up——?"

"Why borrow trouble? He hasn't turned up."

"You are so inexperienced, and I don't know how to talk to you. But" — his tone brightened — "it's not badly set forth in an article." He kissed her and got up, glancing about him, till his eyes rested upon a sober-looking review.·

"It's in this," he said more lightly. "Pure gold!"

She took the review, and glanced at the article indicated.

"Pure gold, is it?"

"Every word."

"Daddy!" she laughed gaily. "It's only half cut. Oh, how I love you when I find you out!"

Desmond laughed too, while his mind took a swallow's flight into the past, till he saw her as a baby.

"I wrote it," he confessed. "But it's unsigned. Mum's the word."

"You wrote it — for me?"

"For you. Every word is addressed to you."

Sheila, slim as any boy, but delicately flushed, opened her pretty lips. In her eyes lay a puzzled interrogation: above them were two tiny wrinkles. She sighed, as if something had stirred within her for the first time. Perhaps she was attempting to behold her famous father as a failure.

"The other things have counted?" she asked slowly.

"Oh, yes, but other things don't count so much with a woman. It's hard to believe you are a woman."

"Perhaps I'm not quite a woman — yet."

CHAPTER V

JOHN MAKES UP HIS MIND

JOHN passed two rather sleepless nights after meeting Scaife. And in trying to see Scaife as he was, it became necessary to take careful stock, so to speak, of himself. He began to wonder if he were lacking in that great quality so conspicuous in his old school-fellow — initiative. High honours at Oxford, he soon discovered, are but means to an end from a political point of view; and his talents were used to further his Chief's interests and ambitions rather than his own. It surprised him pleasurably to learn that his light had been perceived by others. Scaife's affirmation that he was a marked man made an impression upon a character temperamentally modest. He remembered that Warde, his old house-master, had aroused in him ambitions higher than those inseparable from cricket and football. At Oxford, also, his tutor had fired him to efforts which without some such stimulus might have been abortive.

And now Scaife, of all men in the world, was pushing him on to — what?

Upon the Monday Fluff and his lovely mamma returned to Trent House, but, before departure, Fluff confessed to John that he had proposed marriage to

Sheila, and had received in reply a gay laugh and the assurance that he was one of the nicest boys in the world.

"The darling let me down easy," concluded Fluff mournfully, "but I felt an ass. What would you have done in my place?"

John considered. A smile flickered about his lips as he replied:

"I should have asked permission to ring the bell for a glass of sloe-gin."

"I see. You think I have rushed things. Well, I'm frightened of the other fellows. They'll all be buzzing about her when she goes back to Eaton Square. She likes that bounder Scaife. Told me so without a blush."

"Good sign that."

"I don't believe your modern girl can blush. Scaife, who said on Saturday that he had business of importance to transact this morning in the City, is staying on till to-morrow, isn't he?"

"Yes."

"You think I'm prejudiced against Scaife, unreasonably so. You frowned when I called him a bounder. He is a bounder, and as unconscious of his bounds as a kangaroo. Did you see his face when I said that I knew Ormsby, the man who was with him outside Ladysmith?"

"I noticed something."

"He winced. Why? Because he left poor Ormsby in the lurch. Ormsby had planned the whole thing."

"But if only one man could get through the lines——"

"The right sort would have at least shared the credit with his pal. I had the truth from Ormsby himself. He was very sore. I don't think he told anybody except me, and I've told you because the Demon is still diabolically 'slim,' and he means to capture Desmond and you. He's captured the Duffer already. He speaks of him as 'one of the best.'"

With that, the unhappy Fluff shook off the dust of The Corner from his beautifully polished shoes. The Duffer said good-bye at the same time. He intimated with enthusiasm that he was returning to the Mile End Road much fortified by so charming a visit; and he waved a slip of paper, exclaiming: "Scaife has not forgotten the Harrow Mission. I didn't dun him. Jolly thoughtful of the old man, eh?"

"Very thoughtful indeed," said Fluff.

During the rest of the morning Desmond and John were at work, while Scaife played golf with Sheila. At luncheon Desmond asked for particulars of the game. Sheila said enthusiastically:

"He did the long hole in three."

"A fine performance," said her father. He was so fond of golf that uncharitable persons accused him of playing it to the neglect of public business.

"What is your handicap, Scaife?"

"I'm scratch."

"Where?"

"At Sandwich."

"Played all your life, eh?"

"No.   I took up the game when I chucked cricket."

"And you are down to scratch!" he laughed, turning to John. "You hear, Jonathan? This Admirable Crichton gallops *ventre à terre* where we crawl. Scratch!   I feel like a tortoise.   We must have a game to-day.   You will give me four strokes.   After years of energy and patience I stand still at six."

The match took place that afternoon, and was closely contested from the beginning. John and Sheila witnessed it.

"I'll play you for a ball," said Desmond, as they stood upon the first tee.

"With pleasure, sir.   Do you want anything on?" Scaife turned to John.

"Jonathan is going to bet a nice fat half-crown with me," exclaimed Sheila.   "Of course I shall back my Daddy."

"You back me?" said Scaife to John.   John nodded.

At the fourth hole Desmond was one up.   The teeing grounds of the fifth and eighth holes happened to be close together, and Sheila suggested to John that they should sit down upon a convenient bench to watch the play of the next three holes instead of walking with the players.   Desmond drove a good ball straight down the fairway.   Scaife drove forty yards beyond his opponent into the rough.

"If I could keep straight," growled Scaife.   As he spoke his eyes happened to meet John's.   Scaife frowned, and Sheila saw it, and saw, too, some expression in John's face which puzzled her. As soon as the players were out of earshot she said abruptly:

"Jonathan, do you like Mr. Scaife?" Not waiting for his answer, she added quickly: "I remember Cæsar telling me that you hated him. Why?"

Her eyes met his.

John wriggled in the grip of temptation. The why and wherefore of his former hatred of Scaife lay pat upon his tongue's tip. Afterward a score of times he wondered whether he ought to have spoken. As he hesitated, Sheila added quietly:

"He likes you, and believes in your future."

"So he tells me."

"And that is why I wonder at your disliking him, because you do dislike him, don't you?"

"I did."

"Then it is past?"

"Yes — it is past."

This, in a sense, was true. Such an unforgettable experience as the Boer War might change any man, however hardened, not to mention a boy. What Scaife had done since — in spite of Fluff's indictment — not only justified but exacted a fresh judgment of his character. Dominating these reflections was the ineffaceable recollection of his jealousy of Scaife, always an ardent flame and still unextinguished. Honesty made him blurt this out.

"Once I was horribly jealous of him."

"Jealous? — you?"

Her eyes seemed to grow in size. John explained:

"I was jealous of his friendship with Cæsar."

"But you were Cæsar's greatest friend."

"I was never sure of that till after his death."

"Of course that ended the jealousy forever and ever?"

The girl's persistence was exasperating. An older man might have retorted: "You've set it in a blaze again." Not bold enough to say this, too truthful to affirm that jealousy was dead, John allowed the girl he loved to form a wrong opinion of him by replying with emphasis:

"Nothing can kill jealousy."

"Oh!"

He was quick to perceive that he had fallen in her esteem. She believed, naturally enough, that he was still jealous of his school-fellow's talents and pre-eminence, that he begrudged him worldly success.

"All the same, I hope you will let him help you."

"You advise me to accept this Verney-Boscobel offer?"

"My advice is worth nothing, but acceptance means a lot, doesn't it?"

"Yes — a lot."

"Parliament and all that."

"All that and more than that."

"And you hesitate" — her voice was kinder — "because you don't like to accept help from a man you once disliked."

"Perhaps."

She laughed rather scornfully.

"You mean to cut off your nose to spite your face?
And —— "

"Yes?"

"I've said quite enough."

"Please finish."

She answered with spirit, her cheeks as red as his:

"I think it ungenerous and silly. I say so because
we have always been such particular pals."

John made a gallant attempt to regain a lost position.

"Sheila dear, I will accept Scaife's offer to-night.
Silly I may be, but not ungenerous."

Some subtle inflection in his voice, some hint of
intense feeling suppressed, melted her. She looked
at him with affection, holding out her hand.

"It's all right, Jonathan. Was I very cheeky?"

"You were not quite fair."

"Oh! Now we're quits. I pride myself upon
being fair. What a thrust! Most girls are horribly
unfair."

"And jealous, too, sometimes," added John.

"Because of that we loathe to see the nasty, crawly
thing in men we care about. Hullo! Mr. Scaife
has the honour. They are all square again."

"Never played a better match," declared Desmond,
when he rejoined his daughter. "We're both at the
top of our form."

Once more, however, Scaife pulled his drive into the
rough. Sheila walked with her father. It happened
that both John and Scaife's caddies were a few yards
ahead of Scaife, with their noses in the heather, when

Scaife found his ball. John, rather to one side, saw Scaife hit at the ball with his niblick and miss it. A second attempt was more successful. The ball, struck with great strength and skill, soared out of the whin-bush and found a beautiful lie upon the course. Scaife took his brassy and laid it on the green.

"You're dead," said John.

"Looks like it from here."

Desmond, meanwhile, was on the green in three. As Scaife approached, Sheila said with enthusiasm: "What a recovery! We're like as we lie, and Daddy has a long put for a half."

John waited to hear Scaife reply that he had played four. To his amazement Scaife held his tongue. Desmond putted firmly on a very fast green, just missed the hole, and lay nearly a yard beyond it. He glanced at Scaife's ball lying within two feet of the hole, and picked up his ball, saying, "Your hole."

"Thanks," said Scaife, and laughed.

By the written laws of golf it was Scaife's hole. By the unwritten laws he ought, of course, to have informed Desmond that he had played four strokes, when Desmond believed him to have played three. John wondered whether his eyes had deceived him. Had he mistaken the "addressing" of a ball in a difficult lie for an actual stroke? His horrid doubts upon this point were resolved by no less an authority than Scaife's caddy, a boy who often carried John's clubs, and on that account was emboldened to whisper furtively:

"The gen'leman played four strokes on to the green. 'E missed one in the 'eather."

"Hold your tongue!" John replied sharply.

The boy grinned, as if he remembered that John was backing Scaife. The match was finished without further incident, Scaife winning at the sixteenth hole with three up and two to play.

As they approached the house, the victor took John's arm, and murmured pleasantly:

"Have you thought over my offer?"

"Very carefully."

"I hope you mean to accept it?"

John hesitated. He was very young, and instinct warned him to have no dealings with an unscrupulous partner; but the acceptance of this offer meant a bold bid for fortune and Sheila. In desperation, clutching at the weapon his old enemy proffered, and yet realizing that it might be turned against himself, he said firmly:

"I accept — upon one condition."

"And that?"

John's steady eyes met Scaife's sparkling, derisive glance.

"Can you give me your word that you see profit in it for yourself?"

"Of course I see profit in it for myself."

"Then I accept."

CHAPTER VI

PARTNERS

THAT night John Verney, of Verney-Boscobel, and Reginald Scaife, of Dover Street, London, drew up a rough draft of partnership. John's solicitor, when he read this rough draft, allowed an exclamation of astonishment to escape from discreet lips, adding emphatically that Mr. Scaife had been very liberal, very liberal indeed, an opinion shared by Charles Desmond, who affirmed to Sheila (and others) that Scaife had behaved very much like a gentleman. Thereafter he shone resplendent in the Desmond firmament, and it is possible — for we must admit him to be as shrewd a dealer as his illustrious father — that the young fellow had never invested a large cheque to better advantage.

Then John and he spent a week at Boscobel. The Manor was let, furnished, for a term of years, of which about half had expired, and, accordingly, the two men put up at the Verney Arms, where they received excellent entertainment at the hands of a stout, smiling landlady.

The garden of the inn overlooked the estuary, and below the harbour shimmered the pool where the sea-trout assemble before attempting the passage of the mill-dam. John told Scaife that these trout leaping within a few yards of them refused any lure, however tempting. Fly, worm, or minnow were presented in vain. Above the dam, in the fresh water, it was no difficult matter to fill a creel with the beauties. In spite of this information, Scaife fished the pool for half an hour every morning and evening, and upon the fourth day he foul-hooked a fine two-pounder, landed him triumphantly, and announced his determination to fish no more.

"I had to have one," he said.

"But you foul-hooked him."

"I don't care. I got him."

"By whatever lure — fish."

"That's it. I've snagged salmon in Norway when everything else failed. The Caterpillar had a fit when I told him."

"Do you see much of the Caterpillar?"

"We took that Norway fishing together."

John was too polite to express surprise, but possibly he showed it in his face, for Scaife laughed, with a certain grimness.

"Perhaps I tried to snag the Caterpillar. He barred me at Harrow, and I've an idea that he tried to keep me out of the *Celibates' Club*. That made me set to work to capture him. By Jove! he jumped about just out of my reach, like your trout, but in the end he came to my net."

"How did you scoop him in?"

"Ask him. We're quite friendly now."

Scaife laughed again, as he lit a fresh cigar. Then, in a different tone, he continued: "I think I shall commission old Angus M'Vittie to paint a picture of this view."

John gazed at the most beautiful part of his domain. At high tide, upon a midsummer's evening, the estuary might have been mistaken for an inland lake, so placid was its surface. A certain languor diffused itself, as the sun declined into the west. The overhanging woods, reflected in the water, seemed to be asleep. Presently, at the ebb of the tide, the seaweed-covered flats would display their gorgeous livery of green and gold; through them the gracious curves of the river would wind their way to the sea. Boscobel is one of the few estuaries that are perfectly beautiful and sweet-smelling at low tide.

John could not look at his lovely woodlands without feeling an emotion of tenderness. As a boy the poetry of the forest had appealed to him insistently; and always he had the conviction that it was rightly named the New Forest. It remained new throughout the centuries, a virginal Arcadia, never changing, save for the different seasons, holding, as it were, in trust incomparable health and youth and beauty.

Was it not sacrilege to mutilate the fair face of this landscape, to cut down these lovely trees, to turn loose in such a paradise the iconoclastic Scaife?

Then he thought of Sheila, and regret fled from his soul. He repeated vaguely:

"Angus M'Vittie?"

"Yes."

"You like his work?"

"I detest it. His earlier pictures are magnificent.
My father owns three of the best. M'Vittie tried to
buy them back to sell at an enormous profit in America.
His work now is stereotyped. Yes — I'll order a vast
canvas."

"But why?"

"Can't you guess?"

"If you dislike his work — I loathe it myself — I
can't imagine what you are after."

"An 'ad.' of course. M'Vittie will hang a big picture
upon the line at Burlington House. It will be engraved
and photographed. I may have to pay two thousand
guineas for it, but, later, when my object is accomplished, I shall sell it at a small profit to some Yankee
collector. See?"

"I see," said John.

Scaife continued reflectively:

"I shall have it puffed as the masterpiece of our
famous Royal Academician. Crowds will stand in
front of it, and underneath will be inscribed the legend
— 'Verney-Boscobel.' From May till next September
we shall be advertising the sale and subdivision of
Boscobel residential sites. Now, John, admit that
I'm a great man."

John laughed.

"You are. All the same —— "

"Yes?"

"It enrages me to think that M'Vittie's work sells. He's an artisan, a tradesman."

"We think alike about these things," said Scaife slowly. "Your smug fellow rolling down his well-soaped groove exasperates me. Would you believe it, when I gave up first-class cricket a certain member of the Marylebone Club told me in sepulchral tones that I was making the mistake of my life. He was kind enough to assure me that I might, with perseverance, play in a Test-match. Another pal indicated with equal solemnity the possibility of my becoming a Master of Hounds."

"But you like hunting?"

"Two days a week. Upon the other days I want to be after something bigger than foxes. Talking of foxes, Charles Desmond has gone to earth, hasn't he?"

"I'm not aware of it," said John stiffly.

"Oh, yes, you are. Why not treat me as I'm trying to treat you — with confidence? Is there any reason why we should not discuss a public character?"

"Not while I'm in his service."

"You're leaving his service. However, I had forgotten that you were his secretary. Yes — he's gone to earth, and I'm going to dig him out. Mum as usual. Never mind!" He laughed gaily, clapping John upon the shoulder. "I'm your Chief's friend, and he knows it, the wily old dodger. We three are going to have a famous hunt together across the stiffest country in the kingdom. And we shall end up in Downing Street."

He glanced at John keenly, trying to interpret a slightly ironical smile which flickered about a firm mouth. Reminding himself of hard cash paid for John Verney's confidence, he wondered when "goods would be delivered." With engaging frankness he had said to his father: "I am getting at Charles Desmond through John Verney." When John remained silent, he changed the subject and talked of a new dynamo which would furnish Boscobel with electricity at a cheap rate. His knowledge of such matters astounded John, to whom the developments of science were wrapt in mystery. Scaife's omniscience, however, limited itself to matters personal to Scaife. He studied what pertained to the successful conduct of his affairs, being a master of the arts and crafts of minding one's own business. He never wasted time, or money, or words, upon what lay beyond his very extended horizon. Also he had curious reserves. Upon marriage, for instance, and its objects and conditions, he held a discreet tongue. Religion, the consideration of creeds, the exchange of old doctrines for new, the modern philosophies, stirred no enthusiasms. When John approached such themes, Scaife would shake his broad shoulders and exclaim:

"I grab at substance. Bodies interest me more than souls. I should like to give the workers better houses, better food, more soap and water."

"So should I."

"Because I know that, we can trot together."

Invariably he assumed a knowledge of aspirations

and ideas which John had never put into words. Apparently Scaife and John were travelling toward the same goal by different roads. John admitted that Scaife was spending money as he himself would have spent much of the money which once he had expected to inherit. And he tried sincerely to see the good in Scaife, and to believe with the Duffer that the Ethiopian was gradually turning white.

They returned to London By this time every one agreed that a General Election was inevitable. Once more Scaife exhibited his capacity for absorbing and monopolizing information demonstrated long afterward to be correct. To Desmond and John he submitted an immense bundle of papers, figures, and facts, laboriously accumulated, which, supposing that Ireland remained what it was, gave to the Liberal poll an immense majority.

"You are going to publish these?" asked Charles Desmond.

"Hardly. My flag is nailed to the mast. Every paper I control is instructed to predict a victory for the Unionists. Only to you" — he laid emphasis on the pronoun — "do I show the tabulated results."

"I appreciate what you have done."

"It gives one pause, doesn't it?"

"We shall be out for years if — if your forecast is correct."

"Take my word that it is correct. I won't mention what I paid for it."

He laughed. The veteran turned upon him with irritation, muttering: "You take it coolly."

"I try to do so, sir."

With that Scaife went his way, leaving behind the monstrous bundle of facts. Desmond said to John:

"There are moments when this young man frightens me. This" — he tapped the accursed bundle — "must have cost a small fortune, and he seems to have spent it for my benefit."

"He can afford it; the circulation of his papers is leaping ahead."

"He's very extravagant. He tells me that he has commissioned M'Vittie to paint a six-foot canvas of Verney-Boscobel!"

"Yes."

"Rather a waste of money."

"Verney-Boscobel is to be advertised at Burlington House."

Desmond frowned. Scaife's cleverness impressed with uneasiness a man who belonged to the generation which underrates advertisement and prefers old lamps to new. This conservative attitude, combined with great personal charm and high birth, had endeared Desmond to the upper and upper-middle classes. Such an aristocrat, it had been said, would stand by his own order to the death! Upon the other hand, he had an adaptability which delighted the multitude. He accepted facts, however unwelcome, with a disarming smile; he kept his temper so admirably when heckled;

he acclaimed another's success so generously; he apologized with such dignity and suavity. These are great gifts, so great that they blinded even his colleagues to a certain Irish strain of irresponsibility, cunningly concealed. John, possibly, was the only man who realized the Chief's infirmities were increasing. Indecision and procrastination were becoming habitual. John alone knew — Scaife may have guessed as much — how often he, the humble secretary, was called upon to deliver an ultimatum.

Presently Desmond laid down his pen and said abruptly:

"Sheila thinks highly of Reginald Scaife."

"He is rather — dazzling."

"What is his attitude toward her?"

"He admires her immensely."

"Between ourselves, is he in love with her?"

"I don't know."

This was the truth, for Scaife's manner with Sheila remained as impenetrable as a Scotch mist; and she, for her part, betrayed no feeling other than that of friendship. A great lady, wife of the head of the Desmond family, had presented Sheila at Court, and immediately afterward — as Fluff predicted — the young fellows began to buzz about her. At her first ball, she suffered two proposals of marriage from men to whom she had vouchsafed no encouragement. She complained to John:

"Why do they do it?"

"Some of 'em can't help it."

"It's so stupid. A man ought not to ask a girl to marry him unless he's sure that she'll say 'Yes.'"

John wondered whether Scaife shared this conviction. Then he heard his Chief's voice continuing:

"Miss Bargus is Scaife's friend." He added: "But he hasn't quite captured you yet."

"But he has you," said John.

Charles Desmond laughed:

"One must march with the times."

"A dignified progress to the sound of the sackbut and dulcimer — not a gallop."

"You understand me better than anybody else. Yes — a march. Something orderly and — impressive. I have never rushed my fences. Scaife frightens me because he goes so fast."

"If he goes straight he can risk a toss or two."

"Quite — quite. But I can't at my age. And I must take my own line. I won't ride after any man. There are moments, Jonathan, when I wish that I was out of the hunt. I tire more quickly than I used to do, and when I get tired, my boy — physically tired, I mean — it seems to affect my judgment. Often I yield to importunity because I am so bored."

"You would be more bored looking on."

"Yes, yes, in my robuster moments I realize that. We'll talk of this again."

John nodded.

"It would be awful if Sheila made a mess of things. Why can't she take a good fellow like Esmé Kinloch? He'd give her a free hand, and everything else."

"Fluff lets her trample on him."

"I suppose that's it. She told me yesterday that she adored what she calls the great qualities: pluck, initiative, enthusiasm. I've remarked that young women who admire conquerors are generally the most easily conquered. They are eager to render to Cæsar all that is theirs, as well as all that is his."

"Sheila has a lot to give," murmured John.

CHAPTER VII

IN AUGUST the Desmonds went to Scotland upon
a month's visit to Scaife, who had rented Strath
Armyn, an immense place in Sutherland, half
forest and half grouse-moor, with fishing in lochs
stocked with trout, and four miles of a famous salmon
river. John, accompanying his Chief, was made to
understand that he was cordially welcome as a guest.
Egerton, "the Caterpillar," was the fourth man.
Scaife explained that the grouse were to be shot over
dogs, driving being impracticable, whereat the Caterpillar grumbled.

"I can't make out why he's taken this place,"
he said to John, as they strolled down to the loch
upon the afternoon of the first day.

The Caterpillar had not changed much since the
old Harrow days. He crawled now, as then, to his
conclusions, and seldom abandoned them. Tall and
thin, immaculately turned out, he had achieved the
distinction of being the best-dressed man in the
Brigade. During the war, an act of gallantry at
Modder River had gained him the Victoria Cross.
A cartoon, which appeared subsequently in one of
the illustrated papers, bore the superscription, *Conspicuous and Cool.*

"But it's simply magnificent."

"Magnificent? Last year he had Roy, and we shot thirteen hundred brace in four days. Just six men. Topping! Not a petticoat in the Lodge. I hate tailing grouse. And besides, why should Scaife bother about running a big establishment? That's a mug's game for a bachelor. And he's asked Charles Desmond for a solid month, knowing the old chap can't shoot for nuts. Can you shoot?"

"I hit 'em sometimes," said John.

"Have you seen the Demon shoot?"

"No."

"He's one of the very best and keenest. Likes a butcher's bill, too; doesn't carry his Purdey to look at. Mind you, I'm not complaining, or crabbing Strath Armyn, but it amazes me that Scaife should take it. And, look here — this is between ourselves — Scaife had Roy this year, and he swopped Roy for this. Roy! Think of it! The deed was done last June. Now — why?"

"I dare say he'll tell you."

"I shall ask him. Rummy thing, too, to find you his honoured guest. We used to bar him — eh? But he's all right. He did me a turn I shall never forget." The Caterpillar sank his voice. "About four years after I joined the Brigade I nearly came to grief. I'd gone it a bit, and the Governor was deucedly hard up. We thought that I should have to exchange. Just then I met the Demon at some shoot. Jove! I was ass enough to resent his

being under the same roof with me. I'd taken particular pains to keep him out of the *Celibates' Club*.
The Governor was there too. He was civil to Scaife,
because he thinks it's idiotic to be anything else, and
Scaife advised him to buy shares in Scaife's Limited.
The Governor funked it. Scaife told him to apply
for a thousand ten-pound shares, and he hinted that
he would be lucky if he got a quarter of the number,
and also that they would go to a premium after allot-
ment. Well, the Governor wired to his broker, who
wired back: 'Take all you can get.' To cut the story
short, he did get a thousand, thanks to Scaife, who was
Managing Director. The shares, as perhaps you
know, went up and up. Scaife gave us the tip when
to sell. We just doubled our money. I know now
that he did it to pile coals of fire on my head. Afterward I got him into the *Celibates*, and we took a fishing
together."

"In Norway, where he snagged the salmon?"

"Told you of that, did he? Not quite — cricket.
But, bless you, he's so confoundedly keen, and he
gets there with both feet. Never met such a fellow —
a record-beater. All the same, he was a fool to swop
Roy for this. Don't you agree?"

"I have not seen Roy," John replied

To the end of August the sun shone steadily. Even
the Caterpillar admitted that shooting plenty of grouse
over perfectly trained dogs was worth while. The
men shot in parties of two each, and Sheila walked

with the party that included her father. Penelope sketched. Her sketches were admirable, the expression in water-colour of careful training, nice powers of discernment and selection, and consummate talent of never attempting any subject beyond her powers. In Eaton Square, throughout the season, she had remained mistress of the house and situation. She treated Sheila tenderly, and Charles Desmond had been impressed with a kind aunt's desire to conceal the inexperience and occasional tactlessness of a pretty niece. Since Sheila's return, Penelope's solicitude for the comfort of her brother-in-law seemed, if it were possible, to have increased. Upon every opportunity she "spared" him, as she put it.

"Aunt Pen never tells tales," said Sheila to John, "but if we do anything not quite right somehow Daddy finds it out."

John smiled at the "we," which happened to be justified, because upon that particular morning he had forgotten a matter of small importance. However, he said lightly: "She's awfully sweet to you, Sheila."

"You think me a beast to crab her?"

"Disloyalty is not one of your faults."

"I feel that I must speak or burst."

"If it has really come to that — speak!"

"She does go it with Daddy, doesn't she?"

John repeated the words to gain time, wondering how much Sheila had seen.

"Go it?"

"Well, she piles on the agony. It *is* agony to me. You, of course, look upon it as butter."

John nodded again. Sheila continued eagerly: "The amazing thing is that Daddy allows it. Why doesn't he say, in his own nice way, 'Shut up!'?"

"Oh, he couldn't!"

"He must loathe it."

John hesitated, picking his way between three damning admissions. He knew that his Chief did not loathe butter. To be quite candid, he swallowed it with appetite. To hint, moreover, that butter disagreed involved the tacit assumption that the great man was an incomparable actor. John temporized.

"You see, he's so accustomed to it; perhaps he doesn't notice it."

Sheila's expression of relief was almost a caress.

"John dear," she said solemnly, "how understanding you are! Well," she added reflectively, "Aunt Pen butters me, but all the same she means to get rid of me."

"How?"

"Marry me off, perhaps."

She smiled, glancing at him roguishly. Then she said quickly, with heightened colour: "If I can't be mistress in my father's house, I shall be mistress in my own — some day."

"Oh, ho!" said John, and the colour rushed into his cheeks also.

At Strath Armyn Scaife devoted himself to his

illustrious guest. The Caterpillar and John shot together, as a general rule, and upon non-shooting days were despatched to loch and river. At the end of the third day the Caterpillar's mind was brilliantly illuminated. He said to John, as they were smoking after luncheon:

"By Jove! The Demon gave up Roy because of Sheila Desmond — eh, what?"

"Rubbish!"

"I'm sure of it. What a tribute! Thirteen hundred brace of grouse. I should like to know whether he's off with Genesta Lamb."

"Do you mean the dancer?"

"Of course. Cold Lamb we called her till the Demon cut in."

John said, with a violence that surprised the Caterpillar: "Do you mean to tell me that this affair is a — a fact?"

"Be perfectly calm. I don't know it to be a fact."

"Damnable gossip!"

"Why so warm? Call it gossip if you like. Did Scaife never mention Genesta Lamb to you?"

"Never."

The Caterpillar laughed: "Rather fishy that. Anyway, the business must have been squared. I wonder if Genesta took it quietly. From a slight acquaintance, I should say she was one of those charmers to whom a cheque is not everything."

John stared at the sharp peak piercing the skies to the north-west; then he glanced at the Caterpillar,

who was enjoying his pipe. It struck him with
violence that the Caterpillar was a good old thickhead
whose vision never penetrated beneath the surface.
Scaife in impossible clothes, Scaife swaggering as he
used to swagger out of the school-yard, Scaife talking
too loudly, or shooting another man's bird, would
have aroused him to indignation. But the Scaife
who belonged to the *Celibates*, and took Roy, was
eligible to marry any maid in the kingdom.

The Caterpillar went on:

"I'll bet Sheila will have him."

John replied emphatically: "Not if she ever hears
about the other."

"My dear fellow, if a woman is really in love with
a man she surrenders unconditionally."

"Is that your experience, Caterpillar?"

"It's my father's. You'll allow he knows a bit."

John assented, for Colonel Egerton's *bonnes fortunes*
were the undivided property of the gossips. Then
he felt quite sick, as he realized that the Caterpillar
might be right. Ever since Desmond's question:
"Is Scaife in love with Sheila?" John had watched and
waited for a sign. But Scaife had been very clever.
His attentions were marked, indeed, but to the father
only. Then John heard the Caterpillar drawling on:
"Such a marriage would suit Charles Desmond down
to the ground. He's confoundedly hard up. Scaife
will make him chairman of some rich company. If
our party remains in power those two will make things
hum."

"Scaife calls himself a free lance."

"That be damned! Nobody's a free lance in politics. He belongs to the Carlton."

"And never goes there."

"Quite right. Dullest club in London. I'm amazed that you should even hint at Scaife's not being heart and soul with us. Good Lord! if he kow-towed to the Rads, I wouldn't be seen in his company, not even at Roy!"

They went on shooting. John supposed that the Caterpillar had forgotten what was said: but at dinner that same evening Desmond spoke of Arnold Grandcourt, a backslider of parts, a cadet of ancient family, and a man of great personal charm, but now regarded by all God-fearing Tories as Judas Iscariot.

"I'd shoot that fellow with my own hand!" declared the Caterpillar. "And he's my cousin, too, confound him."

Scaife laughed disdainfully.

"I mean it," continued Egerton. "He was one of us: he owed all he had to us: he was born and bred a Tory. The scoundrel has fouled his own nest, disgraced his own order. 'Down with the Beerage and Peerage!' is his cry. It's too thick. Shoot him? Too easy a death, by Jove. The traitor ought to be crucified upside down. He's a Socialist."

"So am I," said Scaife.

A silence followed. Scaife's eyes were sparkling with a sort of furious vitality, an expression familiar to John. Although he spoke quietly, a clarion note of defiance had sounded. Sheila stared at him with fear in her eyes. Desmond carefully examined his nails. The Caterpillar, red with amazement, said hoarsely:

"You?"

"Yes — I," replied Scaife. He had chosen this moment for a confession of faith, because a better opportunity was not likely to occur. These people were his guests; they had just eaten an excellent dinner: and the servants had left the room. He met Sheila's eyes and held them. While he spoke, the colour ebbed and flowed across her cheeks. But her eyes remained fixed upon his with an eager fascination.

"I am a Socialist in the widest sense of the word," began Scaife. "I don't suppose, Egerton, that you know what Socialism really is?"

"Oh — don't I?" replied the Caterpillar scornfully. "Socialism is the determination to enjoy something you've not earned."

"Your own that?"

"My Governor's."

John burst out laughing at the familiar answer.

"You still quote him?" asked Scaife derisively.

"I might quote a more foolish man. Your Socialists are a pack of discontented rascals."

Penelope, ever ready to pour platitudes upon troubled waters, said sweetly:

"Contentment may be found in contrasting our position in life with that of those below us, instead of above."

Scaife, however, ignored this sugar-plum, and addressed the Caterpillar:

"What else does Colonel Egerton say?"

"The tap-root of the trouble lies with the Dissenters. The beggars can't get over the fact that our parsons dine with the squire of the parish, and theirs don't. Socialism is more than half jealousy."

"Have you read any Socialist propaganda?"

"Wouldn't touch the beastly stuff with tongs."

"Exactly. I wonder whether it has ever occurred to you or your father that it is wise to read what the other fellow has to say. You dyed-in-the-wool Tories won't even have a Radical newspaper in your houses."

"Can't have the servants' minds tainted," retorted the Caterpillar.

"The curse of English politics is that the average man won't read both sides of any question, or face a situation he doesn't like. Socialism must be faced. And you and your friends won't destroy it by abusing it or ignoring it."

"I have heard *you* say that, Charles," murmured Penelope.

"What do you call Socialism?" demanded the Caterpillar.

Scaife hesitated, pulling himself together for a supreme effort. And his choice of words, the conciseness of his sentences, showed that he had carefully prepared the theme, and desired to present it and himself in the best light. John realized with intensity

that Scaife was about to make a tremendous bid for
Sheila's interest and favour.

"Socialism," said Scaife, "is the gradual extinction
of all forces which hinder progress. Day by day we
become more civilized, more humane. The people
who refuse to admit that may, perhaps, be satisfied
with existing conditions. But, if you grant that we
are more intelligent, less cruel, less primitive, and with
an increasing appreciation of personal cleanliness,
decent food and clothing, and comfortable houses,
why then, unless you hide your head in the sand, you
must ask: 'How is this progress to be accelerated?'"

"Not by robbin' Peter to pay Paul," growled the
Caterpillar.

"I'm one of the Peters," said Scaife, "and too
selfish to advocate confiscation. If we live to see
such a revolution as they had in France, it will be
brought about by the ignorance, the obstinacy, and
the injustice of the Peters."

"What do you think Paul is entitled to?" asked
Desmond.

"You know the answer, sir. To raise the standard
of intelligence, which flies at half-mast everywhere,
we must feed and clothe starved bodies., The State
must take care of its mothers and children. In
Samarkand we began feeding the children, and then
washing 'em. Fifty per cent. of the poorest were in
an unspeakable condition. I'd like you to examine
them to-day."

"May we do so, Mr. Scaife?" Penelope asked.

"Any time. Some fun has been poked at Scaife's Baths, but you can't clean minds till you scrub bodies."

Desmond said rather apathetically: "We are agreed that things can be improved, but who is to pay for the improvement? The ordinary employer of labour, struggling hard for a profit, hasn't a ha'penny to spare for the weaklings. In the carrying out of your ideas upon a national scale, I ask again: 'Where's the money to come from?'"

"Tariff Reform," declared the Caterpillar. "Make the foreigner fork out!"

Scaife addressed himself to Desmond, who was fumbling at his chin. To John the gesture indicated irresolution.

"Do you believe, sir, that Tariff Reform will prolong the life of our Textile Industries?"

"Possibly."

"Will it not be wiser, sir, to concentrate our energies on doing things better than other nations? When we fail at that our evolutionary race is run. Tariffs can give us a Fool's Paradise for a bit, and that's about all."

John waited for a smashing answer from Desmond, but he remained silent, much to John's surprise and obviously to the Caterpillar's disgust. Scaife turned with an eager smile to Sheila. He looked extraordinarily handsome, and spoke with feeling and sincerity.

"This country has prospered under Tariff Reform and Free Trade. Neither the one nor the other will do away with unemployment. And the well-being of any country can't be measured by trade balance-sheets. The most prosperous nation is that in which there are least starving children. We are thriftless. The statesman who understands his business must educate the proletariat to put by for bad times."

As Desmond still remained silent, John said ironically: "If you want to inculcate thrift and independence, is it wise to save the people the trouble of taking care of themselves and their families?" Scaife hesitated, frowning, and John went on: "Can you name any teacher of Socialism who has suggested means of increasing wealth? There are plenty of nostrums for dividing the wealth made by other people, but have you attacked the problem of the increase of wealth sufficient to maintain the world?"

Scaife said with some asperity: "I want to see every man, woman, and child given a fair chance."

"Who doesn't?" said John dryly.

"Very few. Here and there a duke does his duty, here and there a manufacturer gives to his operatives more than their bare wage, here and there a squire thinks more of his peasants than his pheasants, but the vast majority are indifferent — and you know it."

"I don't know it," John replied. "I believe, on the contrary, that the average squire throughout the kingdom makes unpublished sacrifices for his tenants that they will not appreciate till they have lost them. English gentlemen don't brag about such things as remitted rents and clothing and coal funds. The best work is done by the best men in silence."

Penelope rose. Possibly she preceived that Scaife
had made an immense impression upon one of his
small audience. She may have feared that he might
lose the ground so easily gained.

"These are deep matters," she murmured. "Too
deep for us poor women."

"Aunt Pen, please sit down."

Penelope, smiling sweetly, moved toward the door,
which the Caterpillar opened.

"My poor head is swimming," she said softly.

Sheila glanced at her father, who nodded. The
girl left the room slowly and with reluctance.

When the ladies had gone, Charles Desmond said,
in a tired voice: "Let us leave politics alone."

Scaife replied: "With pleasure. Would you like
to stalk to-morrow? The forester spied a fine ten-
pointer on our ground this afternoon."

The Caterpillar lit a cigar, and presently embarked
upon the never-failing theme of taking nets from the
mouth of salmon rivers. John was thinking of Sheila's
charming face, and her eyes sparkling with enthusiasm.
And he was thinking also of the shares in Scaife's
Limited, puffed by the Scaife papers till they had risen
to a big premium, and then unloaded upon the small
investor. He thought also of Miss Genesta Lamb,
who danced so alluringly.

Trying to sort his conclusions, he became sensible
of an exasperating weariness. He had done a hard
day's shooting, but no harder than Scaife. Yet
Scaife appeared fresh. The Caterpillar continued

"jawing" about sport. Time-worn phrases . echoed in John's head: "The salmon don't get up the rivers as they did," or "In wet years the grouse *will* go to the high ground. One can't exaggerate the impor-; tance of burning heather properly."

Scaife caught John's eye and winked. The wink revealed the Caterpillar as the epitome of what used to be styled in sporting prints, "One of the right sort . doing the thing well."

Scaife's wink said plainly: "Hark to him!"

John harked.

"The amount of grouse on this moor could be trebled by driving. And you can train the birds to fly as you wish them to fly, given, of course, the right condi- tions. There you are again. Circumstances alter cases. I have a pal who for years has made elaborate notes. He jots down the flight of the birds, rain or shine, wind or no wind. Early in the season he comes up to his place, and has a series of drives over empty butts. The pains that man takes is incredible."

"Incredible," repeated Scaife. "You are speaking of the Poodle?"

"Wonderful dog — wonderful! He's given up his life to it. Might have been anything. You agree with me, sir?"

He appealed to Desmond. The Poodle was a peer of the realm, a large landowner, and the husband of a pretty wife.

"He might have been a game-keeper," said Desmond dryly.

"He beats any game-keeper," said the Caterpillar. "Employs the best, too, and gives 'em snuff, by Jove. Attends to the rearing of his pheasants. And when it comes to shooting 'em —! He told me that he practised with two loaders for weeks before the twelfth. I've seen four grouse come over him, and he's downed the lot. Snick-snack, two in front. Change! Snick-snack, two behind! I should like to think that I'd live to do that. Four birds, mind you, coming together! And these damned Rads jaw about driving as unsportsmanlike!"

"Let us join the ladies," said Scaife.

CHAPTER VIII

THE Caterpillar left at the end of the week, taking himself and his guns and his servant to another moor where grouse were not "tailed." Upon the eve of departure, he led John aside and poured more henbane into sensitive ears.

"Drop me a line, Johathan, when there's somethin' doin'. I'd like to be one of the first to congratulate Cæsar's sister — eh? Wonder what Cæsar would have said— what?"

"He would have said that you talk a lot of tosh," said John nervously.

"The little duck will fly into Scaife's arms when he opens them; and there'll be less Socialistic rot when our friend has Charles Desmond for a papa-in-law. You mark that."

He was whirled away in Scaife's car, which returned with the Duffer, looking the worse for much wear and tear in Whitechapel. Scaife had said:

"I hope Duff will be able to come to us."

Sheila exclaimed: "How awfully kind of you to ask him!"

"Capital fellow, Duff," remarked Charles Desmond

"I got him the offer of a snug living, but he refused it."

"Some men prefer work on the frontier," cooed Penelope, with a malicious side-glance at John.

The Duffer brought a prehistoric hammer weapon, which had belonged to his father, and an old portmanteau stuffed full of the shabbiest garments. Arrayed in these he took the heather, with beaming eyes and red hair bristling with anticipation of many "rights and lefts" and wily old blackcock to be "downed" without mercy. The fact that he was a shocking bad shot never damped his enthusiasm. "Must leave a bird or two for John," he explained with his cheery grin. In the same spirit of optimism he missed his first stag, standing broadside at eighty yards, and confounded the discomfited stalker by exclaiming:

"Could any man hold straight on such a splendiferous beast?" But as a fisherman he was more successful. He belonged to the "chuck and chance it" school, and knew nothing of educated Test trout and the fine art of presenting a dry fly to them. Out of loch and burn he filled his creel, and brought to the gaff more than one fine salmon.

John spent much time with him. And he had to listen to panegyrics of Scaife delivered with fervent conviction. The Duffer's work was so dear to his heart, and filled it so absorbingly, that he saw everything and everybody in relation to it. No zealous worker amongst the very poor can escape the conclusion

that their appalling condition is a fact grotesquely
out of proportion to other phases of life.

Daily intercourse with an old friend who persisted
in believing the best of his fellow-men affected John
profoundly. Indeed, this month in Scotland, with
everything to remind him how enchanting life may be,
was the most bitter-sweet he had ever spent. He saw
Sheila by day; he dreamed of her by night. In his
dreams, she eluded him: he could never come up with
her. Was she slipping from him into Scaife's toils?
What he had suffered when Cæsar forsook him he
suffered again with intenser pangs. He still hugged
the conviction that he had never indicated his love
to his Chief's daughter, and, hourly, he tried to persuade himself that Scaife was nothing to Sheila and
Sheila nothing to Scaife, and yet Penelope Bargus
seemed to pronounce a benediction whenever she
looked at the pair. And the Duffer said, with endless
repetition, as of a priest mumbling interminable *credos:*

"The best thing that could possibly happen! Each
the complement of the other! Warms my heart to
think of it."

One day, John found himself alone with Sheila.
Her father had returned to the Lodge before luncheon
to nurse a knee slightly strained by hard walking.
John shot well, although he was aware that Sheila
must be making comparisons between his performance
and that of Scaife. The heath lay to the left of the loch,
and commanded a view of the forest where Scaife
was stalking. The Duffer had gone fishing.

Presently the ghillies brought a bag containing luncheon, laid it beside John, and withdrew. Two hundred yards away were the head-keeper, the other ghillies, and the dogs, some splendid Gordons and Laveracks. A round hill, brilliantly purple, rose between the loch and the loftiest mountain in that part of Sutherland. The peaks of the mountain were gray, and its face was gray also, seamed and seared by the ineffaceable wrinkles of Time. From their altitude, about a thousand feet, Sheila and John could see other peaks, the sentinels of this vast, wild country, through which the red deer roamed at will from sea to sea, from forest to forest. In the rutting time a lordly stag might travel a couple of hundred miles without jumping a fence.

"Isn't the colour wonderful?" said Sheila.

The colour scintillated, as if the landscape were some huge opal. In the distance a pale blue haze hung between the lower and upper ground, and out of it sparkled the reds and yellows and greens of moss and bracken and grass. A score of lochs shone with a pale silvery radiance; through the heather a thousand rivulets ran joyously to lake and sea. The air was fresh and crisp, with a touch of frost tempered by the midday sun.

They were sitting beside a burn, which tumbled from rock to rock in a series of miniature cascades. It sang loudly as if exulting in its escape from the durance of the mountain, and mad with ardour to reach the pleasant valleys.

Sheila said softly: "You like this, John?"

"It's heavenly."

"You are fond of simple pleasures?"

"Too fond, perhaps."

Then he saw that she was staring at the distant forest, and at the same moment a rifle-shot was faintly heard.

"Another stag," said John. "Scaife has 'got in' early."

"It seems rather barbarous that we should come to this fairyland merely to kill things, but Mr. Scaife says they are preserved for that only, which is true enough."

She frowned slightly, and began to unfasten the bag, while she exclaimed with a child's laugh: "I hope there are plenty of rock-cakes and apples."

John told himself that she was still a child. She wore a short walking skirt, which confirmed the impression of immaturity, and her face might have belonged to a pretty boy.

"How solemn you look!" she said, and laughed again.

The lightness of her laughter moved John to sadness, as he realized her inability to see beneath the surface and at the same time her unappeasable desire to do so — the voracious curiosity of youth. Throughout luncheon she chattered, happy and absolutely at ease with her companion. Moreover, she insisted upon buttering John's bread, mixing his whiskey and water, and, finally, filling his pipe. The wind happened to be blowing strongly, and John discovered that he had but four vesta matches. Sheila, sitting with her back to the wind, opened her coat.

"I'll shelter you from the blast," she said.

John, kneeling before her, lit the first match, which flickered and went out.

"You must get nearer," said Sheila.

The second attempt was successful. John lit his pipe, and he was so close to her heart that he could hear the beating of his own.

"Thank you," he said hoarsely. But Sheila was not looking at him; her gaze had wandered once more across the broad strath to the hills beyond, where Scaife was stalking.

"John," she said, with a change of voice and manner, "there are such lots of things I want to know. I can't talk to Aunt Pen. She's very sweet, but somehow counsels of perfection make a sinner of me. Daddy, too, treats me like a child."

"What do you want to know most particularly?"

"Myself."

"Oh!"

"I'm so different from you. I take things at a run. You crawl."

"I have to," said John grimly.

Instantly her eyes melted with compassion. She touched his hand.

"Oh, Jonathan, I'm so sorry. I had forgotten. But you are all right now?"

"Am I?"

"Of course you are. And you see yourself quite plainly, don't you?"

"Occasionally."

"You encourage me to confess that I don't always feel the same person."

"You are a crowd — so am I."

"Are you really? I've always thought of you as the same old Jonathan, always, always the same."

"The same stupid old bore."

"Never, never! But you — a crowd!" She laughed, and then instantly her face became grave again. "How do you account for it?"

"Easily. Our bodies are houses of which spirits, ruly and unruly, take possession."

"The unruly spirits are the most amusing."

"At first. They are the most difficult to kick out afterward."

"I shall think of myself as a haunted house."

In the silence another rifle-shot was heard.

"Scaife must have wounded his beast with the first shot," said John.

Sheila frowned again. More than three quarters of an hour had elapsed between the first and second shots. It was extremely unlikely that in so brief a time another stag could have been spied, stalked, and slain. Perhaps, while they were eating and laughing, some poor beast, shot too far back, or with a broken leg, had been dragging its mutilated body through heather and peat-hags!

"That will haunt me," she answered vehemently.

Without pausing, she continued: "And I want to enjoy the present, to make the most of every minute."

"It's natural enough."

"Natural to be selfish?"

"Natural to enjoy."

"That's what Mr. Scaife says, but he's made me see the seamy side, too. Whenever he talks about the submerged tenth, I feel mad keen to get into the lifeboat. Another part of me, just as strong, perhaps stronger, is in a horrid funk."

"Most of us are in a funk when putting to sea in a storm."

"I don't think Mr. Scaife knows what funk is."

"Possibly not."

"He frightens me sometimes. Why was he called the Demon at school?"

"During his second term he lay in wait for a hulking bully and half killed him with a cricket stump."

She gave a little shiver of fear, as she murmured: "Yes, he would do that. He told me the other day that you prevented his being expelled. I asked — how? And he answered: 'John will tell you.' Tell me now."

"It's such ancient history."

"But I want to know."

After more coaxing, John related the incident:

"Scaife had been given his fez, which was supposed to exempt him from fagging. One of the Fifth had a spread in his honour, and some whiskey was drunk. There was a bit of a shindy, and a monitor sent for

Scaife, who refused to go. In a fit of excitement he
drank more whiskey. He had to be put to bed, and
our house-master came in. He asked for the truth,
and I told him that I didn't believe Scaife to be drunk
— and I didn't at the time — but what struck conviction to the soul of our house-master was my blurting
out that I *would* tell a lie to save a pal."

"And Mr. Scaife was really drunk?"

"Well — say half drunk and half mad with rage."

"And now"— she leaned forward, looking at him
with a half-smile upon her face —"would you tell a
lie to save a pal?"

"I suppose so," said John.

"You know you would — a big one, too. And it
would be successful. Well, I hope you'll never try
to deceive me."

"Not likely."

She considered, with her head a little bent, and on
one side. Her smile had subtlety, the expression of
Monna Liza, the smile essentially feminine which is
provoked by an inner vision not vouchsafed to men.
She saw John sane and sweet, as clean in mind as
Scaife was clean of limb. Then she said gravely:

"I could forgive anything except deceit. Hullo!
here's Donald coming to bid you arise and slay."

The keeper strode up, saying excitedly:

"There's a shootable beast lying doun above us."

"A stag? Let me look at him!" exclaimed Sheila.

This part of the moor was never stalked till late in
September, when some stags from a forest which

marched with Strath Armyn were sure to come over. Occasionally a wanderer might be seen earlier.

Donald pulled out his glass, and tried to indicate the exact position of the stag. John heard him saying: "Ye see them peat-hags above the runner?"

"I see miles of peat-hags."

"Tak' the white rockie. Ye'll be seein' that?"

"I see twenty white rockies."

"He's under the knobbie, where the wee bit green grass runs into the hags."

"I have him — I have him!" exclaimed Sheila triumphantly. "What a splendid fellow!"

"He's a monster," said Donald. "It's a peety we haven't a rifle wi' us."

"But I have a camera," said Sheila. She looked askance at John, wondering whether he would sacrifice his afternoon's grousing.

"Could we get in?" demanded John.

"I canna say. He's in a verra commanding poseetion — the brute!"

"I should like to try," said John.

A minute later they started, Donald leading the way. It was necessary to ascend the hill, and then approach the stag down-wind from above. This was the only chance of getting really near the stag, and the wind — which plays queer pranks upon hillsides and corries — was likely to upset the most carefully laid plan. In any case, a long "crawl" was inevitable.

"He'll be verra suspeecious," affirmed Donald.

After half an hour's sharp walking, they were near enough to distinguish points. Donald guessed him to be a ten-pointer at least. He kept moving his head restlessly.

"The midges are disturbing the b-brute," said Donald. "He may be up and awa' any meenit."

Presently, to their dismay, they discovered that farther advance was impossible. The stag commanded all approaches. They lay in the heather and let the midges work their will.

"He'll be feedin' soon," said Donald.

"There's a storm racing up," said John. "Look at the loch!"

To the right, half a mile away, the loch was already lashed into a caldron of foam. Beneath the fury of the wind the water seemed to rise up in feathery clouds which swept over the heather.

Donald knelt down to face it. Sheila and John crouched together as the rain fell torrentially, blotting out the stag and everything else.

"The b-brute canna see us," said Donald. "We may get in the noo."

He began to run uphill, the others following more slowly, for the force of the wind nearly swept Sheila off her feet. She clung to John, and as he held her tight he could feel her body throbbing with excitement.

"Isn't it glorious?" she exclaimed.

Presently they reached a small hollow, into which they sank panting and wet to the skin. They could hear Donald swearing in Gaelic, as he squeezed the water out of the knees of his sodden knickerbockers.

And then, suddenly, the squall passed and the sun streamed out from behind the masses of black cloud. The savage gloom which seemed to have settled eternally upon the landscape vanished as if by enchantment. The wonderful colours, the purple of the heather, the azure of the sky, the green of the grass, shone with ineffable beauty. And the change communicated itself to the face of the girl. A woman revealed herself to John; the child had run away, frightened by the elements.

"I suppose life is like this," she whispered in an awed voice.

Donald pulled out his glass, carefully protecting it from moisture with a waterproof covering. He spied every tussock and hummock near the stag, trying to determine how near they could crawl.

"If we reach yon knobbie —" he said doubtfully. The stag seemed to be staring at the hollow which hid them. "We'll no do it," he added regretfully.

"We must risk his catching us," exclaimed Sheila. "Ah! He's up!"

The stag rose and stood at gaze — truly a magnificent beast. Within a minute, he turned his broad back upon those watching him, and began to feed. Donald made a sign. He wriggled out of the hollow in a serpentine progress uphill. Sheila and John followed noiselessly. The heather was sopping wet after the squall, and the wind blew cold, but little they recked of that discomfort. The thrill of the pursuer approaching his quarry had gripped them. Inch by inch they advanced, in full sight of the stag should he turn his head. Fortunately he didn't. The three reached sanctuary behind the white rocks which Donald had indicated nearly an hour before. They were above him. Donald tried the wind with a bit of cotton-grass. Sheila saw him shaking his head and muttering to himself "The b-b-brute!" They went higher.

Then began the perilous descent down-wind. Sheila loosened the strap of her camera-case, for the stag was out of sight, and — if he were moving — they might come upon him suddenly. All went a-tiptoe, treading where the heather was softest. A stone dislodged, the crackle of a twig, the swish of a too wet boot, would send the stag galloping over the march.

Donald paused, with finger to lip.

"He's lyin' doun," he whispered.

Not sixty yards distant John could see the fork of an antler. Donald sank to the ground, signing to his companions to crouch also. Sheila prepared the camera, while John looked upon sparkling eyes, flushed cheeks, and the admirable lines of a slender figure. And he saw that she was transformed into a boy again, with a boy's enjoyment of the passing minute.

Donald pointed to the knobbie just below. Then he slithered toward it. It seemed incredible that the stag should not hear them. Nevertheless, they reached the knobbie, and peered over a fringe of heather. They could see the back of the stag's head. Sheila adjusted her camera.

"Roar him up," she commanded in a whisper to Donald.

Donald uttered a faint roar, and the stag turned his head without rising. Donald roared again, so convincingly that the stag answered with a louder roar as he rose and faced them, a superb Royal, with a head as wild as the corrie in which he stood. The antlers were almost black, with gleaming white tips, a full yard in span, and a few inches more in length, with the triple points finely outlined against the sky.

Snick!

The stag snorted with surprise. Then he galloped away, back to his own forest, with a story to tell, maybe, of two men and a girl who had stalked him well and truly with nothing more alarming than a square black box.

"Aren't you glad he's alive?" said Sheila.

But Donald looked rather disgusted.

"He'll no come back," he murmured.

They returned to the Lodge to find the Duffer entertaining Miss Bargus with a vivid account of a desperate struggle with a salmon, which in the end had escaped, carrying with it a new Jock Scott. The Duffer affirmed that it must have been a seventeen-pounder at least. In the small study Charles Desmond was writing. Scaife had not come back from the forest.

John went to his room to change. In front of
a glowing peat fire was his bath.   Sitting in it, refreshed
in body and mind, he told himself that he had enjoyed
his day enormously.   Everything had gone right.
He had killed his birds, now much stronger on the
wing, well and cleanly; he had been alone with Sheila
for several hours, and he was experiencing that sense
of well-being which regular exercise, fine air, and
pleasant intercourse are likely to beget in any healthy
young fellow.   He thought of Sheila's expression:
"I can't make myself out."   Obviously, she was not
quite sure of her feeling toward Scaife.   Being her
father's daughter, Scaife's success in everything he
undertook must have impressed her tremendously.
But she admitted that he frightened her.   Nevertheless, he had begun to dominate her thoughts and
speech.   She lugged him in, quoted him, exalted him
— with a pretty, slightly pathetic air of interrogation
— as if she wanted to know more, as if some friendly
spirit was warning her to look well before she leaped
into the gulf.   Presently a servant brought letters,
but John let them lie undisturbed upon the table.
He cared to gaze at nothing less enticing than Sheila's
face which he saw in the heart of the peat fire, and
Sheila's lips, half opened as they murmured: "I'll
shelter you from the blast."

He had finished dressing, when he heard Scaife's
door violently slammed.   A moment later an electric
bell tinkled.   John tied his black tie, slipped on his
dinner jacket, and glanced at the pile of letters.   As

he did so he heard the discreet step of a servant in
the passage outside. He opened the door. The butler
was taking a tray to his master. John waited till the
man came out, and then beckoned to him.

"Mr. Scaife is back?"

"Yes, sir."

"Any luck?"

"Bad luck, sir. Mr. Scaife wounded a fine stag,
followed it, missed it again, followed it all the afternoon, and lost it over the march."

"That doesn't often happen to him."

"No, sir. Can I do anything for you?"

"Nothing, thank you."

The man withdrew with an odd expression upon his
face. He looked frightened. His plump cheeks were
pale. He fidgeted with his fingers as he stood, otherwise impassive, in front of John.

John sat down to read his letters. He opened
a postal telegram first, and stared at the curt message
with stupefaction.

Colonel Jalland died suddenly this morning.

It was signed by the secretary of the New Forest
Conservative Association. Jalland had represented
John's division in Hampshire for many years, and,
being an old and infirm man, it had been understood
that he would retire at the next Dissolution. After
the deed of partnership with Scaife was signed, John
had consented to be put forward as Jalland's successor,

and, during a long conversation with the secretary of
the Conservative Association, it was agreed that
a serious contest impended, and that the campaign
would be strenuous. Throughout the division the
Liberals had been hard at work. Their man was a
carpet-bagger, but a brilliant speaker and a veteran.
Colonel Jalland, as master of the New Forest Hounds
and a large landowner, had qualifications to represent
his constituency, but, secure of his seat, he had not
lifted finger or voice to assure that seat to a successor.

Amongst the letters was one from the secretary,
confirming the telegram, and urging the necessity
of John's presence without delay. It concluded:
"I have made several engagements. Things are
much worse than I supposed. This by-election will
be made a test. Some big guns will open fire at once."

John jumped to his feet, tingling with excitement.
This clarion call meant emancipation, the inalienable
right to fight for the woman he loved. He repeated
her dear name softly, adding his own to it.

"Sheila Verney."

A delightful vitality seemed to stream through his
veins, a new strength which made him rejoice in the
conviction that he could surmount all obstacles between him and Sheila. Words came, the opening
sentences, marshalling themselves in his mind. The
questions long considered, the themes selected and laid
aside, the flotsam and jetsam of political controversy
unconsciously sifted and hoarded, now assumed form
and colour, rising up from some inner zone of conscious-

ness, obedient to command, but inspired first and
last by Sheila.

Before extinguishing the candles on the dressing-
table, he glanced at a new John in the glass, the John
who had worked seven years for this blessed moment.

Crossing the passage, he tapped at Scaife's door.
Scaife answered irritably: "Who's there?"

"John Verney. It's something important."

Scaife growled out: "Come in."

John entered. Scaife was lying upon a sofa; his
boots had been taken off, but he was still in stalking
kit. By his side was a tumbler half full of raw whiskey.
Before John could speak, Scaife rapped out an oath.

"I've had a damnable day! Lost the best stag of
the year. Hit it twice, too, by God!"

He said this with a brutal satisfaction that could
not be mistaken. Then, gulping down some whiskey,
he added: "The cursed rifle missed fire."

He poured out more whiskey. John saw that his
host was half drunk. Probably he had emptied his
flask during the long tramp home when most men feel
suicidal after wounding and losing a fine beast. Probably, also, he had eaten nothing since breakfast.
Then he laughed recklessly.

"Have a drink, old man?"

"No, thank you. Oughtn't you to eat something?"

"Couldn't eat anything." With John standing
looking at him, he plunged into a recital of his mis-
adventures. The damned stalker had blundered;
the damned stag had caught 'em; the damned

sun was blazing along the barrel of the damned Mannlicher! . . .

At the end John said quietly:

"You are quite right not to come down to dinner."

Scaife sat up.

"What d'ye mean? 'Course I'm coming down to dinner. Dinner! Why shouldn't I come down to dinner?"

John hesitated. Some voice, not his own, seemed to be saying: "Don't be a fool! Let him come down to dinner! Let him drink champagne on top of raw whiskey. Let Sheila see him as he is, and as he may be again and again. This is your day. Make the most of the shining hours. One great opportunity has come to you, bringing another. Seize it!"

But instead he said impassively: "Whiskey upon an empty stomach has been a little too much for you."

Scaife jumped up and staggered. He sat down laughing.

"Fact is, when I get mad with rage, drink affects me. Don't you worry!"

He laughed again. His rage had passed. A robustious self-confidence took its place. He took John affectionately by the hand.

"What's your important business, old man?"

"Our member, Colonel Jalland, is dead."

"Is he? That seems important business for him, not you."

John explained.

"You must go to-morrow,"said Scaife, more soberly. "We'll drink your health to-night. And you can count on me, old Jonathan. I'll come down and stir up your foresters. I'll scratch the moss off 'em. You see."

A clock upon the mantelpiece struck eight.

"I must dress," said Scaife. "I'm going to prove to you, old man, that I'm the best pal you've got."

"Scaife," said John impressively, "go to bed. You are worn out; you have a headache: your guests will understand. Don't let the ladies see you to-night!"

"I tell you I'm sober as a judge."

"I tell you, you are as drunk as a lord."

The men confronted each other, their two wills in opposition. John saw that Scaife would be deaf to further persuasion. He saw sparks of rage glow in Scaife's eyes; he saw his strong, too animal jaw set with the determination to do as he pleased: and then, believing firmly that he would prevail, John felt rather than perceived that Scaife was weakening. A moment later he sank back upon the sofa, saying heavily: "My head is splitting. I shall go to bed." As John nodded and turned to leave the room, Scaife called after him:

"You'll vamp up the right lie — eh?"

John nodded.

CHAPTER IX

H E FOUND Sheila alone in the drawing-room, playing the piano. She played charmingly, with great taste and feeling, old-fashioned airs, folk-songs of many countries. John stood beside her, studying her face, which seemed to be losing its look of girlish immaturity. Presently she stopped playing, and, in her turn, glanced at John, perceiving at once that something had happened. She rose from the music-stool, laid her right hand upon John's shoulder and said softly:

"John, you are excited."

"Yes."

"You have news? Is it good or bad?"

"Both." Then he told her of Colonel Jalland's death, and that he must go South. She listened attentively, without taking her eyes from his. Then she said:

"This means that you are leaving us."

"Yes."

"Oh, John! How dreadfully I shall miss you!" She sighed, and then glanced at him.

"Of course you are glad?"

"Glad to leave you." He spoke in a low, constrained tone, but his voice trembled, and Sheila heard it. "Hardly!"

She waited a moment before she said provokingly:

"You will be elected; and Mr. Scaife says that there is a fortune at Verney-Boscobel; and the Chief expects you to marry a nice girl with enough money to lift the mortgage from the dear old Manor."

John, seeing the faint derision in her eyes, answered rather explosively:

"Do you suppose me capable of making a marriage of convenience?"

"Many people do it."

"Do they? Well, I'm incapable of it."

"You will never make a marriage of convenience?"

"Never, never, never!"

"Nor I," said Sheila demurely. "But you have always seemed so matter-of-fact, so — cold."

"Cold?" repeated John. His face flushed, for he remembered at last that he was free, and that Fortune was smiling upon him. Without reflection, spurred to speech by her slightly mocking smile, he said impetuously: "Do you think I don't know what love is?"

"Oh, you know what love is?"

Then he realized what he had done, and knew that the little rogue had beguiled him into a dangerous admission. He tried to assume a nonchalance which in no wise became him.

"Yes. Why not?"

She moved from him, crossing to the fireplace, where she rested one foot upon the fender.

"I see no reason why you shouldn't love. I hope your love is returned. Do I happen to know the person who has inspired this — this wonderful love!"

From pink John's cheeks turned to red, as he replied hesitatingly:

"The person doesn't know — or guess."

"That's not an answer to my question. Do I know the girl? I suppose she is a girl?" As John held his tongue, she added falteringly: "Oh, John, I thought we were real pals; I thought you trusted me. Evidently you don't."

When his eyes fell before hers, she gave a scornful laugh, and went back to the piano, humming a tune. The desperate John pursued her.

"Sheila."

"Yes?"

"Shall I tell you whom I love? Shall I?"

"As you please."

He hesitated for an instant, but his voice rang out clear and steady, with all the quality of a fine bell.

"I love you — I've always loved you, ever since you were a child. I've never cared a hang for any one else. I couldn't. The Chief thinks I'm ambitious. I'm ambitious for you. I loathe the idea of cutting Verney-Boscobel to ribbons. But it meant, perhaps, you. I hate going away from here, because it means leaving you."

The music in his voice thrilled her. She closed her eyes for an instant. A faint exclamation fluttered from between her parted lips.

"I think of you by day and night, Sheila. When you were in France, you always came to me in my dreams."

"Oh!"

He saw that she was pale and trembling. In a sorrowful voice he continued: "I ought not to have spoken. But I'm leaving to-morrow. Forgive me."

"But there is nothing to forgive. If you want me, dear, I'm yours."

He gazed at her stupidly.

She smiled, as she murmured: "And, of course, I knew you cared for me all the time."

He caught her to him, kissing her eyes and lips, but even at this supreme moment he noticed that she accepted his kisses without returning them. What surged within him was as yet unborn in her. Very gently she released herself, whispering:

"The others may come in at any moment."

"What shall I say to your father?"

"Nothing; I'll say it."

"He must be told to-night."

"Of course. After dinner he will go to the study. I shall pop in. You must give me a few minutes."

"He may be very angry."

"John, we have him on toast. He has said again and again that you must marry a woman with money. Well, I have a nice little fortune which my godfather left to me. And Daddy has told me that I must marry the right man. I'm sure you're the right man. You're exactly right, dear Jonathan. Wait a moment; I want to find something."

She turned over a number of magazines and newspapers, piled high upon a table in the corner of the
room.   Presently, with a triumphant laugh, she held
up a review.

"I knew it was here," she said.   "Now, listen to
this!"

Standing in front of John, blushing with excitement,
she read the following passage from the article written
by Desmond, and particularly recommended to his
daughter's consideration:

> "The vital question of the proper selection of a mate, with
> a due regard to heredity and environment, with a due regard, also,
> to character, temperament, and a common interest in similar occu-
> pations and pastimes. . . ."

"What is this?" asked John.

"Daddy's own words — pure gold — which I have
read, marked, learned, and inwardly digested.   I
shall floor him with this after he has had his coffee
and his cigar.   You see?"

As she spoke, she appeared more like a mischievous
boy than a woman in love.   John said anxiously:

"Sheila, are you quite sure?"

"Sure of what?"

"That you love me?"

"Didn't I say that I meant to marry you the first
day we met?"

"You have remembered that?"

"Always."

A moment later, Penelope sailed into the room,

followed by the Duffer. When Charles Desmond appeared, John explained curtly that Scaife had left upon the hill a wounded stag and brought home a bad headache. A few questions provoked by Scaife's indisposition were put to flight by the news of Colonel Jalland's death. Throughout dinner nothing else was discussed, and John was made to understand that he had become the hero of the hour. Scaife, so to speak, dwindled into an attenuated shade. When Sheila remarked pensively: "I'm glad that Mr. Scaife was so affected by the wounding of his stag," John replied: "Yes, yes, it upset him terribly."

Charles Desmond related some electioneering experiences.

"Once," he began, "an unspeakable Scot was heckling me, and as he was remarkably well informed upon a subject of which I knew little, I could see the favourable impression that I had produced on the audience slowly oozing away. In short, my dear Duffer, I found myself up a tree with no branches, and a bear below waiting to annihilate me."

"Awful," said the Duffer.

"I am quite sure," Penelope observed, "that you slid down that tree, dear Charles, with your usual grace and agility."

Sheila glanced at John. Her expression said plainly. "More butter!"

Charles Desmond continued with a gracious smile of acknowledgment:

"I had an inspiration. The fellow heckling me was at the other end of the hall. I said in a loud voice: 'Will the gentleman kindly come forward?' He did so. I advanced to meet him, laughed, and shook him by the hand. 'Sir,' said I, with a slight Irish brogue, 'it's delighted I am to meet a foeman worthy of my steel.' He was so astonished that he became dumb. The audience cheered both of us, and quite forgot that I had not answered his main question. The touch of blarney did it."

"I've not kissed the Blarney Stone," said John ruefully.

The Duffer laughed, but he added half apologetically:

"Is blarney necessary?"

"It's part of the game," said Charles Desmond. John murmured: "I hope I shan't be badly heckled."

"We shall stand by you. They tell me that Reginald Scaife on the stump is a wonder. You are certain to get in."

"But if there is a Dissolution I shall have to stand again within the year."

"That is rather hard luck, but it can't be helped."

Presently the ladies retired. The Duffer discreetly followed them.

"Now that we are alone," Desmond said, "I should like to touch on one or two matters." His voice was grave, and John fancied that he detected a slight inflection of nervousness.

"Certainly, sir."

"Are you going to preach Tariff Reform?"

"No."

"I am glad of that," Desmond declared. "How about education?"

"I remember what Lecky said: 'In England extreme enthusiasm for education is combined with an utter disregard for the opinions of the educated classes.'"

"Absolutely true. The fact that you are a distinguished Oxford man is against you. Don't touch the burning questions till you are forced to do so. Travel along the line of least resistance. I have always done so."

John nodded, as Desmond continued with a geniality which could not quite conceal his uneasiness:

"To be quite frank, you and I must prepare for changes. We can no longer rely on party shibboleths. The country is becoming daily more democratic." Then, hurriedly, perceiving from the expression of John's face that the ice was rather thin, this practised skater skimmed on: "Attack the Opposition. Describe them as split up into factions with conflicting interests. Give the Little Englanders grape and shrapnel. Your people know you, John, and your manner my dear fellow, is very reassuring. You speak with conviction. Yes, yes, deal with the facts."

"I should prefer that."

"I look upon this election as mine, Jonathan. I am as keen about your victory as if you were my son."

When he rose, he held out his hand, which John grasped.

As soon as he reached the study, Charles Desmond lit a fresh cigar. The prospect of John's election pleased him, and sorry as he would be to lose a clever and indefatigable secretary, it was just as well, perhaps, on Sheila's account that John should go.

He was thinking of Sheila, trying to envisage her as Scaife's wife, when he heard her tap at the door. He had come to the conclusion that the member for Samarkand was likely to win whatever he wanted; and Desmond was reasonably sure that he wanted Sheila. Scaife might be persuaded to buy a house in Arlington Street, something distinctive, a mansion with traditions, hard to come by, but a valuable asset. St. James's Square might do. To establish a new party meant entertaining upon a princely scale. It was more than ever necessary to "feed the brutes." How well the Whigs had understood that!

"Come in," he said.

Sheila entered. Desmond's uplifted eyebrows expressed surprise, but he failed to notice that Sheila was carrying a review soberly bound. She perched herself upon the arm of his chair, and began to stroke his hair.

"I want to talk to you," she began.

"What about?"

He could not see that her eyes were twinkling mischievously.

"About the proper selection of a mate."

"Oh, indeed?"

"With a due regard to heredity and environment, and —— "

"What rubbish is this?"

"Pure gold, every word of it.   Your own."

She waved the review before him as if it were an oriflamme.

"Bless me!   Yes, yes, I had forgotten."

"You told me to read it carefully."

"And I hope you have done so."

"I have.   It's opened my eyes."

"Good!"

"To the appalling dangers of marrying the wrong man.   You want me to marry the real right man, Daddy, don't you?"

"I do, I do."

"Well, I've found him."

Charles Desmond chuckled.   Then he turned and kissed the face so like Cæsar's.

"That's splendid," he said.

"You can guess who it is?"

He chuckled again.

"I think so."

Sheila jumped from her perch, ran to the door, and opened it.

"You can come in, John; it's all right."

Charles Desmond jumped up almost as quickly, confronting John and Sheila, who stood before him, looking uncommonly like culprits.   His eyes were sparkling angrily; upon his fine forehead blazed a flush of amazement and indignation. Sheila faltered out: "Daddy, aren't you pleased?"

"Pleased? Have you two dared to become engaged to each other?"

"Acting upon your advice," said Sheila.

"My advice?"

"You advised John to find a wife with a little money and you told me —— "

Desmond held up his hand, enjoining silence, as he turned to John. "I'll deal with you, sir, first. You have taken advantage of a silly and inexperienced girl."

"He hasn't," said Sheila.

"I trusted you. It's inconceivable that you should have betrayed that trust."

"He didn't."

Sheila continued vehemently:

"Do you think I'm going to stand here dumb, while you accuse him of making love to me? I made love to him."

She laughed softly, pursing up her lips into a tiny grimace.

"I knew how it was with him from the beginning. He adored me when I smelt of bread and butter. And when I came back from Paris, when he saw me with my hair up and in my new frocks, he gave himself away whenever he looked at me."

"Nothing of the sort," said John firmly.

"But he would have held his tongue and left us, if I hadn't hurled myself at his head. There!"

Her father, apparently unmoved, said dryly.

"Have you anything more to say?"

"Yes, lots; but I'll wait and hear what you say first."

The Chief turned to his secretary.

"You are not in a position to support my daughter."

"Not yet," said John.

"Is there any reason why I should not dismiss you, here and now?"

"There's me," faltered Sheila. She slipped to her father's side, placed her hand upon his arm, and said imploringly: "Darling Daddy!"

"Let go."

"I can't. My head is going round and round."

Then he saw that she had become as white as milk, and that her limbs were trembling. He felt her weight upon his arm.

"Pull yourself together, Sheila," said John. Then he added anxiously: "I believe she is fainting."

Together, the two men supported the limp figure of the girl to the sofa. Placed upon this, Sheila began laughing and sobbing.

"Hysterics," exclaimed Desmond. "I must be firm with her." He bent over the sofa, and said angrily: "Stop it! Stop it, I say!" Then, finding that the sobs were increasing instead of diminishing, he muttered to John: "Can't you do something?"

"Am I likely to succeed when you fail?" said John.

A pause followed. Desmond smiled faintly. The

pleasant, genial expression came back to his handsome face. He bent over the sofa and murmured: "Sheila, you poor little thing, I didn't mean to be unkind."

Sheila sobbed bitterly.

"Shall I fetch Miss Bargus?" demanded John.

"Not yet. I've upset her. I never spoke harshly to the child before." He kissed the tip of her ear, all that was visible of a face hidden in the pillow. "No — confound it! — blandishments are wasted. Why, the whole room's shaking!"

John said tentatively: "Let me try."

"Try what?"

"Blandishments."

"Certainly not, but speak to her, tell her to be reasonable."

John knelt down beside the sofa.

"Sheila?"

Sheila exposed one third of a tear-stained face, and murmured: "What a hateful world it is!"

"What does she say, John?"

"She says it's a hateful world."

"I was so happy this afternoon," added Sheila, struggling to a sitting posture, and wiping the tears from her eyes.

"For pity's sake, don't go off again!" entreated her father.

"Cæsar always hoped that I would marry John," she faltered.

Desmond's face softened. He said tenderly:

"My dear child, if you are strong enough to go to

your room, please do so. I'll talk matters over with John."

"You won't be horrid to him?"

"No, no."

She kissed him and glanced at John, shrugging her pretty shoulders, which shone white out of a dark gown, as she said solemnly: "I never felt so miserable in all my life."

With that she left the room.

"You see — a child!"

John nodded.

"A baby! I never realized how young she was till to-night." He paused. "I married too young; a blunder! Look here, John, forgive me for what I said just now in the heat of the moment. I ought to have foreseen this, but — didn't."

"Nor did I," said John.

"The little baggage forced our hands. Well, my boy, you are leaving to-morrow, and perhaps it's as well. There must be no engagement for a year at least. After that, if you are both of a mind, and if your affairs have mended somewhat, we'll see."

"Thank you, sir."

"Shall you or I make this plain to the little rogue?"

"You can trust me to do that."

Next day Scaife drove John to Lairg, taking with him no chauffeur. He prided himself upon being independent of chauffeurs, and understood to perfection the working of his car. Also, as he remarked

at starting, he wished to talk with John. As soon as
the car was running properly, he said cordially:

"You did me a service last night. I shan't forget
it. As a matter of fact, I take jolly good care of myself. It's obvious that I must be as fit as a fiddle to
do what I do. But yesterday my temper got the
upper hand. And you saved a scene. We won't
mention it again. Now about this election of yours.
The cadging for votes must begin at once. I shall
cancel my shooting engagements and join you within
ten days. By that time you'll be ready to tackle the
towns. What towns have you?"

"Lymington and Romsey are the most important."

"I suppose Desmond told you to go for the
Opposition?"

"He did."

"The old campaigner knows the value of abuse.
Give 'em — Hades!"

"Being quite beyond reproach in our own heaven,
we can do so," replied John.

Scaife said seriously enough:

"You're much too squeamish, Jonathan. I remember you refused to use cribs at Harrow. I got
my removes by using 'em, and when I told my old
Daddy about it, he declared that I'd taken after him."

"What's bred in the flesh comes out in the *Bohn*."

"Not bad that. Don't forget to crack a few jokes
with your rustics. And, look here, can't you catch a
few Socialists?"

"They don't play about in the Forest."

"I suppose not." He eyed John with something of the interrogation which Charles Desmond had exhibited; and he was thinking: "Can we carry this parson's son with us?" Aloud he said keenly: "Of course you must offer the poor man something."

"Which he hasn't earned?"

"He must be offered something, I repeat."

"When you come, I shall present his best friend." Scaife laughed.

"Your local popularity ought to get you in."

"I don't know that I am popular."

"That's rot," said Scaife roughly. "I didn't trot in and out of Boscobel for nothing. The affection of your tenants is a trump card. I shall make use of it, I warn you."

"But how?"

"In the papers I control. This carpet-bagger is an ugly old devil. I shall print his photograph beside yours, with appropriate comments."

"Scaife, I don't want to snag success."

"Pooh! All's fair in love and politics."

"I don't think so."

"Well, in this case there'll be no need for any snagging."

At Lairg the station-master told Scaife that he had received his telegram, and that a coupé to Inverness had been reserved. When John protested, Scaife slapped him on the shoulder.

"It's my affair. I knew you would want to be alone."

As the train left the station, John, leaning out of the window, could see Scaife smiling and waving his hands. The very train seemed to be obeying him. Years ago, at Harrow, John had dreamed of Scaife infinitely magnified — a Titan. To-day the dream seemed to have become reality. John beheld himself a Gulliver dandled in Brobdingnagian arms.

Throughout the long tedious journey to Perth he ought to have been planning his campaign, but he could think only of Sheila. She loved him — not Scaife! The unexpectedness of it was intoxicating.

CHAPTER X

PASSING through London, John bought a present for Sheila. Under the circumstances he could not send her a ring, which he would have liked to do, or any valuable trinket; but he managed to expend what was for him a considerable sum upon a very perfect Caughley dish of the famous willow pattern. Sheila had a modest collection of old English pottery, not being able to afford porcelain. The dish carried upon it the pretty story so familiar to collectors. Chang, the secretary of a Mandarin, whose house is on the right of the dish, falls in love with Li-Chi, his chief's daughter. The lady sends a message that she expects Chang when the willow-leaf begins to fall. John knew that Sheila would understand that he, in his turn, hoped to appear as an accredited lover before the leaves fell twice in the New Forest. According to the Chinese legend, the lovers married and lived happily till they died, when the gods changed them into two doves, which are sometimes to be seen flying together in the Caughley reproductions.

Then he told himself that for Sheila's sake he must give undivided energies and attention to his election. Of his first essay there is nothing dramatic to record.

To quote *Scaife's Daily*, the Unionist "romped in."
His opponent, a Lancashire cotton-spinner, with the
preposterous name of Towlerson, was a veteran politician of much ability, who had bought a small place
in the New Forest some two years before the election.
Old-established families, like the Mottisfonts, the
Bowkers, the Pundles, and the Jallands, spoke of
Towlerson as "impossible." They called upon the
carpet-bagger and his wife — and that was the end
of it. John, upon the other hand, was beloved — as
Miss Pundle put it — by the friends who had known
him all his life. His loss of fortune had inspired an
immense sympathy throughout the Forest. Admiral
Pundle voiced the sense of the division when he went
about muttering: "We must help John over his first
stile." Immense posters revealed two men — one
young, smiling, and good to look at; the other almost
grotesquely old and ugly. Beneath the two figures was
inscribed the question: "Are you going to vote for
the man you know, or for the stranger who was defeated in his own country?" Towlerson had been
beaten in a big fight in Lancashire.

To John's dismay and exasperation, the campaign
was fought upon personal lines. Like many another
gallant fellow, he found himself at the mercy of too
zealous friends. Scaife roared with laughter when he
saw the candidate's blushes, and, indeed, the blushes
of an ingenuous young man secure many votes. At
one of the meetings the unfortunate Towlerson ven-
tured to observe that he had nothing against Mr.

Verney except his inexperience. "He has never been tried," he concluded. A voice from the back of the hall shouted: "You have, old man, and convicted too, by golly!" Then it transpired that Towlerson, in his hot youth, had suffered durance vile as a first-class misdemeanant for some offence connected with strikes. John alienated some supporters by saying publicly that his opponent's incarceration had illustrated his courage, which was true; but Scaife, who spoke after John, remarked derisively that none would begrudge Mr. Towlerson the "courage of his convictions."

Throughout the contest little reference was made to Free Trade or Tariff Reform. John "romped in" because he was Verney of Verney-Boscobel, and because Scaife rubbed this fact into the electorate.

"You owe much to Scaife," said Desmond, after the election.

When the result was announced, Towlerson came forward and congratulated John with dignity; but he looked worn, and John felt much sympathy for him and his wife, who had worked very hard. Tears glistened in her faded eyes as she murmured, faintly smiling: "We shall try again, Mr. Verney."

After the election the Radical papers asserted that Towlerson had been ill-treated and maligned. Towlerson achieved a master-stroke by denying this. He submitted that the Foresters were justified in choosing a young man of parts whom they knew intimately. He hoped that the day might come when his new

neighbours would, perhaps, know and like him a little
better.

Some pleasant weeks followed, but the approaching
General Election and the ever-increasing apprehension
of a Liberal victory began to engage the attention of all
Unionists. Meantime, John had not seen Sheila
since the morning when they parted at Strath Armyn.
She was paying visits to her relations, and from place
after place she wrote charming letters to John, which
were answered by return of post. John never questioned her loyalty. She was morally bound to him;
he was morally bound to her. Whenever he thought
of her as his, he became conscious of an increase of
strength. Sometimes he had an odd feeling of regret
that she had been won so easily. There had been no
fight, and he had expected a fight — a long fight with
the odds against him.

Parliament was dissolved in mid-winter, and immediately John knew that his second contest was
likely to be quite other than the first. Scaife and Desmond had no time to devote to a man who, surely,
would be re-elected, and, as each day passed, it became
more and more evident that the temper of John's
own people had changed. For no reason assignable, he
had become less popular. His opponent, on the other
hand, must have divined that the pendulum was
swinging toward him. He was received with unmistakable enthusiasm.

Then one of John's supporters made a grievous
blunder. The fact that she was a woman mitigated the

offence without diminishing the consequences. With indiscreet zeal, she attempted to catch votes by waving the red rag of John's gentility in the face of the electorate. John was a gentleman! Towlerson's supporters grasped the opportunity. An immense poster, a clever caricature of John as an overdressed "blood," adorned the boardings, with the legend: "This is a *Gentleman*. If you vote for the working man's representative, you won't get into Society!"

Upon the morning after this appeared, *Scaife's Daily* burst upon the world the now historical pronouncement of Scaife's allegiance to the People. He had been unopposed in Samarkand. In a remarkable speech to his constituents he pointed out that as an employer of labour his sympathies were, and always had been, with the workers. Henceforward he would fight under the Radical banner. This declaration was made at the moment when it had become certain that the Liberals would be returned with an overwhelming majority. Scaife wrote a short letter to John:

"My dear old Jonathan:

"You, I know, will understand that, as an honest man, I have been driven to sacrifice my independence. I loathe party politics as much as you do, but the country is not ready yet to cut loose from thraldom. The Conservatives have played havoc with two glorious opportunities to advance upon true Progressive lines: first, when Lord Shaftesbury passed the Factory Acts, and, secondly, when Randolph Churchill indicated the possibilities of a magnificent Tory democracy. Anyway, I am obeying my conscience — and there is nothing more to be said.

"Yours, as ever,

"Reginald Scaife."

By the same post came a longer epistle from Sheila. John tried to read between the lines of it indignation at Scaife's defection, but he concluded that Scaife had been able to justify his action both in Sheila's eyes and in the eyes of her father.

The Caterpillar, who seldom put pen to paper, wrote a few lines also. He was fond of saying that if he lacked brains to think things out, he knew enough to associate with those who did. What he wrote, therefore, may be taken as a crystallization of what was said at the *Celibates*.

"Scaife," he wrote, "swaggered into the club this morning, and five fellows got up and marched out! I hope he liked it. I sat tight, because the Governor and I are beholden to him, and you can't get away from that — worse luck! He had the cheek to ask me for my opinion. I gave it to him. 'Surely,' says I, 'you must realize that you're going straight to hell.' That rather staggered him, so I rubbed it in. I went on: 'You may deceive a lot of people cleverer than I am, but you won't deceive Old Scratch — and don't you forget it!' He tried to laugh it off, but he was impressed. Of course, he's ratted because our people wouldn't give a peerage to the old man. At least, that's what they say. Anyway, he's labelled now as a d —— d demagogue. What the deuce are you going to do with him as a partner?"

John took that question to bed with him, and passed an uneasy night. What was he going to do? And what would Desmond do?

Desmond was being acclaimed at the moment by such papers as the *Scrutator* as the pattern of what a Conservative Free Trader should be. Also he had won his old seat, although with a reduced majority. Even the *Morning News* admitted that Charles Desmond embellished the House of Commons, now to be transformed — as a wit put it — into the House of Awfully Commons.

Meanwhile, John's own fight was becoming more arduous. Despite the comforting optimism of his agent, he was beginning to consider the possibility of defeat. Towlerson seemed to have acquired a happy knack of finding the right word. He had "starved." He had "walked the streets of Liverpool without a penny in his pocket." When these facts made their teeth meet in the tough intelligence of the Foresters, John was beset with absurd and irrelevant questions, such as: "Ever been hungry, Mr. Verney?" Or with scathing irony: "Price o' bread never made no difference to 'ee, did it?"

One elector, whom John had often employed, remarked: "I bain't goin' to vote for 'ee this time, Master John. I voted last time — yes, I did. But I allers votes first for one side and then for t'other. 'Tis only fair, seemin'ly!"

At this second election Tariff Reform had become the dominant issue, and John's arguments in favour of it as applied to England were not quite convincing — and he knew it. Towlerson was a dyed-in-the-wool Free Trader of enormous experience. Moreover,

the Unionists presented no comprehensive scheme, and
suggestions for tinkering with this industry or that,
economic experiments fortified by the absurd assumption that Protection would wipe out unemployment,
were torn to tatters by a man who possessed encyclo-
pædic knowledge of the textile industries.

John faced the hecklers gallantly, but his agent
complained that he lacked ginger.

"Pitch it stronger," he said, with some warmth.
"Promise 'em plenty of milk and honey. You lost
a lot of votes by insisting that thriftlessness is the
curse of the English labourer."

"Isn't it?"

"Of course it is. But sticking your thumb hard
upon the soft spot of a baby's head won't make it
stop howling."

"You believe in soothing syrup?"

"For the howling babies, yes. They are babies.
Argument is wasted on 'em."

"They seem to derive some nourishment from
Towlerson's."

"I say — 'Strip and sail in.'"

John smiled derisively.

"I feel rather bare, I can assure you."

"I go into these fights feeling that I want to hit
every Rad on the nose. They think you don't care.
They're beginning to see you as the fine gentleman.
I should like to flog that woman!"

During the last three days the Pundles and the Jallands and the Mottisfonts took the field, some in

motor-cars, others in more antiquated equipages. Word had been passed round that the issue was trembling in the balance. Fury inflamed John's neighbours and friends, but, alas! they rushed into the combat better armed with enthusiasm than argument. Many Tories raised the moth-eaten banner: *Down with the Carpet-Bagger!* But Towlerson was no longer regarded as a carpet-bagger. The story of his conviction as a disturber of the peace redounded very much to his credit when it came to be sifted. Finally it leaked out that his operatives in Lancashire had shared in the profits of a prosperous business, and that Towlerson was really entitled to call himself philanthropist. Hide-bound Tories admitted that he had taken his licking like a man. The result of the poll was declared at Lymington.

John's supporters gathered in force and splendour upon the balcony of the Angel Hotel, which is next to the Town Hall. Mrs. Giles Mottisfont, a smart London lady, appeared in a startling costume of dark blue and yellow, John's colours. Admiral Pundle, of Pundle Green, stood beside her, twising his heavy white moustache. Sir Giles Mottisfont, the smart lady's father-in-law, kept on saying to those about him: "We've done our best — eh? I think the Forest is to be trusted — what? Look at our people, sir!"

"Our people" seemed to fill the wide street. Certainly blue and yellow flamed everywhere. The scarlet of Towlerson was encouragingly absent. An incident illustrated the temper of the crowd. At

one of the windows a boy and a girl were seated side
by side. The maid flew the popular blue and yellow;
the youth sported a scarlet rosette. Suddenly the
youth tried to snatch the maid's colours; and a very
pretty struggle followed, ending with the victory of
the girl, who captured the red badge and flung it
disdainfully into the street below. The crowd cheered
tremendously. Sir Giles murmured complacently:
"Yes, yes, straws indicate the direction and strength
of the current. We deserve success, because we have
earned it." He expanded his fine chest, smiled mag-
nanimously, and became rather red in the face. From
the crowd below came a shrill voice: "Don't you git
too excited, old feller, or you may bust yerself!"

Behind drawn blinds, in a large room upon the first
story of the Town Hall, the votes were being counted
and recounted. It was unofficially announced that
the result would not be made known before two o'clock.
And then everybody seemed to realize that the finish
would be thrilling. Admiral Pundle went for a stroll
through the ancient town, being unable to stand still
in moments of excitement. As he walked, he eyed
with approval the solid appearance of the Georgian
houses, and the general air of time-mellowed respec-
tability. He descended slowly to the river, and gazed
sentimentally at the fine landscape upon the farther
shore. As a collector of prints, he had a nice eye for
delicate tones. When he was entreated to repair the
leaky roofs of his cottages, he usually pleaded his constitutional inability to destroy the exquisite colouring

of Time. He owned some property in Lymington, a few houses here and there, very picturesque but sadly dilapidated. He looked at them now, stroking his moustache and reflecting: "Only a Vandal would alter 'em."

Men touched their hats to him as he strolled and women bobbed. When he had passed, the men growled out: "Rare old pincher, he is," and the women added: "A fine figure of a man still." Twice during this stately progress the Admiral paused to ask hoarsely:

"They can't turn out a Verney, can they? Impossible — hay?"

That a Verney might be turned out by a Towlerson because he and his old friend, Sir Giles Mottisfont, had failed to do their duty in that particular station of life to which it had pleased Omnipotence to call them did not occur to him. Upon the contrary, he and Sir Giles were convinced, each in his degree, that by them nothing was left undone which ought to be done. The Admiral — unlike most sailors — shone conspicuous in the hunting-field. He looked magnificent on his old bay hunter; he had the finest hands in the world. Beholding him, even the thoughtless reflected sadly that the veteran belonged to a generation that bred the real right thing. When he died, everybody would attend his funeral, and gentle and simple would murmur regretfully: "We shall not see his like again."

The comedy of the matter lies in the fact that hitherto the Admiral had imposed his self-complacency and self-satisfaction upon others. He had been taken at his own valuation, swallowed whole, gulped down, perhaps with a twisted mouth or a winking eye, but ultimately absorbed and assimilated as stout nourishing stuff.

Within half an hour he returned to the balcony. Sir Giles led him apart and whispered portentously:

"That damn fellow is creeping up."

"They can't turn out a Verney."

"No, no. I'm going to order a glass of sloe gin; will you join me?"

"With pleasure."

Outside, the crowd had grown rather sullen, tired of waiting so long. Oddly enough, there seemed to be more red rosettes. And then, with dramatic significance, the window above the room wherein the votes were being counted was flung up, and a long red riband fluttered forth. Hoarse cries arose instantly. What did this mean? Sir Giles, craning his short neck, beheld the detestable streamer, and exclaimed loudly:

"What damnable impudence!"

"Towlerson for ever!" yelled a voice.

Mrs. Giles Mottisfont whispered to Mrs. Pundle: "There are more red rosettes. I'm certain of it."

A pencilled note from John informed Sir Giles that the majority in either case would be very small. The autocrat of many acres gasped.

"I won't believe it," he said gallantly.

Inside the room, where the votes were being counted, ten tables had been placed, and at each sat the counters, one a Radical, the other a Unionist. The votes were done up in neat packages of twenty-five. Through the closed windows one could hear the cries of the excited crowd. The atmosphere grew intolerably hot and stuffy.

John's agent, an eager little man, not unlike a weasel, darted from table to table, jotting down figures. Towlerson sat beside his wife. John saw that more than once she touched him with her hand, and nodded encouragingly. The strain was so great on her that she had to do something.

The High Sheriff was also present, ready to announce the result of the poll. Presently, after many whisperings, he came up to John and held out his hand. "You've just pulled through," he said. "Nearest thing I ever knew."

"Have I?" said John.

Somehow, this second triumph was not so intoxicating as the first. Then he saw his opponent coming toward him. And at that moment one of the officials exclaimed in a loud voice:

"There has been a mistake."

"A mistake?"

The High Sheriff muttered something unparliamentary. "The votes at one table have been done up in packages of twenty instead of twenty-five."

"What difference does that make?"

"We have estimated the final result by packages, Mr. Sheriff."

"Mr. Verney polled twice as many votes at that

particular table, two packages to one, if not more. It may make a difference."

"Do them up properly," said the High Sheriff testily.

John saw his agent licking his pencil and frowning. Then he began to scribble, and the frown upon his sharp face deepened. When a few more minutes had passed, the High Sheriff said curtly:

"Mr. Towlerson has a majority of eleven."

John pulled himself together, and smiled at Towlerson.

"You see, we do know you and like you better," he said pleasantly.

Towlerson gripped his hand, as the High Sheriff threw up the big window to the right, and asked the candidates to stand one on each side of him. The crowd began to roar, but the High Sheriff imposed silence, and then the result was made known. Once more the protagonists shook hands, but the crowd refused to believe their ears.

"Verney for ever!" they shouted.

Towlerson tried to speak, but quite in vain. Then John asked for a hearing. He was very pale, but something in his face quieted the rioters.

"I have been beaten in a square fight," John declared:

"No, no," shouted the good people of Lymington.

Further speech became impossible. Even upon the balcony of the Angel, county magnates were seething and raging. Consternation was depicted upon every flushed face. The agent appeared amongst them, and said contemptuously, in reply to a question from Admiral Pundle:

"How do I account for it? Easily. You all slacked; took the result for granted."

Sir Giles Mottisfont said in sepulchral tones:

"There has been dirty work done by somebody."

Admiral Pundle shouted fiercely:

"We shall demand a recount."

"There has been a recount. That's what delayed us."

"This damned fellow has bribed a lot of voters, sir. Don't talk to me, sir — I know. We'll have a Petition."

"In my experience," said the agent coldly, "I have never assisted at an election fought with such courtesy and honesty on both sides."

"There's John," said Mrs. Giles. "What an ovation he's getting!"

Presently, the defeated candidate was carried to a motor, which was hauled round the town. Men cheered, women wept. Lymington, in short, went mad with excitement and disappointment.

Twenty minutes later, Sheila was reading a telegram in Eaton Square:

" Beaten by 11.—JOHN."

CHAPTER XI

A FREE-TRADE LEAFLET

JOHN went up to town next day, and called upon the Desmonds in the afternoon. He neither looked nor felt unduly depressed, because he had cheered himself up with the reflection that Fortune seldom comes to a man with both hands full. Sheila was his, and the estuary lots were booming. Moreover (thanks to Scaife again), he had let the Boscobel shooting for a sum nearly twice as much as he had hitherto received.

Trinder, with a melancholy smile, ushered him into the library, and a moment later Sheila rushed into his arms.

"My poor darling Jonathan!" she cried.

"Poor? I am rich beyond dreams of avarice in the possession of you. Hang the election!"

She kissed him repeatedly: and then sat beside him, holding his hand and patting it with a gesture oddly maternal. Her greeting, her sympathy, her desire to comfort him, could not possibly have been warmer. When John laughed, she said with pride:

"You are a good loser."

"It was a knock," John admitted, "but we rather slacked. I've learned my lesson."

Then he saw that she looked pale and thin. He took her face between his hands and stared at it.

"I say, aren't you a bit thin?"

"Am I? I dare say. This election has not been very fattening for Daddy and me. By the way, Jonathan, Mr. Scaife is upstairs and full of plans for you."

"Upstairs — is he?"

She added hurriedly:

"Of course Daddy and I are convinced that he is absolutely sincere. He found it impossible to vote for Tariff Reform, and at Strath Armyn, you remember, he told us that his sympathies were with the people."

"Has he talked much to you?"

"Now and then. He talks very well."

"No doubt of that."

"Even Daddy listens attentively to what he says."

"Sheila, you have not been ill, have you?"

"What an idea! I've never been ill in my life."

"You wrote me such delightful letters."

She blushed again. Was it with pleasure or embarrassment?

"I'm glad you liked them."

"Mine were rather dull," continued John. "You see, I couldn't write exactly what I felt ——"

"Nor could I," she interrupted.

"And so I stuck more or less to politics and business. The politics are rather knocked on the head, but the business — I say, Sheila, do you know that I'm going to make pots of money?"

"How splendid!"

She spoke enthusiastically, adding: "Please tell me everything." As she said this, she remembered that John seldom spoke of himself and his future. Scaife, on the other hand, had filled her mind with his personal hopes and ambitions, possibly the most subtle flattery which a clever man can offer to a pretty and intelligent girl. It annoyed her slightly that Jonathan should be so reserved. Was it just possible that he considered her to be too immature for such confidence? An older woman would have known that John's silence was due to his modesty, and the sense of his limitations. Sheila said impulsively:

"You know, John, it's worried me a tiny bit that you have never talked to me really intimately about your — ambitions." She paused before she brought out the high-sounding word.

"My ambitions!" He laughed, pressing her hand. "Why, Sheila, how could I count my chickens when I hadn't even the eggs to hatch 'em from?"

"I see. Now you have the eggs."

"Also, talk is generally rather cheap, but most particularly futile when there is nothing to talk about."

She made a tiny grimace, displaying the dimples upon each side of her mouth.

"It's delightful talking about to-morrow."

"I have had to concentrate my attention on to-day. But now"— he drew a deep breath of

satisfaction — "I can talk about to-morrow.   In fact,
I feel justified in asking your father to consent to a
formal engagement."

"Oh! How I wish he would!"

As she sighed out the words, John told himself
that the loss of his election was indeed a trivial matter.
In a warm voice, drawing closer to her, he began to
speak of their possible future.   "We shall be able to
live at Boscobel."

"At Boscobel? At the Manor?"

"No, no, not yet. It's let for another five years.
But we can build a charming bungalow overlooking
the estuary, high up amongst the trees. I've found
the very place, under the 'singing' pines. I lay there
gloating for half an hour last Sunday."

"Wasn't it rather cold?"

"Cold? I was thinking of you. We shall be as
happy as larks."

A wrinkle showed between her brows. Did John
really take it for granted that Charles Desmond's
daughter could be perfectly happy buried alive in the
country?

"Two Arcadians. Forest lovers," he added, with
a flying allusion to a book that had delighted him.

But he perceived faint shadows in Sheila's eyes.

"There will be any amount to do," he went on,
not quite understanding her silence.

"For me?" she asked gently.

He stared at her in silence, not at a loss for words,
because his heart was overflowing with them, but

dumb with the difficulty of picking and choosing. The deep and tender issues of life had been enshrined so long that he hardly dared to reveal them. He tried to behold in her the mother of his children, but saw only the virgin, who might still pass as a pretty boy. He flushed as he noted the delicate texture of her skin, the eyes so limpidly pure. Some instinct urged him to speak with ardour of the work which she might find to do. As he hesitated, Sheila said with eagerness:

"Don't you want to go into Parliament and to get office and all that?"

"All that may come."

"May?" She repeated the word impatiently. "It won't come unless you plot and plan for it. If you bury yourself at Boscobel, you will become just like those people you wrote about — the Pundles and Mottisfonts. I thought you were mad keen about politics. The loss of one election is nothing. Father lost his first election."

"He had money to pay for a second. I have had two contests in less than six months. The development of Boscobel will fill up my time and my purse. There's not much left in it."

"Oh, Jonathan, I am so sorry. This *is* a disappointment."

As she spoke Charles Desmond entered the library, followed by Scaife, who seemed — so John fancied — to have expanded. He began to look what he was sometimes called — a Pillar of the People. His tone toward John was admirable. He asked for details with a solicitude almost fraternal.

"What turned the tide against you?" asked Desmond.

"An electioneering trick that was rather slim."

"Let's hear about it."

"Upon the eve of the polling a leaflet was circulated. Towlerson wrote to me and said that he had nothing to do with it.   I believe him."

"This leaflet, my dear boy ——?"

"Contained a truth ten times harder to expose than any lie.   Here it is."

John handed a sheet of paper to Desmond.

Under Protection				Under Free Trade			
Prices copied from a Grocer's Ledger				*Prices at a Lymington Grocer's To-day*			
	£	s.	d.		£	s.	d.
Loaf sugar, per lb. .	o	1	o	Loaf sugar, per lb.	o	o	2¼
Moist sugar, per lb. .	o	o	9	Moist sugar, per lb.	o	o	2
Tea, per lb. . . .	o	8	o	Tea, per lb. . . .	o	1	4
Yellow soap, per lb. .	o	o	10	Yellow soap, per lb	o	o	3
Currants, per lb. .	o	1	1	Currants, per lb. .	o	o	3
Raisins, per lb. . .	o	o	10	Raisins, per lb. .	o	o	4
Salt, 14 lbs. for . .	o	4	9	Salt, 14 lbs. for .	o	o	4 .
Candles, per lb. . .	o	o	9	Candles, per lb. .	o	o	4
Coffee, per lb. . . .	o	3	4	Coffee, per lb. . .	o	1	o
Starch, per lb. . .	o	o	11	Starch, per lb. . .	o	o	4½
Pepper, ¼ lb. . . .	o	1	o	Pepper, ¼ lb. . .	o	o	3½
.	£1	3	3		£0	4	10¼

Desmond read it, and exclaimed: "Diabolically clever!"

"It was too late to answer it. The prices under Protection were taken from a ledger, *verbatim*. The

electors were not told that the ledger was seventy
years old."

"How infamous!" exclaimed Sheila. "Isn't it?"
she turned to Scaife.

"That sort of thing Miss Desmond, is not confined
to the Radicals. I could tell you stories about rabbits
stuffed with half-crowns by church-going Tories."

"Would you stoop to these particular methods?"

Scaife laughed easily.

"My remarks are general, not particular."

"But mine are particular. Would *you* publish
a lying leaflet like this? Would you?"

"No."

"It was a stab in the back."

"It laid me out flat," said John.

He went away a few minutes later, promising to
return for dinner. Scaife accompanied him to the
door.

"Can you come to my rooms, Jonathan? I've
a lot to say to you."

"All right," John replied.

A taxi took them to Dover Street.

Scaife had a large flat at the top of one of the newer
buildings, which included, amongst other improve-
ments, an express lift, a "lightning elevator," as
it was termed by the enterprising Yankee who "in-
stalled" it. John was shot upward with a distressful
feeling that he was leaving the lower half of his body
upon the ground-floor.

"Jolly, isn't it?" asked Scaife. "I love this lift."

"You're a lightning elevator yourself," said John, as he stepped from the cage. "I'm quite giddy."

They entered the flat, and Scaife said quickly:

"By the way, where are you staying?"

John named a modest hotel, in which the name of Verney was something more than a number.

"Lord! that prehistoric place! Why not camp here?"

"You're very kind, but ——"

"Kind? What rot! I'll tell my servant to fetch your things. I supposed you'd be staying in Eaton Square."

He glanced sharply at John, who said:

"I'm not beloved by that polished corner of the temple — Miss Bargus."

"Look upon this as your hotel."

"Thanks, and thanks again; but I'll remain where I am."

"Right! Pick your chair. I'll be back in a jiffy."

During his short absence John examined his surroundings. The room exuded Scaife, illustrating him in different moods and tenses. It was papered in red, a warm, clear tint as sanguine as the vital fluid. But the cabinets and chairs were of ebony, carved by some famous Chinese craftsman, a genius in expressing the grotesque. Some of the carvings were horrible, because they seemed to be alive and writhing. Upon the walls hung Scaife's collection of prints: each a gem, and immensely valuable. Between these and the furniture and Oriental porcelain the contrast was very striking. The prints were of beautiful women, and children posed against the idyllic backgrounds of Gainsborough and Watteau. Low bookcases surrounded the room, and upon these stood half a dozen striking bronzes representative of strength either in action or repose. The desk was large and massive, and kept in scrupulous order. John had time to read the titles of many of the books. Biology and sociology stood beside military histories and the biographies of great Captains. Poetry was absent. And to mark Scaife's defiance of the conventional, a map of the town of Samarkand was hung between two beautiful Cosway drawings. Above the picture-rail were heads of stags, all fine specimens. Women of taste entreated Scaife to hang these elsewhere. He refused gaily. "They are so much potted fun," he would reply. "I remember each stalk. That fellow"— he would indicate a fine ten-pointer — "defeated me three times. I thought he bore a charmed life, but I nailed him at last." Above the chimney-piece was a magnificent portrait of Scaife's father, a burly, broad-shouldered, heavy-jawed, Rhadamanthine autocrat painted by Sargent.

The man's overbearing, domineering character was emphasized by a tremendous chin. Potential violence glowered in deeply set eyes; his reputation as a "pincher," the employer who boasted that he scrapped worn-out machinery and weak men, was exhibited by a pair of thick, tightly compressed lips. Here was a "getter," who had given nothing away. The pleasure

of getting apart from giving may appear recondite
to some of us. John wondered whether it pleased the
father that his son should be known as a generous
giver.

He recalled his first sight of the Colossus, who,
curiously enough, had never come down to Harrow
to see his son. One day, shortly after he had entered
Desmond's service, John rushed into the grill-room
of a famous restaurant to eat a belated luncheon.
The room was almost deserted, but a big man happened
to be sitting alone at the table next to John's. Evidently he had finished his meal, for his coffee-cup was
empty, and a small tray was piled high with ashes.
He leaned his great head upon his hand and stared
fixedly at the table-cloth. The face was so congested,
of so deep a crimson in colour that John apprehended
apoplexy. Beckoning to the head waiter, he whispered
anxiously:

"Who is that? Is he ill?"

"It's Mr. Scaife, sir, the great contractor." Then,
with unconscious humour: "He's always like that
after lunch."

"Heavens!" exclaimed John.

The head waiter added a word of explanation.

"He doesn't lunch with us often, sir. When he
does —" A gesture indicated Gargantuan repasts.

After this, John was unable to think of Scaife's
father save as an animal gorged.

Scaife came back and found John still staring at
the portentous face upon the canvas.

"Fine thing," he said carelessly. "Sargent brought out the tiger in the old man."

"I hate to hear his son say so."

Scaife chuckled.

"I pulled your leg, Jonathan. I like to make you squirm, just once in a blue moon. All the same, it's true. The tiger in him made him what he is. I hated him when I was a kid; then I learned to admire him; to-day I love him. How do you like this room?"

"There's something uncanny about it. A child left alone here when the light was failing would be terrified."

"You're a child still, old man. Have something to drink? No. Then let's get to business. The loss of this election means that you can devote yourself to Verney-Boscobel."

"Yes."

"We'll make things roar down there this spring and summer. Old M'Vittie is painting a glorious 'ad.'"

"Does he guess that it is an 'ad'?"

"Of course. I say, I'm planning an auction of small lots. A brass band, luncheon, and then a walloping sale. Yankee tricks."

"Are wind instruments necessary?"

"There's nothing like brass. Our lots are going to sell like hot cakes, because"— he eyed John with twinkling eyes — "because — I — am — such — a — hot — lot — myself."

"You will pull my leg out of all shape."

"You limp where I run because you're inexperienced. It's not enough to lead a horse to the water; you must make him drink. I can make him drink, my dear man. By Jove! I can make him drunk."

He laughed loudly.

"You make me drunk."

"That's a very pretty compliment. You know I've talked this over with your solicitors. They cordially approve. In fact," he chuckled, "I made old Manson, who drew up your mother's marriage settlement, believe that the idea of the band is his. Perhaps you would prefer to sell out — now?"

"Now?"

"This minute. I'll buy the land bordering the estuary, and run the show on my own. Name your price! I'll scribble a cheque before you have time to wish you had asked a bigger figure."

"I don't want to sell out. I'm tremendously interested in this development."

"You're going to cut politics?"

"They've cut me."

"Deeply?" asked Scaife.

John answered curtly: "More deeply than I like to admit."

"It's a pity your ideas are so reactionary: we could find a seat for a Progressive."

John laughed, and the talk rippled back to the estuary.

Once more John was staggered by Scaife's grasp of detail. During the election the member for Samarkand had been ubiquitous, speaking twice or thrice each day, writing letters of exhortation, and managing his papers with consummate ingenuity. Nevertheless, listening to him now, it would seem that he had spent laborious nights exercising his wits upon builders' estimates, and a thousand and one trifles connected with the sale and subdivision of land.

Presently John took his leave, and went on to a very select club in St. James Street, which for several generations included a Verney in its list of members. His uncle, the explorer, had put down his nephew's name shortly after John's birth, and the young man came up for election when he was unknown in London, and therefore without enemies. John liked the quiet of the place, its excellent library, its irreproachable service. But the only intimate friend of his own age who belonged to the club happened to be Fluff. The hall-porter said solemnly:

"The Duke of Trent and Lord Esmé Kinloch are in the morning-room."

John nodded, noting the man's reverential tone. A Duke still inspired the ancient awe and obeisance. John hung up his hat and coat amongst other hats and coats, not of the newest nor smartest.

The Duke greeted him. Then, laying his hand upon John's sleeve, he said:

"We were so very sorry."

"Sorry?" Fluff repeated the word. "Sorry? We simply chattered with rage. I am certain Scaife is at the bottom of the mischief."

"That's absurd," John exclaimed irritably.

"I feel it in my bones," Fluff declared with conviction. "Somehow or other the Demon burked your chance."

"An electioneering trick burked my chance," John replied. He produced the leaflet, and handed it to the Duke, who adjusted his pince-nez. Fluff read it, looking over his father's shoulder. The Duke returned the leaflet to John. Then he said quietly:

"We mustn't be too virtuously indignant over this. The system is all wrong, of course, but our own hands are not quite clean."

John laughed.

"Scaife mentioned Tory rabbits stuffed with half-crowns. I couldn't fight this, sir, because it was so nicely timed. Every elector received a copy on the morning of the election."

Fluff said angrily: "There you are. Capable distributing agency at work. The affair positively reeks of Scaife."

To this John replied with heat: "You forget that Scaife is my partner. He has joined the Radicals — and that is his affair — but he's incapable of stabbing any man in the back, as Sheila puts it."

"Sheila said that, did she?"

"Yes; and before Scaife."

The Duke nodded, frowning at Fluff.

"My dear Esmé, you oughtn't to hint at such things even in jest."

"In jest? I know my Demon."

"Are you staying with Charles Desmond?" asked the Duke.

"No," John replied.

Both men were too well-bred to express the surprise they felt. The Duke's eyebrows went up.

"Come to us," he said kindly.

John refused the invitation as civilly as possible. The Duke rose.

"I've got an appointment. You boys want to talk together." As he pressed John's hand, he added: "Let us see you at Kinloch for some spring salmon-fishing. Propose yourself, whenever you like. Good-bye."

He hurried away, an overworked man who considered the welfare of innumerable dependents before his own.

"So you saw Sheila, eh?" Fluff asked.

"This afternoon. I'm dining there to-night."

"What's the matter with the little darling?"

"What do you mean?"

"She's thin, pale, worried. Why?"

"I can't account for it."

John had told himself that Sheila, being so ambitious, was terribly upset by his defeat. The failure of her lover must have been exasperating; then he remembered that girls do not grow thin in a few hours. To the last minute she had been quite confident of his success.

He heard Fluff saying deliberately:

"There's something in the wind. The knowing ones are shaking their heads over Charles Desmond. Scaife has spread his nets in Eaton Square."

"Well, why shouldn't he?"

"And I am convinced that he has a bad influence over Sheila, the sort of influence he exercised over poor Cæsar."

John was startled, but his face remained impassive. Fluff continued with agitation: "He's constantly with her. People are gossiping. I love her; I've told her so a dozen times; and if there's no chance for me — and there isn't — I'd give her up to a decent sort, but I swear I'd sooner see her dead than married to that devil."

John met his friend's eyes. They were still limpidly blue, with the flickering flames of youth dancing in their depths. Suddenly, John remembered with compunction that he had never set quite its proper value upon Esmé Kinloch's friendship. He had taken from the boy more than he had given. At this particular moment he felt the want of a friend; the desire to speak out, so long suppressed, became overpowering. Then Fluff broke down the last barrier:

"You know, Jonathan, I could stand it if Sheila were fond of you. How you withstood her beats me. Your heart must be asbestos."

"I do love her," said John slowly.

"What?"

"And she cares for me."

Then he told the tale, without any embellishment or exaggeration, but he saw that Fluff's eyes were wet with emotion.

"I was forced to tell you," he concluded.

A long silence followed. John did not look at Fluff, but presently he felt the boy's hand grasping his, and in his ears was Fluff's voice, not quite steady, but full of affection.

"I knew from the beginning I was hopelessly out of it. Do you believe me when I say that I am glad for her sake as much as yours that she has chosen a better fellow?"

"I am not that, Esmé."

"You are, you are. So she cares for you, and the whole thing is a secret. I dislike that."

"We promised to wait."

Fluff shuffled: then he said with constraint:

"But this damnable gossip?" As John made no reply, he continued nervously: "Scaife has not cut loose from Genesta Lamb."

"Genesta Lamb?"

"The dancer. You must know about her?"

"The Caterpillar repeated some gossip."

"He rides with Sheila, and motors with that woman. It's too thick."

"Miss Lamb bears a good name. Even the Caterpillar admitted as much."

"Where did her diamonds come from?"

"Paste, probably."

Fluff laughed scornfully, but his tone was serious

enough when he asked: "What are you going to do?"

"I trust Sheila."

"That sounds very fine."

"Her father and Miss Bargus can take care of her."

Fluff laughed again. He had ceased to look youthful.

"Miss Bargus wants to remain mistress of that house. Desmond is occupied with his own affairs; and now these Radicals are on top he'll have to hunt a new job. Have you read to-day's paper?"

"Yes."

"And skipped the most interesting part — the advertisements? I thought so. It may surprise you to hear that Charles Desmond is announced as the new chairman of the Sangan Para Rubber Estates."

"But why not?"

"It's a company of Scaife's. He owns a controlling interest in the shares."

"What of it?"

"Can't you see the slimness of our gentleman?" As John made no reply Fluff continued: "I hear things that you don't. Desmond is confoundedly hard up. He's always been extravagant, entertained too much, and all that. It wouldn't surprise me a little bit to be told that the Demon had lent him money. He has put more than one fine gentleman upon his legs when he was tottering."

John thought of the Egertons. Then he said abruptly:

"I am in the dark about that, but I refuse to see ghosts. Scaife has treated me with extraordinary generosity. It is he who has made marriage possible. Politically, he may have honourable designs upon Desmond. He has never concealed his independence. Because I hated him once, I try to do him justice now. We don't see eye to eye about everything. His methods are not quite mine or yours."

"I should hope not."

"Oddly enough, he offered to buy me out this afternoon. I was invited to name my price."

"I hope you named a thumping figure?"

"I didn't, because I want to have a hand in the development of my own land."

"Scaife knew that too. He was bluffing."

"Fluff, I can't discuss him like this, not even with you."

"All right. Are you going to discuss him with Sheila?"

"Of course not."

With that he rose to go, but Fluff accompanied him. They walked together up St. James Street and into Piccadilly. Presently they passed a shop which exhibited photographs of celebrities.

"There's Genesta Lamb," said Fluff, stopping.

John's curiosity made him stop also. He stared at a singularly handsome face, and one of the most shapely figures in the world. John had seen Miss Lamb dance, but he had never examined her features with an eye to divining her character.

"Her face is sly," Fluff declared with emphasis.

John perceived a subtle expression about the long, slightly closed eyes.

"Has her own way too," muttered Fluff.

The chin indicated a strong character. Costly furs softened its bold outline.

"Sables, not mink," commented Fluff. "Do you think they were paid for out of a dancer's salary?"

CHAPTER XII

BLUDGEONINGS

FROM a certain portentousness in Trinder's tone when he mentioned that members of the family were dining in Eaton Square, John guessed that Lord and Lady Wrexham had come to town; but he was not prepared to see Mrs. Starkey, Charles Desmond's elder sister, who had married a famous Anglican preacher, now the Bishop of Penzance. John liked Mrs. Starkey, who, on her part, had a genuine affection for the young man; but he had to admit that his late Chief's sister was a lady of imperious will, and without that tact which should be as a guiding star to the wives of our spiritual peers. John knew also that for many years civil war had raged between Lady Wrexham and Mrs. Starkey. To hear either lady pronounce the name of the other was quite enough for any understanding person.

Penelope received John very sweetly.

"You have all my sympathy," she murmured as she placed her cool fingers in his hand.

Mrs. Starkey made him sit down beside her. She was wearing, as usual, a gown of severe cut. A necklace of bog-oak beads surrounded her thin neck. Lady Wrexham was in purple velvet, displaying many diamonds. Lord Wrexham, a very imposing veteran of the "beerage," was talking to Charles Desmond on the hearthrug. The Bishop of Penzance, the most courtly of ecclesiastics, listened smilingly to the octogenarian's scathing indictment of Radical electioneering. Presently he said in his silvery voice:

"We are all stout Tories, my dear lord. Let us keep our powder for the enemy. Charles, I'm sure, must be heartily sick of politics."

"I am," said Desmond. "For the moment I am vastly more interested in rubber."

"Saw that you'd wandered into the City. They'll fleece you, Charles; take my word for it."

"I've not much wool left."

Sheila came in, still pale, but looking lovely in the simplest of white frocks. She nodded to John, and went up to her father, slipping her hand upon his arm. John tried to compose himself, but Sheila's words in regard to the ratification of a formal engagement, her sighing "I wish he would," went singing through his head. His depression passed; he felt delightfully happy and gay. She wanted him — God bless her! Mrs. Starkey whispered: "She was always a pretty child, but to-night she looks beautiful."

"Doesn't she!" John replied with enthusiasm, and he felt Mrs. Starkey's eyes boring through clothes and skin and flesh.

"You two are great friends."

"Yes," he said, with more composure.

"I am told that she refused young Esmé Kinloch. Why?"

John's impassive manner veiled his words as he asked indifferently: "How should I know?"

"You might know. Between ourselves, I take it that there is somebody else. There must be. Esmé Kinloch is very attractive. Yes, yes, I am positive there is somebody else." She sank her voice as she added: "Is it Mr. Scaife?"

"No," John replied with emphasis.

"I am delighted to hear that."

Trinder announced dinner.

John took in Sheila. When he felt the pressure of her hand upon his arm, he whispered: "I hope I shall have a chance of speaking to the Chief to-night."

"Do," she murmured. Then, hastily, as if he were an ordinary guest, she added: "I wish we had an more amusing party for you."

John glanced into her face, but her eyes did not meet his. The feeling of exultation began to ooze from him. He wondered why Sheila — so frank, so candid, so ingenuous — should puzzle him. Surely she must know herself to be his "party."

They sat down to dinner, but before the fish was eaten John became aware that a skeleton sat at the feast. Desmond tried to infuse sparkle into the talk, but he was certainly bored, although none but his former secretary and Penelope became aware of it. Mrs. Starkey and Lady Wrexham sparred for an opening, and contradicted each other with acerbity, which made Sheila whisper to John:

"The pertinacity of some people makes one tired, doesn't it?"

"It's a wonderful quality."

"You are always so philosophical."

"Am I?"

He had a fugitive glimpse of a pout as she nodded. He considered the question, feeling anything but philosophical.

Sheila went on inquisitively:

"When did you learn to take things easy?"

"When I discovered that it hurts more to take them hard."

"I can't imagine you in a rage. I met a Sicilian girl the other day. She told me that her father, who is a man of importance, bangs his head against the wall when he loses his temper."

"Sicilian heads may be thicker than ours."

"I remember doing it when I was a tiny. It hurt, but it did me good. How I hate bottling things up!"

He laughed, but she turned reproachful eyes upon him.

"Are you thinking of us?" he asked gently.

"Yes."

"What fun the uncorking will be!"

"Your cork will come out quietly, Jonathan."

John glanced at the wine in his glass. "The best champagne," he replied, "is not that with the most fizz to it."

"I hate this waiting."

"So do I."

"You would wait patiently for seven years."

"Fourteen, if necessary, for my Rachel."

He spoke in a whisper, but the smile left her face, and there was a pathetic droop to her mouth which he failed to interpret. Sheila and he drifted back into the general conversation.

After the ladies went upstairs, Lord Wrexham attacked the port, which he pronounced to his liking. Then, with his usual abruptness, he said to Charles Desmond: "I'm told that you wouldn't give Scaife's father a peerage."

Charles Desmond sipped his wine, and Lord Wrexham continued irritably:

"Is it true, Charles?"

"He didn't ask *me* for one. Have you got a biscuit?"

"I was told at the Carlton this afternoon that they hold you responsible for the defection of the cleverest young man in England."

"Do you know Scaife?"

"No."

"I thought not."

The Bishop said mildly: "I do, as a philanthropist."

Lord Wrexham snorted. The Bishop continued:

"I was impressed with his sincerity. Any rich man can sign cheques; but he went amongst the miners, and satisfied himself about their pressing needs. A very remarkable young man."

"John knows more about him than any of us."

Lord Wrexham turned round in his chair, and stared.

"Do you?" he grunted. "Well, is he a humbug, as some of them say, or not?"

"He has been most generous in his dealings with me," said John quickly. "I know that he regards himself as one of the people. He is adored in Samarkand. That ought to silence some critics. He plays cricket and football with Duff's East-Enders. He has left us, but did he ever belong to us?"

Then, somewhat to John's astonishment, Charles Desmond spoke with emphasis:

"Thank you, Jonathan." He turned to Lord Wrexham. "Reginald Scaife is a striver. That should appeal to you, because the young men of to-day are so slack."

"The fools kill Time without reflecting that they are tampering with Eternity," remarked the father of Penelope Bargus.

"Excellent," said Desmond.

"I must steal that as a text for a sermon," murmured the Bishop.

Lord Wrexham smiled graciously, and said in a milder tone:

"Without offence to you, Charles, I stick to my conviction that 'you could have kept Scaife in our fold. Personally, I refuse to credit Socialists with principles. This young spark will fire our tricks. He has already announced his intention of reforming *us*." He glared at his colleague in the Lords.

"We need reforming, my dear Lord Wrexham," said the Bishop.

"If you have finished your wine, I can give you a good cigar," said Charles Desmond. "Smoke it here. I must have a word with John Verney in the library."

As he spoke, he pushed a thin box of cigars toward Lord Wrexham, and then rose. John followed him, wondering what was coming. Had Sheila spoken to her father? He perceived that his former Chief was fidgeting with articles on his desk.

"I also want to speak to you, sir," said John boldly.

"Do you?" Desmond blinked at John, as if endeavouring to see him more clearly. Then he offered him a cigarette and lighted one himself.

"What have you to say?"

"What Scaife calls the boom has begun at Boscobel. We have raised prices. I cannot doubt that the mortgage on my home will be lifted before long. I had no idea that estuary land was so valuable. Also, I have let the shooting at double the usual figure."

"Well?"

"Doesn't that make me more eligible as a son-in-law?"

"Yes."

"Under these brighter conditions I thought you might see your way to announce a formal engagement."

"My dear boy, I should be less worried if I could see my way to do that. Sheila is fond of you, and true as steel. She recognizes — as I do — the moral obligation. But a mistaken sense of honour tyrannizes over her, as it did long ago over me. Her affection for you, is rooted, shall we say, in delightful memories and associations. You were Cæsar's friend; and I — well, I have tried to treat you as a son. You are dear to me, John Verney. Before God, I wish that you were the right man to marry my child."

"Why am I not?"

"Because she has no passion for you, and I suspect ——"

"Yes."

"That some one else has aroused in her the feeling which a girl ought to entertain toward her future husband."

John felt that his hands were trembling, and with an effort he managed to control such outward manifestations of the storm within. It has been said that Desmond's voice possessed the quality of impressiveness. His successes in the House of Commons were achieved, partly, it is true, by eloquence, but to a greater extent by an appeal to the higher motives, which do and must animate politicians of the better sort. The baser sort spoke of this compelling persuasiveness as "blarney," but others were exalted by it to issues higher than themselves. John knew that Sheila — impulsive, highly sensitized, passionate as a child in her likes and dislikes — had never thrilled beneath his voice or touch. But he had hoped that this would come. Indeed, the realization of his inability to awaken what must be dormant had restrained his own thoughts concerning her. He had hardly dared to envisage her as wife. He writhed beneath the new-born reflection that he had blundered in not appealing to the clay which cannot be separated from the spirit. Such an opportunity had been his. When she fluttered to his arms he might have taught her the alphabet of passion.

"Whom do you suspect, sir?"

Charles Desmond stood up, turned, and crossed to the fireplace. For the first time in their long intercourse the youth in the one perceived the age in the other. Desmond's face expressed the drab wisdom of experience confronted by the ardours and enthusiasms of inexperience. At the moment the elder man was repeating to himself one of the saddest lines in French literature:

Malheureuse est l'ignorance, et plus malheureux le savoir.

In silence Charles Desmond gazed into the fire. When he faced John he looked worn and harassed. John rose to meet him, clenching his hands, but holding himself upright.

"Reginald Scaife is, I think, the man."

"Has he spoken?" John demanded.

"How can you ask such a question? Would she let him?"

Desmond continued: "I invited him here because there were questions of moment to be discussed, and because I took for granted that Sheila cared for you.

I accepted that as a fact, and pigeon-holed it. After Scotland she was separated from me, paying a long round of visits. She came home looking rather worn. She avoided talks with me. I supposed that she blamed me for not sanctioning an engagement, for she detests concealment of any kind. Then Scaife was in and out all December. They rode together."

"I heard of that," said John; "but I trusted her absolutely."

"Your trust was not misplaced. She is ready to marry you to-morrow — if you hold up your finger."

"I can make her forget Scaife."

"Are you sure of that?"

The two men stared at each other unflinchingly. Desmond added, with a sigh: "I thought that I could make my wife love me. She married me under pressure from her mother. I found out afterward that she had cared for some youngster in a marching regiment. Can you make Sheila forget an overmastering personality?"

"I can try. She came to me, sir. I was first then."

"Were you? I have asked myself that question. Did she rush to you because she was afraid of the other, unable to analyze new and conflicting emotions?"

"I shall fight for her," said John incisively. After a pause he added: "As I fought for Cæsar."

"For Cæsar?" repeated the astonished father. "What do you mean?"

"You never knew. I had to fight for Cæsar's friendship. And the odds were against me. In the end, when Cæsar wrote me that letter, I knew that

I had won. I read that letter always on the anniversary of his death. It will mean more to me now. You see, I had made so certain that Scaife had conquered, but he hadn't."

"You will hold Sheila to her engagement?"

"She is free to choose the man she loves best. I shall try to teach her to feel for me what I feel for her."

Desmond gazed at his son's friend with a keener interest, for he beheld a different John. He saw divested of the mask that convention imposes upon certain men a glowing face, and eyes sparkling with resolution. He asked himself: "Has John power?" It seemed incredible that this quiet, self-effacing man should attempt to enter the lists against Reginald Scaife. Holding out his hand, he said slowly:

"If Sheila marries the man she loves, I am content. Do your best."

"I shall," said John grimly.

"What will you say to the child?"

"I shall find the right words."

A few minutes afterward they were in the drawing-room. Sheila sang two or three songs, including a duet with John. The lovely voice he had possessed when a boy was now a passable tenor, nothing more, but he sang with taste and feeling. As he bent over Sheila, she asked nervously: "Have you had a word with Daddy?" He nodded, trying to smile. She murmured quickly: "Are we to proclaim our engagement?" As he placed the duet before her, he whispered: "Not yet. I'll call to-morrow morning."

Something in his tone made her glance at him. Did she also behold a new John? He saw that her cheeks were flushed, and the first notes of the duet were not attacked with assurance.

John walked back to his hotel. The east wind blew strongly, but the night was fine, giving promise of a frost before morning. The nip in the air fortified his resolution to fight his ancient enemy to a finish; the strength of the wind when he met it squarely, on turning into Piccadilly, braced his sinews. He had to push against it.

Passing Dover Street, he paused. The impulse seized him to walk a few yards out of his way to gaze at Scaife's windows, to peer through them and beyond them into the heart of his rival. The whim seemed absurd, but he obeyed it. Lights, he perceived, twinkled in the top story. John stood upon the pavement opposite the building, looking up. As he stood there a landaulette glided past, turned slowly, and drew up at the door across the street. Inside the motor an electric light shone upon the face of a woman. John recognized Genesta Lamb. She was leaning back, as if tired after the nightly performance. Her eyes were closed. John noticed the firm lines and curves of the face, the delicate nostrils slightly dilated, the red lips too tightly pressed together. She was wearing the sables not to be mistaken for mink. Upon an ungloved hand sparkled a splendid ring.

John saw the door open, but the lady did not move.

Evidently she was sending a message which demanded an answer. John resisted a sudden temptation to play the spy. He walked back toward Piccadilly, but the motor overtook him before he had turned the corner. As it sped smoothly by, John perceived that Miss Lamb was alone.

He reached his hotel as midnight was striking. From the clock-tower at Westminster floated the familiar chimes, and then the deep booming note of Big Ben. It seemed to be calling him out of the millions, summoning him to join the six hundred about to assemble from all parts of the kingdom. The instinct to fight for his own hand gathered force as the great bell rang in another day.

Upon the table in his room lay three letters. The envelope of one bore a Duke's coronet, but the writing was not Fluff's, nor his exquisite mother's.

John opened it, and turned to the signature. The Duke had never written to him before.

My dear John:

I understand from Esmé that you are no longer the private secretary of Charles Desmond. Your re-election seemed such a matter of course that you may, perhaps, find yourself with nothing in particular to engage your attention. Can I persuade you to come to me as my secretary? The work is hard, but the pay is good. Esmé is no keener than I about your acceptance of an offer which naturally you must consider as a stop-gap. Most of the work would be political. The Duchess hopes with Esmé and me that this may be a stepping-stone to the House. At any rate, as my secretary, you would be near, if not on, the battle-field.

Yours very sincerely,

Trent.

CHAPTER XIII

JOHN passed a restless night. From time to time he dozed, but only to wake with a start of distress and horror. A malign power seemed to be hovering about him, ready to attack whenever its victim slumbered. He remembered that he had suffered a similar nightmare at Harrow. Scaife had then assumed colossal proportions, towering between John and Cæsar, higher than the spire of the church upon the Hill. Presently, John got out of bed, slipped on a coat, and sat down beside his fire, to resolve the problem of his future relations with Scaife. The man could not be avoided; and John refused to consider retreat. He wanted to fight, in the same spirit with which many a gallant ancestor of his had buckled on the sword. Never before had these primitive instincts so strongly manifested themselves.

And yet, at the same time, he was sensible of an overpowering depression, such indeed as may have possessed the Verneys who fought to the bitter end of Naseby for a losing cause. This was mainly physical, the result of his accident, but none the less overpowering, inasmuch as the measure of his weakness constrained him to overestimate a rival's strength.

Desmond's words repeated themselves in his brain. If he held up his finger —— !

The finger of a hand not quite clean. With bitter humiliation he told himself that he had accepted Scaife's money against his finer instincts, and because of that Scaife in his turn had been accepted by Desmond and Sheila. Had he said boldly to his Chief: "I know this man to be unchanged. I see through his apparent generosity. He wants to 'snag' you, and he will do it, as he 'snagged' your son long ago. He is unscrupulous in small matters. He's a win-by-any-means fellow, unable even to resist cheating at golf! Keep him at arm's length! Let us have no dealings with him whatever."

That is what he ought to have said.

With increasing humiliation, John indicted his advocacy of Tariff Reform, when he sought re-election. He had besmirched himself again by preaching a policy in which he had little faith, because he wanted Sheila. And now he wanted her more desperately than ever, and she would come to him, if — if he held up his finger. Having gone so far, why should he not press on, regardless of a conscience which had already shown itself to be expediently elastic?

Her face, so alluring in its dimpled youthfulness, so charmingly suggestive of a woman's beauty yet to come, beckoned out of the shadows. Her mouth, with its enticing curves, seemed to say: "My lips are yours if you want them." And he did want them with an intense longing that made other desirable things of no account.

And then, swiftly, he was at grips with temptation of a more subtle, insidious kind. The manhood which shrank from imposing passion without the certainty of a response urged him to rescue an ingenuous girl from marriage with a bogus paladin who sooner or later must reveal himself as of the baser sort. If he lifted his finger, Sheila would be saved from Scaife!

Having thus soothed conscience, he began a delightful journey through that blessed country where, awake yet dreaming, we are able to drape our dreams with the shining tissues of reality. He had travelled far upon a pleasant road, hand in hand with Sheila, when in fancy he bent down to kiss his wife, and to his horror beheld loathing, not love, in her soft eyes. The dream had become a nightmare.

Suddenly, he sprang to his feet, trembling, almost strangled by his emotions.

"My God!" he exclaimed, unconscious that he spoke aloud, "have mercy on me! Take this burden of doubt from me!"

Almost instantly the prayer was answered. He discerned, mistily at first and then with increasing clearness, the right path; and felt some power stronger even than love for Sheila drawing him upward and onward to the peace that endures. His will, strengthened in the past by many unremembered acts of self-denial,

became once more dominant. He could think with
the lucidity which precedes right action. Whatever
happened he would cut loose from Scaife. And on the
morrow, if he failed to inspire ardour in Sheila, and the
certainty of that failure gibbered at him, he would
leave her free. As the Duke's secretary, he would
remain in London near Sheila. He would begin again
to woo her, and he would fight for her, squarely, with
clean hands, against all comers.

Sheila received him in the library. Knowing what
he did, he wondered at her self-possession. Then, as
he held her hands, she turned her faintly flushed
cheek to his lips.

He kissed her, thinking he might never do so again.

"I'm sure it's all right," she whispered.

"And if it shouldn't be?" he asked. As he spoke
he released her, hardly able to trust himself. It was
not all right, but if it had been —— Once more devils
possessed him. The turned cheek had been cool, and
he wondered whether she had felt his burning lips. She
was really fond of him, a comrade with whom, surely,
one could face whatever life might hold. Was he
a fool to ask for more? Was he not, in a sense, dis-
loyal to doubt that an intense emotion would be
aroused later? The temptation to marry her assailed
him with increased violence. A mist suffused his
sight. Sheila seemed to be melting away, dissolving.
Then the mist lifted, and he saw her with penetrating
vision. She stood before him willing to surrender

without conditions, but the conditions had left scars. John saw the scars.

She sat down, saying quietly:

"You are here to settle things, Jonathan. Daddy told me that he had left it to you, and" — she smiled — "to me."

He nodded, adding abruptly: "I told the Chief that I was in a position to marry you."

"That is enough."

"Enough to settle — dates?"

Some inflection made her look upward. He stood beside her, and the winter's sun shone palely upon his face.

"Dates?"

"Would you object to an early date?"

"Something *under* fourteen years." She glanced at him with a pretty shyness which tempered yesterday's admission that Rachel was tired of waiting.

"Easter?" said John, tentatively.

"If *you* can get ready." It might have been Cæsar chaffing him.

He sat down, and took her hand, gazing at the third finger.

"I've not dared to buy an engagement-ring."

Her voice became serious again.

"That shows you are not quite sure of me, Jonathan."

He was silent, wondering what he should say. How could he explain that he had never been sure, except, perhaps, for five enchanted minutes at Strath Armyn? The temptation to shirk explanations assailed him for the third time, when she whispered: "I shall love the ring that you will buy me."

"Sheila," he began hoarsely — and at the change in tone she winced — "I have never been sure of you."

She sprang to her feet, staring into eyes which no trouble could make unsteady.

"What?"

"Because of that I must ask — Are you sure of yourself?"

"I don't understand."

"I think you do."

As she remained silent, he continued: "My love is the stronger because I had to suppress it, because, from the beginning, I knew that I must work and wait. It was hateful waiting, but delightful working for you. Other women are shadows, you are substance. Perhaps that is *the* test. Every sense is quickened by my love. Is it so with you, Sheila?"

As he put the question, he saw fear, not love, in her soft eyes.

"Am I the first man on earth to you?"

"I want to marry you," she faltered.

"Because you can't live without me? Is that the reason? Sheila — don't answer! It isn't the reason. You would marry me, because you are loyal. You are fond of me, you trust me, you feel, perhaps, that you would be safe with me; but — do you love me as I love you?"

"It may come."

The words were almost inaudible.

"Yes — it may," he repeated fiercely, "but I shan't marry you till it does. I have made a mistake. I see it too late. This morning, for the first time, I have moved you; I have made you — feel! That encourages me to begin again."

"Begin again?"

"You are free, and so long as you remain free I shall hope to read some day in your eyes what you can read any day in mine."

"You refuse to marry me?"

He drew her toward him.

"Till the time comes when you can whisper to me: 'John, I love you with heart and soul and body.' If I married you now, I should loathe myself; and you might end by loathing me."

There were tears in his voice, and when she looked up swiftly, trembling with distress and irresolution, she saw tears in his eyes. He kissed her hands, and hurried from the room.

At Trent House that same afternoon John accepted the Duke's offer. The Duke said a word about Verney-Boscobel which might present claims not to be ignored.

"I shall sell my interest."

"Is that wise, my dear boy?"

"It is necessary."

He had determined to submit the valuation to arbitrators. His solicitors expressed surprise when he mentioned that Scaife had asked him to name his own price. Old Manson, with a vast accumulation of experience, said dryly that Mr. Scaife must have something up his sleeve.

"He is generous in money matters," John murmured evasively.

"Apart from business, does he owe you anything?"

"Nothing," John replied in a tone that closed the discussion.

Alone, he sought for a motive that might illumine Scaife's apparent eagerness to buy him out at a big price. Was the offer mere bluff, as Fluff suggested, designed to impress John with the conviction that his interest in the development of the estuary lands might be worth undivided attention? In a word, did Scaife want him out of London? Had he scented a rival? Unable to answer such questions, he wrote to Scaife that he had changed his mind, and suggesting arbitration as a sound method of arriving at a just valuation. Scaife sent a telegram in return, asking John to come to his flat next day.

That same morning there was a paragraph in a Society paper announcing John's appointment as private secretary to the Duke of Trent.

"What does this mean?" demanded Scaife, shaking the paper in John's face. He spoke cordially, but John felt that he was annoyed.

"It means work in London instead of work at Boscobel."

"But I was counting upon your giving time and

brains to our enterprise. My offer the other day was hardly meant seriously."

"I took it seriously."

"Sit down, and let's thrash it out. I detest mysteries. Why are you so keen about work in London?"

"I shall tell you. It explains, if it doesn't justify, my chucking Boscobel. To be perfectly frank, I don't think we could work together. And now you will reap nearly all the profit, so my conscience is clear."

"Why do you want to work in London?"

"To be near Miss Desmond."

"Miss — Desmond?"

"At Strath Armyn, last September, I became engaged to her."

"Engaged to her? You?"

For an instant the tiger in Scaife displayed teeth and claws. John continued: "Mr. Desmond insisted that there should be no announcement. Of course the moral obligation remained."

"You Verneys freeze tight to moral obligations!"

The sneer betrayed him. John asked: "Do you suggest that I would hold anybody to a contract entered upon too hastily?"

Scaife answered pleasantly: "I beg your pardon, Jonathan. The suggestion was outrageous; but I've seen a lot of Miss Desmond lately. We are friends. We have often talked of you and your interests. But lately she has not mentioned your name. And, now, you spring upon me this astounding news of an engagement."

"The engagement is broken."

"What!   You retire from the field?"

"Not till I'm beaten."

"Beaten?   By whom?"

"I think you can guess."

Scaife laughed.

"I see that I must be equally frank. This is the Cæsar business all over again."

"Yes."

"I shall try to win her, John Verney."

Then John said steadily:

"Are you fit?"

"What the devil do you mean?"

"You ride with Miss Desmond; you motor with a dancer."

"We'll settle here and now about Miss Lamb. She is a young lady of spotless reputation and a great friend of mine.   I'll introduce you to her, if you like."

John flushed. In the Harrow days Scaife had possessed this humiliating power of making him feel youthful and foolish.

"Scaife, I wish to God that I really knew you."

"I'm delighted to talk about myself, or to write about myself, or even to have myself written about, but I'm a tough subject to dissect.   You stand for the old; I for the new.   You thought me a devil at Harrow. You think me a devil still, only fit to motor with a dancer.   I'm a humbug, posing as the People's Friend and all that.   Gad!   How easily I read you!"

"You are not a humbug," John admitted.

"Thanks! Well, John Verney, what have we in common which draws us together? I'll tell you — ambition. Success, in whatever you undertake, appeals to you as it does to me. We are equals in brains and tenacity of purpose, but I'm the stronger physically, and I'm not hampered with a conscience. It's going to be a good fight, but, frankly, you were an ass to release the young lady from her engagement."

"Good-bye," said John abruptly. His voice was not quite steady when he added: "You have always puzzled me, another reason for dissolving partnership. If I have ambitions, I shall remember that you made them possible."

John went out, without looking back. Scaife, with an odd smile upon his dark, handsome face, followed him to the lift. As John was stepping into it, Scaife said lightly:

"By the way, Miss Lamb is dining with me to-night. Would you care to join us?"

"I've got another engagement."

The lift dropped like a stone falling down a well.

CHAPTER XIV

THE LIONS OF SAMARKAND

JOHN had paid many visits to Harrow since he left the Hill for the "dreaming spires" of Oxford. The place remained delightfully the same, and his welcome from old friends unmistakably sincere. Since health and strength had come back, he liked to play cricket in the Yard, or a mild game of fives with Warde, or squash with some not too active Manorite. He might feel stiff the next day, but his spirit seemed more supple. In less robust moments, he would stroll to the Tower, where he had read Cæsar's last letter, and gaze across the Uxbridge flats and meadows, hardly conscious of the years that had passed.

He spent this week-end with Warde. The school had reassembled after the Christmas holidays, and John experienced that rejuvenating emotion which invigorates each new term. Already the blackbirds had begun to build in the shrubbery near the Tower.

Upon Sunday afternoon he occupied a chair in "Speecher," and listened to the organ recital. But at evening service, afterward, he refused the offer of a stall next to the head-master, and sat in the north transept, below the brass plate which recorded the date

and manner of his friend's death. The inspiring statement, "*Killed in Action*," never failed to thrill Cæsar's
friend. Nothing was left of that gallant youth but
this small piece of brass, which when at Harrow he
had coveted.

To the story of John's defeat by Towlerson, Warde
listened sympathetically. At the end he said: "My
dear boy, you are a bad beginner. You never fight
hard, till you're in danger of a licking. But, when your
blood is up, Tom Sayers would call you a customer."

This greatly comforted John. On the Monday
morning he wrote a letter to Sheila.

"I am writing this from Harrow, where I received
Cæsar's letter, when I thought that I had lost all belief in friendship and love. In a few hours I shall be
in London again and at work there. Sheila dear,
remember that I am still your lover. I am faithful
because you inspire fidelity. It is your merit, not
mine. . . ."

Sheila read these lines at breakfast, next morning.
She was going to ride with Scaife, who would be waiting
for her, as usual, opposite the Achilles statue, as
splendid a figure of youth, strength, and vitality, as the
son of Peleus himself.

Charles Desmond and Penelope had left the dining-
room. Sheila read and re-read John's letter, and she
wondered: "Can I inspire fidelity?" But she was not
thinking of John when she asked this question.

Upon the following Wednesday John took up his
new quarters in Trent House, a vast Palladian mansion
overlooking the Green Park. Fluff had returned to
Paris, carrying with him the knowledge that Sheila
was once more free. Upon the eve of departure he
muttered gloomily to John:

"We haven't got a chance. . . . All the same,
you must prevent her taking that devil. Watch
him night and day! Sooner or later he'll display
the cloven foot, and it will be your job to show it to
Sheila. By the way, Scaife paid for Genesta Lamb's
sables."

"How on earth did you find that out?"

"My mother's sables and Miss Lamb's were bought
at the same shop."

"Scaife asked me to meet her at dinner."

"Bluff again! Jonathan, I'm sure you overestimate
what you owe to Scaife."

"I pay my debts," John replied.

For several days after Fluff's departure, John was
immensely busy, prodigiously so, for the Duke seemed
to have a finger in a thousand pies, not pulling plums
out, but putting them in. About a week later, John
saw Sheila for a few minutes at a ball, and she managed to whisper: "As you won't marry me, I've made
up my mind to become Daddy's secretary. You should
see Aunt Pen's face. I suppose the day will come when
she must resign."

"I suppose so," John admitted vaguely. Something
in his tone roused Sheila to ask:

"Don't you ever try to read women? You are very acute about men."

"I tried to read you."

"Which cost me a good husband."

A band happened to be blaring, so he was able to answer passionately: "Don't joke about that!"

"But I'm not joking," she protested. With a glance at his face, she continued: "Marriage frightens me; it appears that we Desmonds are unlucky in our love-affairs. You told me, once, that love was not everything."

"I was a fool to tell *you* that," said John bluntly.

She looked at him, as if, like her father, she had envisaged a different John. At the moment a young fellow claimed her for a waltz.

Later in the evening, John exchanged a few words with Charles Desmond. He had noticed that his former Chief looked fagged during the rare moments when he was not talking with one or other of his innumerable acquaintance. Presently he beckoned to John, and, as soon as they were alone, said abruptly:

"So your partnership with Reginald is at an end?"

This was the first time that Desmond had spoken of Scaife by his Christian name.

"Yes."

"It has annoyed him."

"I can't help that, sir. After all, we made a poor team. Scaife is too speedy for me."

"Speedy? What do you mean by speedy?"

The tone was slightly autocratic.

"Well" — John tried to laugh it off — "his methods are transatlantic."

"You meant more than that?"

The interrogation was so sharp that John flushed, wondering whether Sheila's father had heard of Miss Lamb's sables. Fortunately John was able to reply with sincerity that he was thinking of Scaife's schemes for advertising Verney-Boscobel. Smiling pleasantly, he spoke of the band, and the luncheon, and the auction to follow.

Desmond listened, half frowning. At the end he said quickly:

"You have not quarrelled?"

"Oh dear — no."

"The Duke speaks highly of you. Your big chance will come, John; that is certain. But cutting loose from a powerful friend was unwise."

With a nod, the great man moved on, leaving John slightly oppressed. Desmond invited confidence, which the younger man withheld. John wondered what had restrained his tongue.

Meanwhile, Scaife, who had arrived late, was waltzing with Sheila. He danced admirably, steering his course with extraordinary ease and skill. Of innumerable partners, Scaife — so Sheila told herself — was the only one with whom she felt absolutely safe in an overcrowded London ballroom. She could half close her eyes, and let her mind drift whither it pleased to the rhythm of the music and the alluring movement of the waltz. Other men, who danced nearly as well as Scaife, would spoil an otherwise fine performance with foolish prattle. Scaife made no such blunder. When the music stopped, he walked with her to a couple of chairs near an open window, sat down, and said:

"I've got news for you. I wanted to tell you first. My father has been offered a peerage."

"Will he accept it?"

She was still slightly out of breath, and rather astonished, for she had met the Colossus, and by no effort of a lively imagination could she envisage his vast purple countenance surmounted by a coronet.

"Of course. Why not?"

Impulsively she blurted out a valid objection: "But you will be smothered in the Lords!"

His eyes were sparkling with triumph, for her words showed that she was thinking of his interests.

"Thank you. I am very greatly honoured" — his voice indicated an emotion hitherto suppressed — "by your thought for me; but" — he laughed genially — "my old daddy will live forever. He has an iron constitution; never been sick or sorry in his life. Perhaps it will strike you as rather odd that I have not considered the future so far as it concerns me, because that future seems so remote. You are perfectly right — I should be smothered in the House of Lords." His voice changed, and became hard and defiant, as he concluded curtly: "I should loathe it."

"I wonder why your father wanted it?"

"He has always wanted the things hard to get. I am like him."

She smiled, playing with her fan, and avoiding his eyes.

"You have certainly got what you wanted."

"So far — yes. I hold that a man of marked strength of character can get anything if he wants it hard enough. I grasped that conviction when I was at Harrow. I wanted your brother's friendship, Miss Desmond. That was not easy to get. Boys are prejudiced, you know, even the best of them. As a new boy, I was regarded as in the outer darkness socially, and Cæsar was a very bright, particular star, I can assure you."

"What else did you want at Harrow?"

"You will laugh when I confess."

"I can't see myself laughing at you."

"Thanks again. Well" — he threw up his handsome head, expanding his great chest — "I wanted to be Captain of the Eleven and racquet player, and the hardest footer-player of my time. And even then I wanted to be Prime Minister of England."

"That is quite possible."

"You think so?" He emphasized the pronoun.

"My father thinks so, which is more important."

"Not perhaps to me."

He saw that the fingers which held her fan trembled, and she moved restlessly. Instantly he dropped the personal note, with a hint that he would confess more at another time.

"Some day, Miss Desmond, I shall tell you of other ambitions. I wonder if I can persuade your father to come to me again in Scotland?"

"You must ask him," she replied.

A few days later a cartoon appeared in *Punch*, entitled "The Lions of Samarkand." One lion wore a baron's coronet, and the other grasped a new broom and a large sponge. The Duke of Trent showed it to his secretary, and asked Sheila's question: "Did you know old Scaife wanted that?"

John laughed. "We must admit, sir, that Scaife *père* is the king of beasts. The son, I suppose, reckons it a prize to be played for."

"And paid for," added the Duke, with a chuckle. "The old lion had to fork out thirty thousand pounds. He paid the bill without growling. Have you read this?"

He indicated a long article in one of the weekly papers, a biographical panegyric.

"Esmé would accuse the son of writing it. Did Charles Desmond tell you that Reginald Scaife approached us about this peerage?"

"No?"

"Yes; he went to our Chief Whip and said, 'I've been working for you tooth and nail, haven't I?'"

"I can hear him," John remarked. "'Tooth and nail' is good."

The Duke nodded, looking at his secretary with

a melancholy smile — the smile of a man set far above the necessity of petty scheming, and possessed of a sensitive nostril in regard to it. He continued:

"The Whip was very polite, and expressed his gratitude so prettily that Scaife was emboldened to mention what he wanted and to add, with effrontery: 'How much?'"

"And then——?"

"Well, unluckily Somebody is a Scot, and the Butcher of Badavarchy is anathema in Scotland. Strictly between ourselves, there was a rather dramatic interview between Scaife and one who shall be nameless. I can only add this — Scaife pushed his claims too hard, and Somebody was obliged to ring the bell. The cub of Samarkand went out snarling horribly. Possibly the affair might have been worked through Charles Desmond. What do you think about that?"

John hesitated, and then said:

"Scaife wants to marry Sheila Desmond; if she knew that there had been a bargain — well, she is nice about such matters."

The Duke smiled, and John was left to wonder whether his kind friend had designedly placed a weapon in his hand. He was tempted to use it shortly afterward, when he met Sheila at Hurlingham, where Scaife happened to be playing polo. Sheila, evidently, had read more than one appreciation of lions.

"Mr. Scaife is simply splendid," she declared with enthusiasm. "Look at him now."

Scaife, in command of the ball, was galloping down

the ground.   The back upon the other side, one of
the steadiest players in the kingdom, calmly awaited
a furious charge.

"Scaife ought to pass," said John critically.

As he spoke he remembered half a dozen games which
Scaife had attempted to win regardless of the claims
of others upon his own side.   The back saved a goal,
because Number 1 chose to ignore the existence of
Number 2.

Sheila turned a flushed face to John.

"You are sure he ought to have passed?" she asked.

"I think so."

Sheila murmured with an accent of defiance:
"But how natural not to!"

As John maintained silence, she continued less
defiantly: "Is it a weakness when a strong man, with
tremendous confidence in himself, does ignore others?"

"Certainly."

"You cannot put yourself in his place."

"I have tried to do so."

"You are not quite fair to him.   It worries me that
you and Esmé Kinloch should not be proud of an old
school-fellow's success.   Big men do him justice.   Only
the little men belittle him.   Two or three have dared
to hint that this peerage was bought."

"Such privileges are bought and sold."

"Then they cease to be privileges.   Can an honourable man buy honour?"

"I take it you made the Lilliputians feel smaller
still?"

"Didn't I just?"

Sheila laughed joyously, and, to John's relief, began to speak of something else, becoming at once the kind "pal" of former days. But he saw that her eyes were focussed upon Scaife, and once, when he was unhorsed, a little cry escaped from her, succeeded by a sigh of relief, as Scaife vaulted into his saddle.

"He bears a charmed life," said John.

"He told me that. He has never been hurt."

Then once more, as if with deliberation, she turned the talk. But, within a minute, two ingenuous youths approached, stamped as Lilliputians from the tips of their varnished boots to the shining "toppers" which surmounted their amiable pink faces. At sight of Sheila, they halted, smiling and raising their hats. One said, with the gravity of an expert:

"I shall never ask the bounder to play for me."

John beheld sparks of indignation in Sheila's eyes, but she held her tongue. The other youth added blandly:

"Ratter and rotter."

Sheila said, with tightening lips: "Whom are you speaking of?"

"Of the Honourable" — he mouthed the adjective — "Reginald Scaife. Poisonous fellow — eh?"

"Why?"

"Good Lord! Have you been watching him this afternoon? Selfish beast! Dangerous brute, too. That toss he had was entirely due to his fouling the other chap. He's a wrong 'un, and no mistake."

"Will you do me a favour?" said Sheila, with frigid politeness.

"Rather. Delighted. What is it, Miss Desmond?"

"I want you to repeat to Mr. Scaife's face what you say behind his back."

The Lilliputians grew crimson, but it must be admitted that one escaped with dignity.

"He's a friend of yours, Miss Desmond? Just so. Then I'm awfully sorry I spoke. I can't do you this favour, because my fighting weight is only nine stone ten."

He lifted his hat, and vanished.

"Let us have tea," said Sheila hurriedly.

The game was over, the victory remaining with Scaife's side, and indeed won brilliantly by him at the last moment. As he rode off the ground, a tall girl waved a parasol. Scaife pulled up, and John saw that Miss Lamb was patting the pony's neck, and presumably offering congratulations to a conqueror.

"Who is that?" asked Sheila.

"Don't you know?"

"Her face seems familiar."

"You have seen her dance."

"Of course. How stupid! It's Genesta Lamb. How handsome she is! Somebody told me that she had an appalling temper."

"With her mouth and chin all things are possible."

"But there seems to be nothing else against her. She goes everywhere. She sat next to an Ambassador at luncheon the other day, and his wife complained about it. But I'm not a bit starchy. I should like to meet her? Do you know her?"

"I have not that honour."

She smiled.

"You're rather starchy, Jonathan."

He answered with vehemence:

"Sheila dear, an ocean lies between you and this dancer. Don't try to cross it!"

"But I like voyages of discovery."

Her slight hesitation, the ingenuous expression upon her face, a disarming smile, were as arrows in the heart of John. He perceived the curiosity of a girl standing upon the threshold of womanhood, the desire, the craving, to look out, to escape from surroundings too familiar, from restrictions beginning to chafe.

"Don't put to sea in a hurry."

"Aunt Pen will keep me in dry dock. Don't worry!"

CHAPTER XV

THROUGHOUT June the Cub of Samarkand, as his political opponents styled him, roared lustily at many public meetings. The Socialists deplored, of course, the father's acceptance of a peerage; but the Independent Labour Party entreated the son to speak on their behalf. In the papers controlled by him, much space was given to the exposition of the Labour movement, not only in England, but in France, America, and Germany. The Unionists watched his performances with an amusement diminishingly corroded by distrust and exasperation. Scaife pranced gaily to the piping of the Radical leaders, and everybody knew that his high kicking would be rewarded sooner or later by office.

During this summer Sheila joined the Women's Industrial Council, and spent much time investigating the conditions of women's work in slums. Charles Desmond laughed with her rather than at her. Penelope murmured suavely that young girls nowadays found it more difficult to make fools of young men, and, accordingly, were driven to make fools of themselves instead. Certainly such a gadabout was hardly fit to be entrusted with serious responsibilities.

"Let the child wade through nonsense to sense," said her father.

She attacked John whenever they met, accusing him of being encrusted with New Forest moss.

"Why don't you join us?"

"I march with my own order."

"March? You are standing still."

"I may seem so," John replied. "Has it ever occurred to you that the hour hand of the clock is the one which registers the real time of day?"

"You are stagnating at Trent House."

"The Duke works harder than Scaife without any hope of reward or recognition."

"Mr. Scaife has opened my eyes, I can tell you."

"Has he shaken the sawdust out of your pretty dolls?"

"Some of it."

"What a pity!"

"You would have me blind?"

"I would have you blind, or deaf, or even dumb, provided —— "

"Yes?"

"That you wanted me as I want you."

Her voice softened as she whispered: "Do you want me as badly as ever?"

"I shall always want you. And I loathe the idea of your touching pitch."

She held out her hands, throwing back her head and laughing as Cæsar used to laugh whenever John became too serious.

"Are they grimy?" she asked.

"Not yet. Why hunt for trouble when it must hunt you some day?"

"How about duty?"

"Is it your duty to nose out miseries at nineteen? You are not trained; you may be able to tell black from white, but the shades muddle you. Do you believe that you see clearly?"

"Not always."

"You are straining eyes and brain."

"I would sooner do that than play with dolls. Anyhow, I can detect humbugs and liars."

"Do you hate them as savagely as ever?"

"More so."

"Poor Sheila!"

"Give me the truth at any price."

"The price might be — prohibitive."

"I repeat — any price."

She frowned and then laughed.

From such interviews John retired, feeling impotent to avert catastrophe. He had visions of Sheila standing at street corners distributing pamphlets, or summoned before facetious magistrates on a charge of breaking the peace. She called herself Suffragist, although she repudiated Suffragette, and she was seen at public meetings in the company of a distinguished and fluent supporter of the movement. Upon one occasion she spoke with eloquence, and next day the Scaife papers reported this maiden effort, praising it as worthy of Charles Desmond's daughter. Later,

Desmond said to John: "We shan't let this go too far;" and John wondered whether the "we" included Scaife.

Meanwhile Desmond had begun to arouse the curiosity of his party. When Parliament re-assembled he assumed a perplexing air of detachment. He seldom spoke except under pressure from the leader of the Opposition, admitting with genial frankness that he was modifying some opinions and setting his house in order. One day the Duke of Trent said to John:

"Has Scaife infected Charles Desmond?"

"Isn't 'infected' rather strong?"

"I'm too busy to pick words. Desmond was never a strong man, and he loves office. They tell me he is always dining with Scaife at the House."

"But why not?"

"It's a straw. By the way, last night I heard that Silverley must retire."

Silverley was an incompetent Under-Secretary.

"Scaife will get his billet," said John.

The Duke pulled at his beard, now streaked with gray. John glanced at him, being struck by a ducal solidity of appearance. There was something of the mountain about this great feudal landlord, and he was regarded as such by the Radicals, who had faith that they might remove him. John knew that he was rooted like an oak in the soil which had belonged to his family since the days of the Tudors. He owned vast estates in three counties and some acres in the heart of London. John knew also how faithfully this

immense trust was administered, and he remembered
Fluff's words, spoken at Whiteladies: "It's no joke
to be born a Duke. Mother says that father is the
overworked land-agent of the Trent property."

"Nobody has greater claims," continued John.

"They are afraid of him. They are afraid of Ezra
Kitteredge and Arnold Grandcourt."

Ezra Kitteredge was a Lancashire lad, round and
rosy, with a beaming smile but vitriolic tongue. His
smile became even more radiant when his disciples
spoke enthusiastically of their great leader as a statesman Impartial publicists remarked, however, that
Kitteredge never missed an opportunity of violating
what is, perhaps, the first principle of statesmanship.
To adjust patiently differences and misunderstandings
between class and class was too dull a task for this
sanguine orator. Indeed, he sincerely believed that
it was his duty to destroy the bridges which had once
linked together the idle rich and the honest poor.
His methods, in short, may be described as smashing.
Arnold Grandcourt, with none of Kitteredge's experience of the seamy side of life, was a smasher also.
Kitteredge had achieved Cabinet rank; Grandcourt
was still an Under-Secretary.

"It's a test case," added the Duke thoughtfully.
"The elder men don't want Scaife. If he is pro-
moted it will be under pressure from the extreme left."

A week later *Punch* published another cartoon, representing Britannia gazing anxiously into a
cradle in which slumbered three robust infants —

Grandcourt, Kitteredge, and Scaife. Beneath ran
the significant line:

"Won't my triplets howl when they sit up!"

Scaife discussed his possible preferment with a
disarming air of having nothing to conceal from an
old school-fellow. Perhaps he knew that John winced,
as he said carelessly:

"When shall we welcome you to the House?"

"Soon, I hope."

"With the Duke on your back."

John detected a note of derision, but he answered
quietly:

"He has promised to help."

"Dead weight!" exclaimed Scaife viciously; "a
weight you can't carry, my good Jonathan. Mark
me! the Dukes have had their innings. 'Down with
the Dukes!' will be one of the cries at the next election."

"Disorder will never destroy order."

"How about the French Revolution? I say, I
wonder if I shall have a mix-up with you?"

"I'm in training for it," replied John.

Scaife laughed, glancing at John's thin figure, conscious of his own fitness. He looked so handsome and
so strong that John felt a humiliating conviction of
weakness. How could he cope with this approved
champion? The same thought must have flitted
through the brain of the other, for he said seriously:

'You know I don't want to fight with you, really.
Even at Harrow I had an instinct to leave you alone,
but you shoved spokes into my wheel."

With that he went off, head in air and shoulders well squared.

By this time John's work with and for the Duke had brought him to the notice of divers personages, political, social, and commercial. His Chief pushed him forward, made him speak and write and act in his own name. He became part of what is most stable in the Kingdom, a factor in the management of property, learning at first hand the extraordinary difficulty of adjustment, of nicely considering innumerable and conflicting claims. It was exactly the training he needed, as the Duke was aware. This practical experience put to flight some of John's theories concerning State-managed enterprises. He discovered that corporations, with directors not above the average, lack not only conscience, but also the ability to run any business as well and cheaply as the picked individual. A very interesting case demonstrated this. The Duke of Trent owned a vast tract of land, which his ancestors had reclaimed from the sea. The property was model in every respect, the soil of the richest, the tenants of the thriftiest. In fine, all that was possible had been accomplished, and yet the property had never paid 2 per cent. upon the sum total invested. The Government offered to buy the property at a price much less than its actual cost. The Duke agreed to sell. But it leaked out that the Government intended to raise the rents upon acquiring ownership, and at once the tenants petitioned the Duke not to sell, and offered to pay the increased

rent to him, expressly setting forth that they distrusted
the State as a landlord.   Eventually the Duke did not
sell.   Moreover, it was made plain to John that the
State was a hard taskmaster.   Daily he was brought
into contact with the men who were "running"
things upon principles, and nine times out of ten he
discovered that the Jack in Office was feathering his
own nest, and generally the object of undisguised
jealousy and hate upon the part of those who had
clothed him with brief authority.   It was hard to
find one Progressive with public money at his disposal
who was using it thriftily in the true interest of the
public.   When Sheila quoted Karl Marx, he replied:

"To find the right individual, and increase his
power, is what is wanted by this nation."

"You would make your precious Duke, who is so
dull, a dictator."

"He is one already.   You would prefer the Lancashire Lad?"

"He knows what the people want."

"The people never know what they want."

"We must educate them.   I wish you would read
some tracts I have."

"Everybody talks and reads too much."

"You don't talk much."

"I have the privilege of listening to you."

"You think me silly."

"I think you perfectly charming."

Then they would laugh and drop troublous problems.
John knew that Sheila was suffering from a complaint

common enough amongst young ladies with nothing
to do at home.   She dabbled in Socialism and the New
Thought (which is so old) because Penelope remained
mistress of her father's house.   Desmond, quite unconsciously, neglected her.   He seemed to be pre-occu-
pied by the desire to increase his income.   He had
declined a political pension, and accepted instead the
directorate of half a dozen companies.   One day he sent
for John, who obeyed the summons with a sense of
something pleasant impending.   Doubtless his old Chief
had good news, a timely hint.   Nature confirmed this
agreeable intuition.   As John crossed the Green Park
on his way to Eaton Square he saw scores of waifs lying
upon the grass, wallowing in the genial warmth.   Here
and there, even at eleven in the morning, couples clung
together under the trees.   One pair kissed and kissed
again with a cheerful disregard of less fortunate on-
lookers.   The man was about John's age, with a much
bronzed face.   The girl was thin and pale, a Londoner,
probably a sweated worker in some ill-ventilated room.
Jack had a smack of the sea about him.   The Nancy
on his knee must have waited patiently for this particular hour.   Both were making the most of it.   John
felt an overwhelming sympathy for all true lovers as
he counted the days during the past year when he
had told himself that the sun would never shine again.

Trinder opened the door with a welcoming smile.

"All well?" demanded John.

"All well, sir," repeated Trinder, as he took John's
hat and umbrella.   "Mr. Desmond is in the library."

John went in. Charles Desmond sat at the vast untidy desk, but he got up as John entered, and greeted him very affectionately.

"Sit you down, Jonathan. Take that chair. How fit you look, my dear boy!"

"I am fit, for me," said John.

"The Duke sings your praises. He predicts triumphs. We are quite of one mind about that."

Desmond's manner was reassuring, and yet John felt strangely uneasy, because he had seen this incomparable actor play a Charles Wyndham *rôle* so often.

"You didn't send for me, sir, to repeat what the Duke is kind enough to say about me."

The warmth passed out of Desmond's eyes and voice as he answered: "You are right; but, as you know, I hate a suddden plunge. Seeing you looking so well, and hearing how gallantly you have tackled your work, I rather took for granted that you had got over your spring madness. Have you?"

"No."

"I am sorry. I hoped it had been otherwise, for I was right from the beginning. I'll come to the point. Last night Scaife asked Sheila to marry him. The engagement will be made public to-morrow. I sent for you to prepare you."

John was too stunned to speak.

"I have been puzzled," continued Desmond. "I wondered why he didn't ask before, but he has explained that satisfactorily. There were reasons."

John waited, but the reasons were not forthcoming.

"He loves her; and she loves him. It ought to be the real right thing. It *is* the real right thing."

"You are absolutely sure that he loves her?"

"There is no doubt of it."

John was unable to twist his lips into any form of congratulation. Desmond continued:

"We must admit that he is a conqueror."

"Certainly."

"Sheila is a creature of ideals. I fancy that at first she fell in love with a hero of her own fashioning, a possibly impossible mate. You take me?"

"Not quite."

"She was ready to meet her paragon before she had met him. She created him, in a sense, and clothed him in shining armour. She used to describe the pieces."

"A breastplate of fire and jacinth and brimstone?" said John ironically.

"Your quotation is extraordinarily pat. She saw the jacinth in you, Jonathan. Perhaps the fire and brimstone were not conspicuous."

"I hid them," John affirmed. "That was my great blunder."

"At any rate she guessed you loved her, and that fired her. You have treated us very generously."

"I have been inconceivably stupid."

"My dear fellow!"

"Inconceivably stupid," repeated John, "because I should have remembered that she was Cæsar's sister. Is the marriage likely to take place soon?"

Charles Desmond's ears, always sensitive to subtle vibrations, caught an inflection in John's voice other than that of interrogation. He frowned, but replied suavely: "Why do you ask?"

"She is so very young."

"That, of course, is an excellent reason for going slow; but you had something else in your mind — hadn't you?"

He spoke rather peremptorily in the familiar official tone which brushes aside unnecessary reticences.

"Yes."

"Well, then, let's have it. Between us there should be entire confidence."

John was tempted to reply: "Has there been such confidence on your side?" But he remembered the difference in age and position, and Desmond's unfailing kindness during many years. As he pulled himself together for an effort abominably distasteful, he remembered also how tenderly the father loved his daughter.

"I believe," he replied, with convincing deliberateness, "that Scaife loves Sheila — he *must*!" he added, with a note of passion. "But are you sure that she loves him as he really is? If she tried to fit shining armour on to me, isn't it reasonable to suppose that she is doing exactly the same thing with him?"

Desmond muttered irritably:

"What do you mean by your 'as he really is'?"

"He is unscrupulous." As the word left his lips
John changed voice and manner. His face, ordinarily
too impassive, glowed with excitement; his finely-
formed hands betrayed agitation. "I know him to be
unscrupulous," he repeated, "unscrupulous in small
things — offences which many men might consider
venial, offences too small to be mentioned separately,
but in their sum significant. Because I know this,
because from the bottom of my soul I believe that if
Sheila shared my knowledge she would not love this
man, I hope that the marriage will not take place
soon — or at all."

Desmond met his steady glance in silence. An
immense experience in dealing with men of various
complexions told him that John was absolutely honest.
Possibly, he had always underrated his former secretary, reckoning him to be physically a weakling, and
seemingly the antithesis of Scaife in the possession of
those bodily attributes which make so largely for
success as the world interprets it. Possibly, also the
statesman during that brief pause was able to snatch
a bird's-eye view of his own career, and to weigh
material gains against spiritual losses. His eyes
softened, and John saw that he was affected.

"I pray that the child may be happy," he murmured.
Then, in a firmer voice, he continued: "The marriage
will not take place for a year. That is settled. For the
rest, I am quite sure that my daughter would not find
happiness with her very perfect knight, if she could
find him in the flesh. It's vitally important for her

to see all of us — Scaife, you, myself — as we are.
As for Scaife and your charge against him, we must
remember that he has not enjoyed our advantages."
He paused, and a smile broke upon his face, as the habit
of compromise assailed him. His assumed geniality
made John wince when he continued lightly: "We
selected our parents, Jonathan, rather more carefully
than he did — eh? I prefer to let my mind dwell
upon the good that he has done. He behaved very
handsomely to you, for instance."

"Yes," said John, realizing that the advantage he
had gained was slipping away upon this swift and easy
tide of words.

"Once I was prejudiced against him myself. I admit it frankly. I never asked him to stay with us,
because he was his father's son. A touch of snobbery
that! I don't think there is anything more to be
said."

A few minutes later John was walking back to
Trent House. The couple on the bench had not moved.
The girl sat on the man's lap with her thin arms about
his neck, and her lips conveniently close to his. John
passed near enough to see the sparkle in the man's
blue eyes.

"I kept the sparkle out of my eyes," he thought.

During the afternoon he wrote a short letter to
Sheila, and sent her some red roses, red because he
reminded himself that once lilies-of-the-valley had
been the preferred flower. Because of this virginal
preference, he had hardly dared to think of her save

as the lily maid of Astolat. His ignorance gnawed at his vitals, consuming him with helpless rage. The primal instincts, so fatuously restrained, seized and shook him. Afterward he knew that during this black hour he had become a man, born again after bitter pangs. What he suffered was still visible upon his face when he met the Duke.

"You are in pain, John?"

They were alone and secure from interruption. A minute before John would have laughed ironically at the possibility of showing wounds to any man. He wished that his mother were alive, believing that from her alone he might have drawn sympathy and solace. And yet, during Mrs. Verney's lifetime, he had seldom carried trouble to her.

"What is wrong, my boy?" the Duke asked; and some tone in his voice evoked John's house-master, Basil Warde, who had brought light when all was dark. John raised a haggard face.

"Scaife is engaged to Sheila Desmond."

"I am sorry," said the Duke. "I am very sorry," he repeated, with an emphasis eloquent of much, coming from him. His manner, painfully shy, contrasted itself with the not quite sincere effusions of Charles Desmond. He added hesitatingly: "I guessed how it was with you."

"Thank you," said John, grateful because his Chief's sympathy found its best expression in silence.

"I can easily spare you —— "

"I feel better, working here with you."

Next morning, Sheila's engagement was announced in the papers, and during forty-eight hours was discussed by everybody, everywhere. The social world acclaimed it, mouthing the Scaife millions; the world political tried to look omniscient, and searched for mares' nests. This marriage meant "miching mallecho," the defection of Charles Desmond from the Unionists. He was seen laughing and joking with Arnold Grandcourt; he had accepted an English-made cigar from the Lancashire Lad's case. The Tadpoles and Tapers could prattle of nothing else.

And then Fluff arrived from Paris. He had wired that he was on his way, asking John to meet him at Charing Cross. Hardly out of the carriage, he said savagely: "I read that damned announcement and applied for leave at once. I have three days. We must blow Scaife bang out of the water."

"With pleasure, but — how?"

"Have you been watching him?"

"Do you mean playing the detective? Hardly!"

"Only a fortnight ago the blackguard spent a week in Paris with Genesta Lamb. Ah! I thought that would stir you up."

Rage and disgust were visible in John's eyes.

"They lay low," continued Fluff, "but by the luck of things I saw them dining together at a little-known restaurant. We have certain facilities at the Embassy, and I availed myself of them. They were stopping at the same hotel."

Then John admitted that he had spoken to Scaife

concerning the dancer, and repeated what Scaife had said in reply.

"And you believed him?"

"I — I hung up judgment."

"Now we'll hang up Scaife."

John had a vision of Sheila's face twisted by misery and shame.

"This is awful!" he groaned.

"We'll call it a lynching, just you and I."

"We must tackle Scaife first?"

"He may bluff us. He's an inspired liar. It's astounding Sheila has not found him out. That buying of the peerage ought to have disgusted her."

"She doesn't know it was bought."

"But you knew."

"I was tempted most confoundedly to tell her."

"By Jove! I should have told her."

"I'm no good at snagging," murmured John. Fluff understood the allusion. He grew pinker.

"Snaggers must be snagged," he remarked viciously. "Charles Desmond's face will be worth seeing when you and I pull out our hooks. I can hear him saying: 'To the Tiber with him!'"

"You are quite sure of your facts?"

"Absolutely sure."

He repeated them again, and then, glancing at his watch, decided to ring up Desmond with a view to making an appointment. As he was dashing off, John laid hold of his arm.

"Look here, Esmé, if this can be proved up to the hilt, have you counted the cost?"

"What cost?"

"The cost to you. Sheila will associate you with this humiliation."

"That reminds me, I ought to do the trick alone. I don't want your chance strangled. My chance never existed."

"We must tackle Scaife first," John repeated.

Fluff considered this, then he growled:

"Is that necessary?"

"Let us give formal notice of our intention to tell Desmond the truth, unless Scaife promises to break off the other connection. Perhaps he has broken it off. It may have been broken off in Paris."

Fluff spluttered out:

"Anyway, is he fit to marry Sheila?"

His agitation communicated itself to John. Suddenly he gripped Fluff's arm, so fiercely that the young man winced.

"Fluff," he whispered hoarsely, "for God's sake, help me to do the square thing. The marriage will not take place for a year. And if — if Scaife has put this woman from him, are we justified in interfering?"

Fluff looked hard at his friend, remembering the fact that he was a parson's son, nourished on high ideals. From the first this had appealed to him tremendously. After a pause he said:

"Jonathan, I want to help you. But don't you agree

with me that any self-sacrifice of yours which might ultimately damage Sheila is rot? I'm speaking brutally."

"Go on!"

"I'd do anything almost to prevent this marriage."

"The 'almost' covers things which can't be done. You see, Esmé, Scaife made my ambitions practicable."

"Not out of friendship for you."

"That, I fear, is true."

"You know it's true."

"Because I know I'm not in a position to throw stones at Scaife."

"What do you mean?"

"I guessed that he was using me for his own ends, and I let myself be bought because I wanted Sheila so desperately. My hands are not clean."

Fluff seized one and shook it with violence.

"John, I love you for telling me this. When a man like you does besmirch himself for the woman he cares about, why, then he becomes human."

John laughed grimly. Fluff quoted a line that had caught his fancy:

"'We are all in the gutter, but some of us are looking at the stars.'"

"Because of that we must do the square thing."

"Shall we go to Scaife now?"

John shook his head.

"A letter would be better. He deals with his correspondence immediately after breakfast."

"Let's write the letter at once."

After several attempts this was done. Fluff insisted that his name should be mentioned.

"DEAR SCAIFE" (John wrote),

"Esmé Kinloch tells me that you were in Paris a fortnight ago accompanied by Miss Genesta Lamb. Kinloch and I must ask for your word of honour that this connection with Miss Lamb has come to an end. Without this pledge, we shall be obliged to lay the facts before Mr. Desmond."

The letter was sealed, and taken to Scaife's flat by a commissionaire. The answer arrived at Trent House next morning in the form of a telegram.

"*Your absurd letter is in my waste-paper basket.*"

Fluff laughed.

"An undefeated scoundrel!" he exclaimed. "Well, Jonathan, now we have a free hand."

"Yes," said John, frowning.

"I shall make an appointment with Charles Desmond for this afternoon."

He hurried from the room to telephone to Desmond, but John sat frowning and staring at the telegram, at a loss to understand Scaife's attitude, and yet uneasily conscious that Scaife was playing some amazing game of his own.

Fluff came back from the telephone, and said: "I've left you out. I told Desmond that I had come from Paris on business of pressing importance. He will give me ten minutes."

"When?"

"At half-past three."

But Fluff had hesitated for a fraction of a second.

"You made the appointment for three," said John.

Fluff blushed. When the friends parted, it was settled that they should leave Trent House together at ten minutes to three.

CHAPTER XVI

AS SOON as they had entered Desmond's house, John saw Scaife's umbrella, which he indicated with a gesture to Fluff. Trinder said discreetly: "Mr. Scaife is upstairs." He looked at Fluff: "I am to show your lordship into the library."

They walked into the room where John had measured Sheila. Desmond expressed a mild astonishment at seeing John.

"John insisted on coming," explained Fluff.

Then the story was told. Kinloch made no attempt to spare the father, who seemed overwhelmed with indignation and anger, as he stammered out:

"The d-damned fellow is upstairs at this very m-moment."

Unable to control himself, he walked to the window, staring miserably at the trees in the square. He had heard, of course, the gossip which linked Scaife and the dancer together, accepting it as gossip, and assuming for granted that any such connection, if it existed, would be severed at the right time and in the right way. Such affairs were always settled quietly by men of the world. At this point a ray of light descended upon him. Scaife might be black or white, but assuredly wise beyond his years in all wordly knowledge. Desmond stood still for nearly two minutes, with his fingers twisted together behind a shapely back. When he turned, his brow was comparatively smooth, although his voice rang out defiantly:

"Upon second thoughts it seems impossible. Have you any objection to repeat to Scaife what you have told me?"

"Not at all," said Fluff; "but I wish that John would go. This is my affair, not his."

"It is very much John's affair," said Desmond with finality. He rang the bell as he spoke, and then went back to the window.

"Go!" whispered Fluff to his friend.

John shook his head.

Two minutes later, Scaife came in with a breezy air of indifference. He greeted John and Fluff politely.

"A charge has been brought against you," said Desmond.

"By our friends here?"

His slightly flippant tone aroused Desmond.

"The charge is serious!" Then, without any preliminary fencing, he continued: "I understood that you went to Samarkand some days ago; but it seems you were in Paris."

"I was in Paris," said Scaife. "What of it?"

"With Miss Genesta Lamb?"

"Yes."

Desmond made an indignant gesture, but his voice remained under control as he asked coldly:

"Then we are to infer ——?" He paused for an instant.

"Infer nothing," said Scaife, with what seemed to Fluff and John brazen audacity. He met Desmond's glance without flinching as he went on: "If I give you my word of honour that there is nothing between Miss Lamb and myself to which either you, sir, or your daughter could take exception, will it suffice?"

"No," said Desmond.

"I was going to say — will it suffice for the moment, till these gentlemen," he sneered, "have left the house?"

Desmond did not hesitate.

"They brought this charge against you. You owe it to yourself and to me to refute it — if you can — before them."

"In that case, will you send for Sheila?"

"Certainly not."

"But she must be told. If I am the sort of blackguard John Verney thinks me, she must be made to see me as such. You can't throw dust in her eyes. She is intelligent, and she is strong." With dignity he added: "I do not yield even to you, sir, the right of protecting my future wife against anything likely to hurt her. It is necessary that she should hear what I have to say."

"I will fetch her," said Desmond curtly. He moved toward the door hesitatingly, and paused on the threshold.

"If you can't clear yourself, you had better understand that this house will be closed to you."

"I understand that."

Desmond went out. Scaife looked at John, but Fluff, crimson in the face, and shaking with rage, exclaimed loudly:

"You are a cad to drag a pure girl into this beastliness — a cad! If you were not a cad, you'd bolt, now — and never come back."

John saw Scaife clench his fists. Then, with a tremendous effort, he restrained his rage and smiled grimly.

"I'm not the bolting sort of cad, my good fellow."

John took Fluff's arm and led him aside. Scaife stood still, as if master of the situation, but his face was very pale, and John found himself at a loss to interpret the expression in his eyes. They waited five minutes before Desmond came back followed by Sheila. As soon as Desmond entered the room, he said curtly: "I have indicated the nature of the charge."

Sheila was trembling, and her eyes were sparkling with excitement. John saw at once that she was frightened, for nothing alarms a maid so much as her ignorance concerning the real man whom she loves. Moreover, from her white face and dilated eyes, John realized that she did love Scaife with the passion which he himself might have aroused in her. She greeted John and Fluff nervously, and then sat down, letting her gaze rest upon Scaife, who, in his turn,

indicated suppressed excitement.   Before Scaife spoke,
he looked at John.   Then he turned to Sheila.

"I am accused," he said curtly, "of carrying on an
intrigue with another woman, when I have the honour
to be engaged to you."

Sheila nodded.

Desmond interrupted.

"I have told her nothing else."

"The name of the woman is Genesta Lamb."

He spoke softly, with his eyes upon Sheila's face.
She nodded again.

"Before I was engaged to you, I told John Verney
that Miss Lamb was a lady of spotless reputation and
a great friend of mine.   I offered to introduce him to
her.   He refused."

"Why did you refuse?" said Sheila.

From the expression of Scaife's face, John perceived
that he had wished Sheila to ask this question.   He
saw also that she remembered the scene at Hurlingham
and what he had said about the gulf between her and
the dancer.

As John hesitated, Fluff rushed indiscreetly to the
rescue.

"What an irrelevant question!   Any man has the
right to refuse to know anybody else without giving
reasons."

"True," said Scaife smoothly.   "I'll answer the
question myself.   John Verney refused to meet Miss
Lamb because — like his friend Kinloch — he hoped
for the worst."

"No, no," cried Sheila.

John flushed deeply, for the well-timed thrust was driven home. He had hoped for the worst, although, unlike Esmé, he had not taken that worst for granted. As he remained silent, Scaife laughed derisively.

· "I won't ask him to incriminate himself, but it seemed to me at the time that my word as between friends and partners should have sufficed."

"I accepted your statement," said John.

"I am glad to hear that. I have tried to be a sincere friend to you; can you say upon your honour that you have entertained the same sincerity toward me?"

There was a pause. John was looking at Scaife, but he knew that Sheila had turned her eyes from Scaife to him, and that she must be expecting an affirmation from him as strong as Scaife's. Temptation gripped him to evade the real question, to plead — as he might have done — that he for his part had desired sincerely to be Scaife's friend. The situation was extraordinarily complex, because John, as we know, had endeavoured to purge his mind of Scaife as he was at Harrow, and to see him as he appeared to Sheila and the world. The conviction that he had always failed so to see him rose up invincibly strong as he met Scaife's scornful glance. As he remained silent, Desmond said irritably:

"Have you nothing to say, John?"

John replied with reluctance: "I broke off the

partnership because I found it impossible to be Scaife's sincere friend."

"I knew it," Scaife exclaimed. Sheila sighed, as she met John's steady glance.

If there was triumph in Scaife's exclamation, pity, distress, and disappointment infused Sheila's hardly audible sigh. She jumped to her feet with startling suddenness. Then, speaking with excitement, she said impetuously:

"I wish to hear no more. Reginald's word is quite enough for me."

She turned bravely to her lover, holding out both hands with a gesture superbly feminine. Those present beheld her for the first time as a woman grown to full stature and stirred to the finest issues. Her beauty revealed itself as far surpassing mere outward comeliness. The triune spirit of Faith and Hope and Love transfigured her. Scaife said hoarsely:

"Sheila!"

"I trust you," she replied solemnly.

He took her hands; and John saw that he was profoundly affected. If he had ever questioned Scaife's love for this tender creature that doubt was now resolved. The strong man trembled and grew pale; the girl had conquered her fears. She smiled serenely.

"You trust me?" he repeated, and John hardly recognized his voice.

"From the bottom of my heart."

As she spoke John prayed that such faith might

not be confounded. Soon he heard Fluff saying savagely to Desmond:

"Is that enough for you, sir?" As Desmond did not answer, the young man went on with extreme agitation: "Does he deny that he took this dancer to Paris?"

"I deny nothing — to you," Scaife replied. "I repeat for the last time that Miss Lamb is my friend, and the man who says a word against her reputation must settle with me, but not here."

"You, not I, have injured that reputation," said Esmé. "I am prepared to shoulder my responsibility in this matter to the last ounce."

Then John spoke out of the fulness of his heart. Fluff's passion of rage fired him.

"Sheila, you must see that we loathe coming here, that we would have spared you if it had been possible. All this is horrible."

Desmond, torn in two between his knowledge of the facts and Scaife's overpowering assertion of innocence, addressed Sheila persuasively.

"Child, you had better leave us; let me deal with this?"

"I cannot go now, Daddy. You" — her soft voice was slightly defiant —"even you condemned him."

"Reginald must refute this monstrous charge."

"I can do so," said Scaife.

"If you can do so," said John quickly, "why have you not done so already?"

"Because I wanted to make sure that the woman I loved would accept my bare word."

Out of the back of John's brain crept the horrid thought: "Have we blundered?" And then an odd silence prevailed, as if each were touched by the hands of destiny and lulled to sleep by a sense of impotence. Scaife alone of the four men seemed to be in fullest possession of all faculties, alert and defiant. Staring at his dark face, John felt that he had been tricked, and that Scaife had lured him hither to humiliate him in Sheila's eyes. Perhaps at this moment a truer knowledge of himself awoke in him, for a great moment engenders great thoughts. At whatever cost to himself, let Sheila be spared! Presently he heard Scaife's voice, clear but ironic:

"I am surprised that Kinloch has not told you, Sheila, that I have given diamonds to Miss Lamb."

At this Sheila winced. Scaife continued in the same mocking tone:

"And sables and a motor."

"This is the last audacity," Fluff muttered.

"You had some good reason for such generosity," said Sheila, in a firm voice.

Scaife exclaimed triumphantly:

"By God! you are a wife worth winning! Yes, I had a reason, the best of reasons. Genesta Lamb" — as he spoke her name his voice softened — "has been hardly treated. I had to share some of my good things with her."

Desmond broke in impatiently:

"What is Miss Lamb to you?"

Scaife paused, tasting his triumph, letting his eyes wander from face to face, before he answered quietly:

"She is my half-sister."

Sheila uttered an inarticulate gasp of relief. John knew instantly that his enemy had spoken the truth, and that this scene had been carefully planned and rehearsed, played with consummate skill to the utter confounding of himself and Esmé Kinloch. Desmond displayed a shadow of a smile. Fluff said loudly:

"I don't believe it."

"The explanation is so simple," Scaife continued. "Genesta Lamb is my father's illegitimate daughter. My sister has a strong will — nearly as strong as mine. Unwisely, she insisted upon secrecy. I warned her that there would be gossip, and perhaps trouble for both of us. But she is like me in that also: gossip and possible trouble merely amuse her. And there was her mother to be considered, once a dancer, but now a very respectable person, who lives in the odour of sanctity at St. Leonards-on-Sea. I admit that I have done foolish things. I have no other sister. I gave Genesta diamonds and furs, and a good time generally. That is all. If you question my facts I can refer you to my father or the family solicitor."

The anti-climax need not be recorded. John and Fluff escaped after some empty words of apology, which Scaife seemed to receive in an admirably forgiving spirit. It was impossible at such a moment to analyze impressions, which remained, however, for future contemplation. Scaife's tremendous triumph overshadowed Sheila's reproachful glances. Desmond's face indicated nothing except relief.

The young men hastened in silence to their club.

"What a mess I've made of it!" wailed Fluff, after a stiff whiskey-and-soda.

John said impassively:

"He planned this. That's the ugly side to it. If Sheila should discover how cheap this triumph really is ——!"

"Cheap's the word," said Fluff, more hopefully.

"We blundered into a snare," continued John. "It was spread deliberately with a cleverness we couldn't expose. Sooner or later Sheila must find him out. That's tragedy. He ought to have answered our letter frankly."

"Suppose Genesta Lamb is not his sister."

"There is the strongest likeness: the same chin and eyes, the same grace and swiftness of movement. Heavens! what a fool I have been!"

"If ever there was a — knock-out ——!"

"What has been knocked out?" asked John. "I'll tell you — several chunks of obstinacy and stupidity. I have blinded myself. Now I see. That's an advantage."

"We can't give our eyes to Sheila."

"Her own are sharp enough."

"But she adores him."

"She adores a perfect knight of her own creation. She forged his armour, and tried it on me, but it didn't fit. Think of her as dazzled by a consummate actor."

"He certainly knows how to take the stage."

John added ironically: "And everything else he can lay his hands on. That is his only weakness. He grabs too much. For the moment he holds Sheila tight. To-morrow he may be snagging office."

"He will hold Sheila tight till they are married."

"They are not married yet."

Fluff exclaimed admiringly: "By Jove, you are a stayer!"

Late that night, alone in his room, John examined a photograph of Sheila. She gazed pensively at him, with the familiar half-smile upon her lips which had always appealed to him — the interrogatory smile of youth curiously aware of its own inexperience. The inscription, "To dear old Jonathan from Sheila," made him feel acutely unhappy. Reaction had set in, and he was physically very tired, having worked hard with the Duke.

Still staring at the photograph, he drew from his pocket a letter which had come by the last post.

DEAR JOHN:

The sun mustn't set without my telling you that I'm miserable because I let you go this afternoon without a word. It was horrid of me. And all the time I knew that Cæsar would have done what you and Esmé did. Jonathan dear, I am so unhappy when I think of the unhappiness I have caused you. I suppose you hate me, but I shall always love you.

SHEILA.

John placed the photograph inside the letter, and held it firmly between his fingers. He was about to tear up both, believing that an act of violence would alleviate the pain that he was suffering. Then he stayed his hand, reflecting that there was no hurry.

He glanced at his surroundings.

The Duchess had chosen for him two charming rooms — a small sitting-room and a bedroom. Trent House was a sanctuary for many members of the Kinloch family. The rooms assigned to John had been furnished long ago for a poor relation, a man of many losses. John could remember him, when he spent an *exeat* from Harrow at Trent House — a tall, lean old fellow with a kindly face, who talked to the boys about salmon-fishing and stalking with what appeared to John fascinating keenness. Fluff had explained that this kinsman managed the Duke's sporting interests. Later, John had learned more. The old man had lost his money, and his wife, and his children. A thousand times he must have sat in John's chair, thinking of these losses. Above the mantelpiece his quiet, pleasant face smiled at his successor.

"You made the best of it," muttered John. "Nothing soured you."

Then he wondered at the savage impulse which had almost driven him to destroy Sheila's photograph and her pitiful letter. From his desk he took another photograph, slightly faded. His heart began to beat more quickly as he saw the gay, delightful face of

Sheila's brother, so wonderfully like her in feature and character. From the envelope which held the photograph he drew forth Cæsar's last letter. He knew it word for word, but he read and re-read two sentences:

Old Jonathan, you have been the best friend a man ever had the only one I love as much as my own brothers — *and even more.* It was from knowing you that I came to see what good-for-nothing fools some fellows are. You were always so unselfish and *straight* . . .

John replaced the letter and picture, adding to them Sheila's letter and photograph. Then he locked the desk, and confronted the question:

"Am I unselfish and straight?"

His mother and his uncle had taught him that nothing else mattered, that other things must pass away, that this alone remained — the record. Of late he had been engrossed with the other things.

He sat still for a couple of hours, fighting hard. Fluff — had he seen him — might well have supposed that his friend was planning a campaign against Scaife. So David might have looked when he weighed his chances against Goliath. But John was fighting a more dangerous foe — his baser self — whom he must conquer or perish.

CHAPTER XVII

SHORTLY after Sheila's engagement, one of the Cabinet Ministers resigned. The event caused more than the usual excitement, inasmuch as the selection of a successor would reveal a secret carefully withheld from the Opposition; for it was still uncertain whether or not the younger members of the Government possessed real power. When the vacant office was offered to Arnold Grandcourt everybody knew that the great Liberal party was dished. The word "Liberal" ceased to be used by the Unionist press.

"It's a Radical declaration of weakness," the Duke observed to John.

Only a fortnight before Grandcourt had delivered a fiery speech in his constituency, the largest of the Midland manufacturing towns. He began by remarking that his countrymen wanted straight talk, and that he proposed to give it to them. The speech, in fine, was a tremendous indictment of landlords and vested interests, a blow delivered at the class to which Grandcourt belonged and which he had abandoned. Upon that account it created a panic. The same speech from the Lancashire Lad might have provoked laughter,

Erza Kitteredge being of the people, and therefore animated by the popular desire to bring about a more equable distribution of property. Till now, outside Lancashire, the Lad had not been taken too seriously. His inclusion in the Cabinet had been hailed by such men as Sir Giles Mottisfont and Admiral Pundle as proof that there were enough demagogues in the kingdom to enforce representation in high places. Charles Desmond was quoted as saying that the Tory squires "deserved" Kitteredge. When Scaife joined the Radicals, he instructed his editors to report Mr. Kitteredge's speeches in full, and shortly afterward the nation as a whole began to realize that the Lad had "come to stay." In the House he was listened to attentively, although regarded by all Tories and the few remaining Whigs as a buccaneer. When a candidate for one of the East End London boroughs, he had exhorted the electors to vote for Kitteredge, God, and Liberty!

The Lad sat smilingly upon the platform when Grandcourt delivered what the Radical papers termed an "epoch-making" speech. Scaife occupied the chair next to him.

Of course, only Grandcourt knows whether he would have made such a speech to his constituents had he known that within two weeks he would be seeking reelection. What followed is of too recent occurrence to be dwelt upon. When Grandcourt, as Cabinet Minister, represented himself as candidate he was opposed by a brilliant Unionist, and ignominiously defeat'

The blow staggered a Government exulting in a huge
majority and the conviction that the manufacturing
classes to a man were on their side.

Immediately Scaife offered to resign his seat in
Grandcourt's favour. The offer was accepted. Samarkand received Grandcourt with enthusiasm, and the
Scaife papers announced that the election would not
be contested.

John was one of the first to hear of Scaife's act of
self-sacrifice. Desmond, naturally, was full of it.
Even the Duke, who detested Scaife, admitted that
the thing had been done handsomely; Sheila could talk
of nothing else.

"I know what the House of Commons means to
him," she said.

Oddly enough — and this illustrates nicely the
forbearance exercised by newspapers when dealing
with powerful rivals — the Tory Press united in saying
pleasant things about the People's Friend. Not a
journalist was bold enough to hint that this was a
bid for increased popularity, and that such an act
constituted an immense claim upon a grateful Government. The Duke, however, saw clearly that Scaife
had become the ally of Grandcourt and Kitteredge.

When John met Sheila, she said with a shade of defiance in her soft voice: "Do you remember that
match at Hurlingham?"

Something of the old pleasant relations had been
resumed between these two. Desmond had said
with his genial smile: "You know that we want you,

old fellow. Nobody else can fill your particular corner."

"Quite well."

"And the remarks about Reggie's not playing for his side."

"Perfectly."

"Shall I tell you a secret?"

"Please."

"I asked Reggie to give up his seat. It was my idea."

John stared at her, realizing that he had perhaps underrated her intelligence.

"That was extraordinarily clever of you."

Sheila repeated coldly: "Clever? What do you mean?"

"Haven't you realized what an immense pull this gives him with the men of his party who really count?"

"You don't accuse him of thinking of that?"

"Evidently he did not think of it."

"As for my cleverness," said Sheila, "I'll confess that I was trying to measure my influence with him. Of course he will find another seat, but he may have to wait, and he hates waiting."

"Anyhow, you have covered him with glory."

"But he never considered that," she persisted, with a flush in her cheeks. Her persistence made John wonder whether she was as convinced of Scaife's altruism as she tried to appear. She continued: "He loathed the idea at first. But the Government were in a tight place. And no other seat of importance was to be had for the asking."

"They didn't ask?"

"Of course not. He did it to please me."

John would have thought no more of the matter, but it happened that he met, a few days later, a rather voluble Progressive upon the London County Council, with whom there were questions to be discussed concerning some of the Duke's rights. The business finished, John was preparing to take leave, when the Progressive said abruptly: "Mr. Scaife is a friend of yours, Mr. Verney."

"We were in the same house at Harrow."

"Does the failing health of the member of this borough interest him?"

"Is Mr. Littledale's health failing?"

"Perhaps I have been indiscreet. I'm sure his Grace knows it. Yes, yes, between ourselves, doctors are urging him to spend a year abroad."

"I see. You want a fighter."

"Exactly; till the last election, we have not had a look in. As you are aware, the Duke was almost able to regard it as a pocket-borough. But we can beat you — we can beat you."

The Progressive rubbed hands not immaculate, and smiled. He boasted that he could be all things to all men. John and John's Chief were, of course, reactionaries, but friends and brothers notwithstanding.

"With Scaife?" said John tentatively.

"We must have somebody as strong as Mr. Scaife. When he was asked to step out of Samarkand, it was understood that a more important constituency would be found."

"Was Mr. Scaife asked to give up Samarkand? Surely there is some mistake. The seat was given up voluntarily. At least, so I have been told."

The Progressive smiled condescendingly, and his left eyelid flickered. It was rather important that John, as the Duke's agent, should think him a big man.

"Of course, it was so reported; but you may take it from me that your friend was asked. I happen to know. And Mr. Littledale's failing health was mentioned at the time. You have rather drawn me, Mr. Verney, but I am dealing with a gentleman;" and his left eyelid flickered again.

John returned to Trent House, marvelling at Scaife's slimness. He had scored all round, established an immense claim upon his party, flattered and pleased his future wife, and disarmed criticism by his modesty and candour.

When he had finished his report to the Duke, John said:

"Did you know that Littledale is seriously ill?"

"Yes," said the Duke. He stared at John, and chuckled. Then he leant forward: "Does that affect you?"

"Affect me?" said John, with some surprise. "Why should it affect me, sir? It is likely to affect Scaife."

"Scaife?"

The Duke's tone expressed astonishment.

"Scaife was mentioned as Littledale's successor."

The Duke laughed, staring still harder at John.

"I wanted to surprise you. And you have surprised me. If they put up Scaife, we shall have a terrific fight. Are you dismayed?"

"I suppose you can find a strong man," said John doubtfully.

"I have found one, my dear boy."

"May I ask his name?"

"Certainly. John Verney."

The Duke liked these mild jokes, and he was delighted to see that John was genuinely confounded.

"I picked you from the moment I heard of Littledale's illness, but I never thought of Scaife as your opponent. I ask again — are you dismayed?"

"Before I answer that, sir, I must tell you something."

"Say exactly what is in your mind, my boy."

"As you know, I lost my last election through an unscrupulous trick." The Duke nodded. "But I deserved to lose it, because I was not so honest as my opponent. I differ from Towlerson on many points, but he is absolutely sincere. Tariff Reform had to be a plank in my platform. It was made plain to me that I must stand firmly upon it — or step off it and make room for another fellow. I ought to have stepped off it."

He paused; the Duke said slowly:

"You have no faith in Tariff Reform?"

"Not as applied to England and our textiles. As

applied to the consolidation of the Empire, as a weapon of defence rather than offence — yes."

"Go on, Jonathan."

"I wanted to win that election." His voice became fuller, vibrating with emotion. "By Heaven, how badly I wanted a triumph! Because I thought it included Sheila, and the possibility of pouring into her lap prizes which, perhaps, she coveted more than I did. Duke, I went into that fight perspiring with shame, pledged to advocate a policy, and a half-baked policy, in which I had no faith."

"I respect you for telling me this."

"I'm by instinct and training and conviction a Conservative. I look upon Socialism as the dullest and most absurd of tyrannies. I'm an Imperialist to the core, although I abominate Jingoism, but I know that the peace of the world depends upon the Powers that can enforce it, and England should possess a stronger Navy, and an Army able to repel any possible invasion. Lastly, I know this man Scaife to be a diabolically clever rascal, and I'm spoiling for a fight to a finish with him. That's about all."

"It's quite enough for me," replied the Duke, smiling, "and I think I can persuade my friends of the Conservative Association that it ought to be enough for them."

From this moment the excitement began. John discovered that his kind Chief had come to an understanding with the Conservative Association some time

before, and that they were more or less prepared to
accept a ducal nominee. John's name, therefore,
was made public upon the day when it became known
that Littledale would apply for the Chiltern Hundreds.
Upon the following afternoon the *St. Stephen's Gazette*
hinted guardedly that Scaife might be invited to
contest the seat in the Radical interest. This meant
the passing over of another patriot, who was hardly
strong enough to contest an election now regarded as
of supreme interest and importance. Grandcourt's
defeat in his own constituency had opened the eyes
of the Government to the fact that their huge majority
in the House could be assumed no longer to represent
a majority as great amongst the electorate. If this
London borough rejected Scaife, matters would be
serious.

When John saw Charles Desmond, the great man
said tentatively:

"You may have Reginald against you."

"So the *St. Stephen's* says."

"Sheila has asked him to refuse the nomination."

John smiled, wondering whether Scaife would find
it as easy to please his future wife when Duty no
longer walked arm-in-arm with Inclination.

"He won't refuse," said John, still smiling.

"I don't see how he can. And, oddly enough, some
of the Scaife buildings are in the borough, and one
of the playgrounds. Did you know that?"

"Of course."

"Look here, Jonathan, are you strong enough for this

contest? There will be tremendous forces against you, and two failures in succession might mean political extinction. The Socialists have withdrawn their candidate. They will work tooth and nail for Scaife. And under the circumstances I can't help you. I remain stanch in my allegiance to Free Trade. I can take no part in this publicly; privately I might urge Scaife to wait for another opening."

"He won't," repeated John.

Desmond eyed him sharply.

"Do you think that this is a put-up job?"

"How could I know anything about that, sir?"

"I asked what you thought. The damnable thing about party politics is that honourable men are ready to impute base motives to their opponents." As John remained silent, Desmond concluded: "I have spoken sorely against the grain."

"You advise me to withdraw?"

"Without in any sense underrating your ability, I reply — yes."

"The Duke has set his heart upon my winning."

"You can't — if Scaife stands."

"I'm willing to try."

Desmond looked rather annoyed. Day by day the conviction forced itself upon his mind that John's failures had aroused an extravagant pity in Sheila, whereas Scaife's success had begun perhaps to pall. At the same time he dismissed as absurd any comparison between the two men as political assets. Scaife dwarfed John. A contest between them could only

end in more disaster for John. He told himself that
he was giving the young fellow sound advice, and it
irritated him that John should not take it. Knowledge of his former secretary being entirely super-
ficial, it never occurred to him that an impassivity
largely constitutional covered an extraordinarily active
will, a will that required the stimulus of contradiction
to work properly. Difficulties, in fine, had accomplished for John growth. The brutal "You can't"
might depress for a moment, but it begot the irresistible "By Heaven, I will!"

John stayed for luncheon and sat by Sheila. He
saw that she was very greatly excited, and torn in
two between affection for an old friend and pride and
faith in a lover. To John's amazement, for he had
taken Desmond's talk with a pinch of salt, she reit-
erated her wish that Scaife (who was not present at
luncheon) should wait for a happier opportunity.

"Father told you that I had asked him to do so?"

"Yes. It's very generous, but you are asking too
much of the keenest politician I know."

Sheila made a tiny grimace, for already politics
had cast a shadow between Scaife and her. Being
essentially feminine and with a strong infusion of
Irish blood in her veins, she leapt to the conclusion
that Scaife had too many claims upon his attention.
Because he was so much to her she had begun to
measure what she was to him.

And often he frightened her. That very morning
he had come to her with a disagreeable story of

a confidential agent dismissed for incompetence. "You say he had been with you six years. Wasn't it horrid dismissing him?"

"If I let that sort of thing worry me, where should I be? The fellow was very impertinent. I had to kick him out of the room."

"Figuratively?"

"Not a bit of it! I kicked him as hard as I could. I was in a devil of a rage."

For an instant John saw a tremor of fear in her eyes, and he had a glimpse of a mind overstrained by the effort to compute power over a masterful man. From certain words that had escaped her, he guessed that the affianced lover had not been so constant in attendance as the suitor. Also — and this was intuition — John guessed that Scaife had aroused an expectation of confidence which he had been unable to satisfy. He smiled ironically, when he thought of Sheila putting certain questions to a Mazarin who loved scheming for its own sake.

He went away much saddened, fortified in his previous conviction that Scaife, in attempting to grab the whole earth, would crush this morsel of delicate porcelain.

"But I can do nothing," he repeated to himself. "If this man is what I think him, let me pray that she may never find him out too late."

During the next week he was busy with engagements from nine in the morning till twelve at night.

The Duchess plunged into the ardours of the contest, and began that personal campaign of canvassing which afforded so much copy to the half-penny press. The Duke owned rows of model buildings in the heart of the borough, and in one of his houses John's headquarters was established.

Then, with a fanfare of jubilation, the Radical Press announced that John Verney would be opposed by Reginald Scaife.

CHAPTER XVIII

BEFORE the writ was issued and the date of
the election set by the Returning Officer,
John and his supporters realized that the
contest must be fought upon general rather than
particular lines, between the friend of the people and
the representative of a great nobleman. From the
first, therefore, it became certain that the personality
of the candidates would count enormously.

Another factor in the situation, which enhanced
the excitement, was the large floating population in
the borough, who would vote as fancy dictated. Both
parties were able to count upon recognized supporters,
for the organization on each side had been admirable,
although the Radicals had shown greater enterprise
and energy.

Unfortunately, as the Duke pointed out to John,
the floating population of any borough is likely to
be indifferent, if not actively hostile, to the claims of
the established order of things, whether such things are
well administered or the contrary.

"They shift, because they are dissatisfied with
existing conditions. Many of these fellows have been
driven out of the country by neglect or injustice.

They distrust authority, because authority has used
them and abused them. Otherwise they would not
be drifting about at the mercy of the tides of supply
and demand."

"I shall talk to them," said the Duchess.

"My dear, I want you to keep out of this."

"But you know, Archie, that I won't — and can't."
The Duke shrugged his shoulders.

"We shall have Bott, of course?" said the Duchess.

Mr. Montagu Bott is, perhaps, the most famous
and capable of the Conservative Parliamentary agents.
And he had served the Duke of Trent loyally upon
many occasions.

"I suppose so. How I dislike the admirable Bott!"

Alone with John, the Duke admitted that the admirable Bott was inevitable. Next day, John met
him for the first time, a Corinthian pillar of a man,
very florid, decorative in manner, with a deep, booming, impressive voice, and soft, pudgy hands, too yield-
ing and plastic. The Duke received him nervously,
with a flicker of humour about his lips. He had
whispered to John: "We must get what fun we can
out of Bott."

"Delighted to be enrolled under your Grace's
banner once more," boomed the basso-profundo.

The Duke shook hands and introduced John.

"Let us understand each other," he said pleasantly.
"You are not under my banner. Mr. Verney flies
his own flag."

"Quite, quite! I take your Grace. But still —

between ourselves — the electorate regards this contest as a fight between a Duke and a demagogue."

"Dear, dear!" sighed the Duke.

"A fight," continued Mr. Bott, warming to his work, and speaking with fluency, "between — if I may say so — the powers that make for good in this nation and the powers that make for evil.   A fight, gentlemen, between Beelzebub and —— "

"Spare me," entreated John's Chief.   "You are too complimentary.   Now — the programme."

Mr. Bott drew from his pocket a small map of the constituency, mounted upon linen, and coloured with red, green, and blue.   The houses marked in red represented the Radicals and Labour men, who had joined forces, the true blues were designated under their own azure, the doubtful voters were suitably bedecked in green.   As Mr. Bott explained, many Irish lived amongst them.

"We must tickle their palates," said the agent. "Ezra Kitteredge is going to gorge them next Friday."

He glanced at John, who wondered whether Mr. Bott would make impossible demands upon him as a caterer for coarse appetites.

"Hot stuff," he added persuasively.   Perhaps, in his turn, he realized that John Verney would not pepper phrases to order.   John said:

"You expect hot stuff from me, Mr. Bott?"

"Hot and hot, if you please."

"I'm a cold-water man," explained John mildly. "I shall endeavour to pour freezing facts upon the red-hot misstatements which the Lancashire Lad is temperamentally unable to avoid making."

"Bravo, John!" said the Duke.

Mr. Bott looked rather astonished, but he said afterward that he had perceived with satisfaction a reassuring fighting flame in John's gray eyes, indicating that he was not quite so cool and impassive as he appeared to be.

"Cold water — lots and lots of it," continued John.

Mr. Bott nodded solemnly.

"You will supply the soap, Bott," suggested the Duke.

Mr. Bott smiled, displaying large white teeth.

"Yes, your Grace, I keep soap in stock, and ammonia also. By the way, Mr. Verney, have you ever heard a story about a certain Captain Ormsby, who prepared the plan by which Mr. Scaife entered Ladysmith?"

"How did you hear that?" asked the Duke quickly.

"It was whispered to me."

"Not by my son?"

"Certainly not."

The Duke looked relieved. Mr. Bott continued blandly: "I happen to possess evidence that the story is true. Captain Ormsby was scurvily treated. If the affair were put before the electors, if —— "

John interrupted.

"Mr. Bott, I refuse to use such weapons."

Mr. Bott retreated gracefully.

"After all," he murmured, "such weapons sometimes

turn themselves into boomerangs. Mr. Verney, I do not jump hastily to conclusions, but I am happy to be able to serve you, and I am of opinion that we can work together."

Nothing of importance happened till the following Friday. Each candidate wisely began the campaign with a carefully worded appeal to his own particular friends. On the Friday, Ezra Kitteredge addressed a big mass meeting of men in and about the docks. It happened by the luck of things that John, who had spoken in a hall hard by, was returning to Trent House with the Duchess and Bott, and the Duchess's car passed the huge warehouse wherein the Lancashire Lad was still holding forth. Above the doorway was a flaming screen. "Down with the Dukes!"

"Let's go in," said the Duchess.

"Your Grace — !" protested Mr. Bott.

"My dear Mr. Bott, they won't down Duchesses, and besides we shan't be recognized. Come on, John! It will be glorious fun."

John, knowing that he was billed to address the same audience in the same place upon the following night, was more than willing to spy out the land. Mr. Bott's protests availed nothing. The car came to a standstill about a hundred yards from the warehouse, and the dauntless Duchess, effectively disguised in a rough ulster and a tam-o'-shanter, led the way.

"We shan't get in," remarked Bott hopefully.

The warehouse being not quite full, the strangers

were admitted without attracting attention. Sheila was sitting beside Scaife. Kitteredge was speaking, and all eyes were focussed upon his round, rosy face, aglow with excitement and passion. The crowd listened in silence to sharp, caustic sentences, rapped out one after the other, with an odd persuasiveness, and then hammered home with violent gestures of head and hands. When delivered of anything particularly virulent, Kitteredge smiled disarmingly, and his bright blue eyes twinkled. His deprecating expression seemed to say: "My kind friends, it really shocks me to expose these naked truths."

Suddenly the speech became personal. The crowd grunted with satisfaction. Dull, yellow faces flushed, tired eyes sparkled, bodies began to shuffle restlessly, swaying hither and thither like cattle about to stampede.

Kitteredge mentioned the Duke of Trent by name.

Mr. Bott, upon the other side of his precious charge, whispered: "Let us slip away, your Grace."

"Not for all the diamonds of Golconda!"

Kitteredge began to raise his voice, which had a peculiarly vibrant and penetrating resonance.

"And now my friends, for whom are you going to vote? For the brilliant representative of progress, for the advocate of a more equable distribution of wealth, for the strong man who has shown in a thousand ways and in a thousand places that he has pity for the weak, or" — he paused and drawled out John's name — "for Mr. Verney?"

The Duchess nudged John delightedly.

"He's selecting the forceps," she whispered.

"He's administered the gas," John replied.

The Lancashire Lad continued in the same compassionate tone: "Mr. John Verney is, I believe, a very amiable young man, very well-meaning, but a reactionary, the puppet of a powerful Duke — a Duke, let me remind you, who drove from his vast estates in Scotland hundreds of thrifty, honest, happy crofters, tearing down their humble homes, ruthlessly wiping them out of existence. And for what? For what, I ask? In order that his Grace and his Grace's noble friends might have a few more red deer to butcher!"

A stout fellow standing next to John shouted — "Shime!"

Kitteredge went on silkily, dropping the Cambyses vein.

"Is there a man in this great building to-night who can speak up in defence of such a tyrant and such tyranny?"

The Duchess nudged John again.

"You can!" she whispered.

"I'm dying to do it, but there'll be awful ructions."

"We'll chance that. Go ahead full steam!"

Kitteredge shared with Napoleon the conviction that repetition is the first figure of rhetoric.

"Is there such a man here to-night?"

"Yes," said John, in a clear voice. "There is."

At once there was an uproar. Everybody tried to

behold John.   The stout man next to him, not recognizing the puppet of a Duke, said hoarsely:

"You've a nerve, mate, you 'ave."

He stared at the Duchess, who wore her thick motoring veil, and then at the large, pink, carefully shaven countenance of Mr. Bott. Kitteredge held up his hand.
ᐧ "Will the gentleman come forward?" he said pleasantly.   "Let us have no disturbance, please." Then he added: "Remember, I asked for this."

John advanced.   Scaife was sitting on the right of Kitteredge.

"It's John Verney," he whispered to Sheila.

Kitteredge lost his smile.   A sense of the dramatic told him that John had taken his stage. Instantly he assumed an air of patronizing kindness and toleration.

"Gentlemen, what a delightful surprise!   Mr. John Verney proposes to answer my question."

At this the uproar began again.   There were shouts of: "Let him speak!" and the counterblast: "Turn him out!"   Once more Kitteredge quelled the tumult, and John somehow found himself standing upon a chair, facing Sheila across a sea of excited faces. He began with that odd composure which so often masks successfully the most poignant nervousness.

"I happen to have met," he said, "some of these happy, thrifty, honest crofters.   Let me tell you about them.   They lived, herded together, in two-room hovels, under conditions of appalling dirt, misery, ignorance and starvation.   The soil upon which their crofts once stood is so stony, so sterile, that the strongest and most capable must perish upon it, and starved men are not strong nor capable. With great difficulty the Duke of Trent persuaded these almost naked Highlanders — I say *almost* naked because they are covered with snow for about five months each year — to abandon their waste places. At large pecuniary loss to himself, he established them upon fertile lands here and in Canada; he fed them, clothed them, lent them money at a nominal rate of interest, and educated their children. He helped them, in a word, to help themselves. I can give Mr. Kitteredge, or anybody else interested, the names and addresses of these crofters who were sacrificed to a few red deer. Let Mr. Kitteredge ask any one of them to return to the happy home from which the Duke of Trent beguiled him. One word more. Last year, as Mr. Kitteredge ought to know, the Secretary for Scotland, in obedience, possibly, to pressure brought upon him by persons who have never seen a red deer, approached the Duke of Trent, and asked him to reëstablish as an experiment certain crofts in the Highlands. The Duke very unwillingly · consented. He offered two thousand acres, part of his own forest. Men were found willing and eager to occupy the crofts; and the Duke tried to select the most capable of the volunteers. What has happened? We have just learned that these thrifty, honest crofters have syndicated their crofts, and propose to let them as an undivided whole to the highest bidder, to let them — as a grouse-moor and deer-forest. "

A roar of laughter brought John's speech to an abrupt close. He had not raised his voice; he had spoken throughout good-humouredly, with a slight smile upon his lips. The words seemed to trickle forth in a cold, fever-dispelling stream. When the laughter died down, the Lancashire Lad made the best of a bad case.

"Mr. Verney," he declared, "is the devoted secretary and friend of the Duke of Trent; so far as the Duke of Trent's crofters are concerned I may, possibly, have been misinformed."

"You have, sir."

"Then I have only this to say: Would to God there were more like him! The trouble lies with the bad Dukes not with the good ones."

John struggled back to the Duchess and Mr. Bott.

The three pushed their way to the car, with some assistance from the stout man, who announced his intention of coming to hear John speak upon the morrow.

As the car purred on its way, Mr. Bott said blandly:

"Mr. Verney *is* a cold-water man. He handled the hose like an expert."

The Scaife papers hardly mentioned this incident; but the Tory press made much of it. Then Arnold Grandcourt delivered a very remarkable speech, remarkable inasmuch as it indicated the exact lines upon which the contest was to be fought. Scaife and Kitteredge and he hoisted the red flag of Socialism in open defiance — so it was hinted — of the more moderate men of the Liberal Party. Not the least remarkable fact concerning this confession of faith was the spectacle of Charles Desmond and Sheila listening to what the late Cabinet Minister had stigmatized again and again as "tosh."

Within a few hours of the polling, as John was sitting alone with the Duke after breakfast, Mr. Bott was ushered in. Obviously something of importance had taken place. Mr. Bott's face was carmine, and his fat pudgy hands were quivering with excitement.

"Gentlemen," he said solemnly, as soon as the servant had retreated, "the Lord has delivered the enemy into our hands."

"Bless my soul!" exclaimed the Duke. "Sit down Bott, and explain yourself."

CHAPTER XIX

MR. BOTT refused to sit down. When great issues were at stake he stood upright, monumentally erect, square to Heaven's four winds. Drawing from a pocket-book a sheet of paper, he asked a question:

"Mr. Verney, what price would you pay for this?"

John stared at a slip of paper, wondering if too much zeal had driven the great agent stark mad. Then he understood, and gasped. The slip of paper was the rough proof of that pernicious leaflet which had burked the second election in the New Forest division. Upon the side of the proof, in faint pencil, were half a dozen corrections in Scaife's handwriting. John handed the slip to the Duke.

"You remember the two grocery bills which blew me out of the water. That was Scaife's work. He deliberately laid a mine, and lied about it to me and to the Desmonds."

"Precisely," murmured Mr. Bott. He had become pink again, and quite composed. The Duke frowned, and said emphatically: "Damnable!" Mr. Bott chuckled, and nodded his massive head, remarking: "Just so."

The Duke looked at John.

"Esmé was right," he declared. "The fellow is a scoundrel and a hypocrite."

"When the facts become known," said Mr. Bott smoothly, "most Englishmen will share your Grace's opinion." Then, in a lighter tone, he turned to John, who seemed dazed. "You have not answered my question, Mr. Verney. What is that slip of paper worth to you?"

"How did you get hold of it?" asked the Duke.

"Ah, your Grace, I flatter myself that my answer explains adequately the position, the almost unique position — if I may be allowed to say so — which I hold as the agent of your Grace and of the Conservative Association. That slip of paper gravitated naturally to me by virtue of that position. It sought me; I did not seek it."

The Duke drummed with his fingers upon the table. Mr. Bott turned to John.

"I paid one hundred guineas for it. The fellow refused pounds."

"What fellow?"

"Your Grace," said Mr. Bott firmly, "I have pledged my honour not to reveal the man's name. Is it not enough to state that I know him, and all about him? He used to be a confidential clerk of Mr. Scaife. Mr. Scaife, it appears, treated the man with brutality; kicked him, in point of fact. The man is a bit of a worm, but he turned. Yes, in his extremity, he turned to — me."

"Revenge."

"Quite, quite; as sweet to men as to women."

"And what do you propose?"

"This, of course, is what journalists term a 'scoop,' a prodigious scoop, gentlemen. Our papers will publish to-morrow morning a facsimile of this interesting proof, and also a facsimile of Mr. Scaife's handwriting. A few words of explanation, the fewer the better, nothing violent, but with an ironical tincture, will suffice. Fortunately, Mr. Scaife has spoken publicly of his very warm friendship for Mr. Verney."

He rubbed his hands, chuckling.

The Duke glanced at John, who was recovering.

"Well, John —— ?"

"We wanted this badly," observed the agent. "You don't think I paid too much, Mr. Verney?"

"No."

"It will turn the scale. I have been nervous. The unprincipled appeal to the greed of the masses, the setting of class against class, the Free-Food fiction, have done their work; but, without any offence to Mr. Verney, I state as my conviction that his opponent's brilliant personality has proved his most valuable asset. He is Napoleonic, and quite as unscrupulous as that great commander. I happen, for instance, to know for a fact that throughout the doubtful districts, and amongst the poorest voters, certain men have been betting five to one *on* Mr. Verney."

"Eh, eh?" said the Duke. "I haven't quite grasped this new trick."

"Five to one and six to one *on* Mr. Verney. If Mr. Verney loses, five or six shillings will be paid a thousand times and over."

"You affirm these men to be Scaife's agents?"

"That would be difficult to prove. The bets have been made. That is all I know. And on that account alone I call our opponent unscrupulous. However, this contest will be his Waterloo."

The Duke looked steadily at John.

John was not conscious of the Duke's glance. He beheld at the moment Sheila, with a newspaper in her hand, Sheila reading the evidence which convicted her lover as liar and false friend. He saw the deepening horror in her eyes; he heard a cry of anguish; he felt in every fibre of heart and mind what she must feel if the proof were printed — the humiliation, the shock, and withering disillusionment.

"A wonderful slice of luck," continued Mr. Bott cheerfully. "Mr. Scaife is seldom caught napping, but it's a mistake to kick a confidential agent, and everything which is thrown into a waste-paper basket is not necessarily burned."

He turned to the Duke for an appreciative nod, which was not forthcoming. John's silence and the ducal frowns began to puzzle and distress Mr. Bott. It was slightly exasperating to admit that anybody, be he Duke or commoner, could puzzle a man of Mr. Bott's experience. In a different tone, with a shade of anxiety running thinly through it, he continued:

"We have no time to lose. This must appear

to-morrow as a bolt from the blue, from the blue," he
repeated, with a happy allusion to the colours of his
party.

"Well, John" — the Duke waved the slip of paper
— "what have you to say to Mr. Bott?"

John took the paper, folded it, and slipped it into
his pocket.

"Mr. Bott," he said firmly, "I shall write you a
cheque for a hundred guineas, but I shall make no
public use of this."

"Merciful heavens!"

"The publication of this rough proof might turn
the election in my favour. I am fully aware of
that. But some friends of mine would be unspeakably
humiliated."

"You are right," said John's Chief.

Mr. Bott sank into an arm-chair. He said afterward: "For the first time in twenty years, I felt
unstrung."

To his credit, however, the agent in him fortified
the man. A brisk argument followed. Mr. Bott
contended that his candidate must consider the claim
of others. This was a contest upon which depended,
possibly, the fate of the Government. Defeat meant
the triumph of Socialism, the rooting of poisonous
doctrine, the sowing of foul seed. Mr. Bott simply
wallowed in metaphor and hyperbole. Finally, he
appealed to the Duke, who had such vast interests
at stake.

"His Grace must see — " and "His Grace, surely,

could not ignore — " Lastly: "His Grace, on second thoughts, would persuade Mr. Verney to change a mind really too fine and delicate for political uses and abuses."

But his Grace shook his head.

"I shall not interfere," he replied. "Mr. Verney's judgment in this personal matter is better than yours or mine."

Mr. Bott relapsed into slang. He could have torn his hair, had he possessed enough to take hold of.

"To have such a shot in the locker — and not to use it. Your Grace, I could sob like a child from sheer disappointment."

He went away muttering inaudible protests, but the Duke shook hands with John.

"All the same," he asked, "that shot will be fired, eh?"

"Sheila shan't marry a liar, if I can prevent it."

"Do you know that she is coming here to-day?"

"Yes."

"Shall I tell the father, Jonathan?"

They looked at each other in silence. Then, very slowly, very reluctantly, with cheeks hot and red, John whispered:

"I don't quite trust him."

The Duke nodded.

"I never did," he answered curtly. With the hesitation of a man who speaks sorely against the grain, he went on: "I have been told confidentially that Charles Desmond will be sent to the Antipodes to succeed Lord

Mountstuart, who, it seems, is most unpopular."
John looked petrified with astonishment.

"Of course, it has been done before. And I'm
not saying that Desmond isn't the right man for the
place, irrespective of party, but I happen to know for
a fact that they had half promised the billet to somebody else. Great pressure was brought to bear by
Kitteredge and Grandcourt. In short, there has been
a bargain. Desmond's attitude astride the fence has
puzzled me. Now it is explained."

"If Sheila guessed —— "

"Let us hope that she won't guess."

"I'm sure she knows nothing about it."

However, since the issue of the writ, John had hardly
seen Sheila. Purposely he had avoided her, well
aware that the sight of him must be distressing. When
they did meet, she had said impetuously:

"John, Reginald hates this election as much as I
do, but his hand, it seems, is forced."

"No doubt."

"I am beginning to hate politics."

"You?"

"Party politics, office-hunting — the, the dirty
work which even clean hands must do."

"You are beginning to find out about that."

"I have eyes and ears. I was furious when Mr.
Grandcourt spoke of Reginald's fighting for his country,
while you were writing Latin verse at Oxford. Reginald was so vexed. When I scolded Mr. Grandcourt,
he said it was part of the game."

"That didn't bother me a bit."

"Things are done by people one would least suspect— " She broke off with heightened colour, and
finished vehemently: "Thank heaven! I am not
connected with them."

This brief duologue had been interrupted, and John
did not meet Sheila again before the Duchess's luncheon
party. The Desmonds arrived late, but at table
John found himself next to Sheila. She looked astonishingly well and happy, a radiant creature, and
John thought miserably of the shot to be fired.

"How glum you are, Jonathan! And yet Reginald
tells me that you may win. It's my duty to pray for
your defeat, but your victory will not worry me very,
very much."

She smiled and laughed.

"Thanks."

"And how do you happen to be here? Reginald is
kissing babies."

"I can't do that before luncheon."

She laughed again, but her eyes lingered upon John's
grave face.

"You don't even laugh at your own jokes."

"They are not good enough."

"Certainly you are very glum indeed to-day."
Her voice softened as she whispered: "Are you sore
at some of Grandcourt's and Kitteredge's speeches?
Reginald, you know, can't restrain them, but he
personally has said nothing to offend you, has he?"

"Not a word."

"I am so glad. I've suffered horribly. It seems terrible that you two should be fighting, but Reginald's feelings toward you are quite unchanged. Tell me; you believe that?"

"I am sure of it," said John.

"Aren't you going to eat anything? Father says that a closely contested election gives him an enormous appetite."

Her eyes softened again as she perceived the trouble in his, and once more she made an effort to amuse him with ordinary chatter.

"Jonathan, do you order the food?"

"Of course not."

"It's so good here, and everything runs so smoothly. How delightful to have and do exactly what one likes!"

"The Duke doesn't have or do what he likes — far from it."

"The Duchess does."

She gazed so admiringly at her hostess that John said with a touch of irony:

"Are you understudying her?"

She hesitated, hardly liking to speak of a future to be shared with another man.

"Do you want to establish a sort of salon — to play the great lady?"

He spoke seriously, trying to test her. He felt a thrill of pleasure when she answered him as seriously:

"That depends."

"Upon what?"

"Well, not on myself. If I have to entertain, I hope I shall do it properly."

"I'm sure you will."

"But I shan't do it to please myself. My idea of happiness is to be with a few friends, not with many acquaintances. Of course, I'm ambitious, and one must expect to make sacrifices for a gratified ambition."

"How much would you sacrifice?" he asked, in a low voice.

"Well, a certain amount of ease of body, for instance. The Prime Minister's wife told me last week that the mere shaking of hands gave her a 'tennis' elbow."

"Would you sacrifice ease of mind?"

He put the question so sharply that he was overheard by another guest, who considered that he had remained silent long enough. He happened to be a statesman of some reputation. Adjusting his pince-nez, he said in a high, drawling voice: "Ambition and ease of mind cannot walk arm-in-arm, can they, Duke?"

"It depends upon the mind," replied his host; "I mean, the quality of it."

"And the quantity of the ambition," added a dame upon the Duke's left hand.

As the gentleman with the pince-nez had intended, a discussion began, during which John and Sheila, being negligible units in a distinguished company, held their tongues. The short-sighted statesman defined, cynically enough, the particular form of ambition which lures Englishmen of the upper class to sacrifice ease of mind and body to obtain high power and place. Finally, he remarked with brutal candour: "If you play the game to win the highest stakes — and successful politicians are unquestionably superbly rewarded in this country — you may have to sacrifice not only ease of body and mind, but ease of conscience also."

While he was holding forth, Sheila crumbled her bread with nervous fingers. Her eyes sparkled angrily as she said:

"Fortunately there are many exceptions."

The statesman laughed, and bowed courteously.

"Charles Desmond's daughter has reason to think so."

With that the Duchess rose, and everybody went into the hall for coffee and cigarettes. John and Sheila sat together in one of the windows facing the Green Park. John was wondering how he should prepare the girl's mind for the shock of discovering that her lover had no conscience. Then he heard her voice, which was so like Cæsar's in its pleasant, kind inflections.

"Was I rude, Jonathan? Did I speak pertly? Oh, he did exasperate me! and I hate generalities. Of course, *he* didn't run very straight, did he?"

"He believes in compromise, but he never compromised himself."

"I have told Reginald — " She stopped.

"Please go on, Sheila."

"I must," she said desperately, and he felt her hand

upon his arm. "Jonathan, you are my oldest friend, and because of that I must speak to you sometimes about Reginald, and yet every time it hurts me and you."

"What have you told him?" said John steadily. He pressed her small hand reassuringly, hardly daring to speak.

"He's aiming at the highest place."

"Yes."

"He may reach the tip-top. Father says so and Mr. Kitteredge, and Arnold Grandcourt."

"Experts all of them."

"Yes, but they — I mean Mr. Kitteredge and Mr. Grandcourt — frighten me. That crofter business. Oh, Jonathan, you did score over that! Well, Mr. Kitteredge half admitted to me that he was playing to the gallery, and Reginald said that if it had been known you were in the hall the Duke's crofters would have been left alone.   And when Mr. Kitteredge went, I told Reginald —— "

"Yes."

"Perhaps I should say that I entreated him for my sake and his to speak what he believed to be the truth regardless of consequences."

"What a counsel of perfection to a politician!"

"And then —— "

"And then?"

"He said that he loathed double-shuffling and misrepresentation."

"Coffee, sir?"

The suave voice of a servant made John jump to
his feet.

"I must run," he said hastily. "There's the last
batch of babies to be kissed. I shall see you to-morrow,
in the morning."

He hurried away, and Sheila wondered: "Why should
John call upon me in the morning?"

Outside, dashing along in a motor, John was thinking: "I must have time. I can't fire this awful shot
till the right moment comes. When I do fire it, she
will be wounded to death, and she'll remember that
my hand pulled the trigger."

Throughout the afternoon, while he was speaking
here and there, talking to all comers, asking and answer-
ing the same everlasting questions, listening to Mr.
Bott's ripened jests, he kept on repeating to himself:
"She'll hate me for ever and ever!"

He returned at six to Trent House, and went to the
Duke's room to report. The Duke said abruptly:

"You didn't fire that shot?"

"I couldn't. I must have time."

"Yes, yes. By the way, Esmé is upstairs. We
weren't expecting him, but he said he had to come."

"I'm so glad."

His pulse beat faster as he hurried to his old friend.
The warmth of John's grip, the glance of his eye,
rather surprised Fluff.

"It does me good to look at you," said John.

"Father says you're the right sort and no mistake."

"He's too kind."

"I'm going to hear you speak to-night. I've never heard you speak, Jonathan. I want to share this triumph."

"Is it going to be a triumph?" John asked doubtfully.

"Either way — for you, so father says, What do you think of the amazing Bot?"

"He is amazing."

"Has he got his knife into the Demon yet?"

"Why do you ask that?"

"I've no reason except this: Bott does get his knife into political enemies. And he has a wonderful nose for buried pasts. I made sure he'd grub up something unsavoury concerning Scaife. Because, mind you, there must be something."

"He did grub up something you had once told me about Ormsby."

"I wonder where he got that. Not from me. By Jove, I hadn't thought of it, but, nicely sharpened, it would be a useful flint, eh?"

"Your father and I refused to throw it."

"Oh, dash it! The chivalrous attitude makes me peevish. A cad should be fought with his own weapons. I remember at Harrow long ago being stoned by a hulking chaw; I picked him off on the shin with a sharp flint — a nailing good shot. When I told father he grinned, and I'll bet he was just as pleased as I was. I hear there's a big sign up. '*Down with the Dukes!*' My cry is: '*Crucify Cant*'!"

"Shall we dine at a restaurant? I'm not dressing."

"Right."

John retreated to wash his hands. Thus engaged, he began to run over a very carefully prepared speech. To his dismay he could not remember a word of it. Hurriedly, he glanced at some rough notes, scribbled upon the back of an envelope. Then he tried again, and failed as ignominiously as before. Hitherto, the act of speaking had been easy, although the preparation of his speeches exacted time and trouble. Always when he spoke he was conscious of seeing the written word. Sentence after sentence would unroll itself. And now, strive as he might, he could see no sentences, only Sheila, crushed and humiliated. The words which came fluently to his lips were the words with which a cruel blow might be softened.

At dinner, he told Fluff that his memory was playing pranks. Fluff suggested champagne. John ordered some.

"It's stage fright," he said, with a faint smile.

"The best artists never quite get over that, old chap."

In the motor John asked for silence. Once more he became sensible of verbal impotence, or worse, for phrases came to him, but hopelessly muddled. The sweat broke upon his forehead. He wondered if he were ill.

"It won't come," he whispered to his friend. Soon an appalling weakness assailed him. He gripped Fluff's arm, saying desperately: "I mustn't make a mess of it. I could wire to Bott that I'm ill."

"Good idea," said Fluff, alarmed at the expression upon John's face, and his extreme pallor. "Fact is, you're worn out. Father hinted as much. And you must be fit to-morrow. Bed's the place for you, Jonathan. Bott and I will manage. Leave it to me. We'll create sympathy for you, a vast surge of it. Gad! I can hear old Bott at work."

"No," said John harshly.

"You're all right again, eh?"

"I mean to fight against this devilish weakness. I've had it before, when I sang in Speecher, 'Five Hundred Faces.' I'll make the speech of my life to-night — or break down."

"You won't break down," Fluff declared confidently.

The admirable Bott met them at the back-door of the immense hall, which was packed with a mixed audience wearing red or blue rosettes. John engaged in talk with a member of his committee, and for the moment Esmé found himself alone with the great man.

"Delighted to see you, my lord."

"Are we going to win, Mr. Bott?"

"It will be a close finish. I say no more. Much depends upon to-night and to-morrow." Then he lowered his voice to an impressive whisper: "You are a great friend of our candidate."

Fluff smiled.

"Let us say that he's a great friend of mine."

"Then I am emboldened to speak. My lord, we hold the trump card, and his Grace and Mr. Verney refuse to play it." He repeated in a tragic whisper: "They refuse to play it."

"What trump card?"

Mr. Bott hurriedly explained. "Between ourselves, he concluded, "I was so sure that his Grace would see eye to eye with me that I had a block made of the incriminating document. And I had arranged with the greatest of our editors to hand over a 'story' (the technical term, my lord), with the block before eleven to-night. It means victory — it does indeed. Can't you say a word? Can't you persuade Mr. Verney to take what all men must admit is an honourable revenge? Here, my lord, is a rough 'pull' from the block."

From his breast pocket he drew forth a proof. Esmé glanced at it.

"May I keep this, Mr. Bott?"

"Certainly. Not a word to his Grace about the block. If you fail to persuade Mr. Verney, it shall be destroyed to-morrow."

"After the meeting I'll do my best."

"The affair, my lord, has given me a raging headache."

"I am very sorry. It seems to have affected Mr. Verney's memory."

"I don't quite take you, my lord."

"He can't remember a word of his speech. It's on the cards that he may break down."

Mr. Bott groaned.

Within a couple of minutes, the Chairman was leading the way into the hall. John entered with him, and enjoyed, as the reporters wrote, a mixed reception. He sat down, while the Chairman made some introductory remarks. Then John stood up. The silence was slightly upsetting to Mr. Bott, who knew that the same audience had cheered Scaife; but John said afterward that he was not sensible of any emotion save that of overpowering "funk."

He stammered out some sort of a beginning, and a voice from behind shouted: "Speak out!" John heard a venomous answer: "He carn't."

"Mr. Scaife," he continued lamely, "addressed you last night in this hall, and he quoted largely from Gladstone, Bright, and Cobden."

"Good men and true all of 'em!" shouted a voice.

John opened his mouth and closed it, having nothing to say. He saw a sea of faces in front of him, and heard a confused murmur, and for a moment which seemed everlasting he wondered what he was doing, or trying to do. Suddenly, speech came back to him. He smiled pleasantly, quite at his ease. Into his voice flowed those delicate shades and inflections which had made him persuasive as a speaker.

"Yes," he replied, in a tone that carried to the end of the big building. "And I am of opinion that the quotations were not the worst part of Mr. Scaife's speech."

A docker laughed loudly, and many of the men who "sported" red grinned approvingly.

"All is well," said Mr. Bott, as he wiped an over-anxious brow.

"Mr. Scaife has told you that the poor should be

exempt from taxation. In your soul, do you believe this to be just? Do you wish to take everything and contribute nothing? In the United States, if an able-bodied man is so destitute that he cannot pay taxes, he works on the roads for a few days. And he does so willingly. Is there a man in this hall to-night who believes that he is entitled to have a voice in the government of the country and yet is so mean that he wishes to be excused from paying a farthing toward the support of that country? If there is such a man, let him stand up, for I should like to see him, if only for the purpose of satisfying myself that he is not an Englishman."

Nobody moved. Bott whispered to Fluff: "He's getting hold of 'em!"

"Mr. Scaife told you last night that he stands for the happiness of England. I stand for the honour of the Empire. And it is my conviction that our honour is gravely imperilled, to an extent hardly measurable by men who have not the time to consider any problem other than the tremendous one of earning their daily bread. This ignorance concerning matters vital to the welfare of the nation must be laid at the door of your rulers, for during the past ten years there has not been a statesman on either side bold enough to tell you the truth, or sensible enough to appeal to the sense which is latent in you."

"How about the Lancashire Lad?"

"Did he tell you the truth about the Duke of Trent's crofters? Did Mr. Scaife tell the truth about the big and little loaf? During the General Election we read in *Scaife's Daily* that the price of the quartern loaf would rise under Protection, and remain where it was or fall under Free Trade. How many of you accepted that as gospel? Well, you have Free Trade, and yet the price of the loaf has risen, simply because wheat has risen. And the law of supply and demand has nailed to the political mast one more vote-catching misstatement. Gentlemen, aren't you getting rather sick of these misstatements? And aren't you a bit 'fed up' — to use Mr. Kitteredge's homely expression — with soft soap? In your praise, last night, Mr. Scaife rose to heights of eloquence which I cannot attempt to scale. As a son of Labour he claimed you as long-lost brothers. He affirmed that he was of Labour, and with Labour, and for Labour. And he ought to be, for between ourselves he and his father have taken no less than five million pounds from Labour. He is the greatest son of Labour in this country, and yet, from my knowledge of his tastes, I find it hard to believe that he really prefers — as he gave you dockers to understand — the smell of bilgewater to that of rosewater."

The dockers laughed, but one shouted out:

"Used to be a Free Trader and a Free Fooder, wasn't yer?"

John smiled. "Are there any sincere Free Fooders amongst the Radicals?" he asked. "You know, perhaps, that we are taxed at the rate of one million pounds a week upon things which we eat and drink and smoke. Would any Radical take the tax off a poor man's beer and tobacco? I don't think so. Mr. Kitteredge will tell you that these taxes are necessary. Perhaps. But ask him next time why the drinker of beer should be taxed, and the drinker of ginger-beer be exempt?"

"When did you cease to be a Free Trader?"

"I ceased to be a Free Trader, gentlemen, when I realized that ultimately Free Trade must leave us at the mercy of one hundred million Asiatics, who are mastering our arts and crafts, and who can live contentedly upon threepence a day. To me the Yellow Peril does not mean Europe conquered by Chinese and Japanese, but it does mean — so far as England is concerned — a tremendous commercial victory for the Yellow Race, which can only be averted by Imperial Federation and Protection. I admit frankly that England standing alone can do without Protection, and I have yet to see a scheme of tariffs which does not bolster up certain industries at the expense of others closely allied to them. But 'Little they know of England, who only England know.' In the past we have made enormous blood sacrifices to win for ourselves and children the greatest Empire the world has ever seen. What are we doing to-day to weld that Empire together and make it impregnable against assault from outside? The greatest military authorities affirm that an invasion of this country is at least possible, and yet of all the great nations we alone have refused to consider home defence as an imperative duty, whether it be voluntary or obligatory. I appeal to you to-night as an Imperialist. I want to see our Empire developed and protected in every sense of the word upon lines similar to those which have made the United States so amazingly prosperous. As between State and State, the United States, gentlemen, is the greatest Free-Trade country in the world, and Uncle Sam's prosperity is due, as you know, to the fact that he possesses all natural resources within a ring-fence. As an Empire, we hold infinitely greater resources, and these must be developed by us with the maximum of efficiency and the minimum of waste. When Japanese and Chinese cheap labour threatens our textile industries, we must find ourselves prepared for the inevitable with our own trained coolies and our own cotton fields. Face this fact without flinching; England alone can no longer compete on even terms with the United States and Germany, but the British Empire can, and must — or it will fall to pieces. Consolidate our vast dominions, and use tariffs as a weapon of defence, not offence. Remember my figures! One — hundred — million men, patient, laborious, and far more ingenious than the average English mechanic — one hundred millions, my friends, who are learning to do your work, and who can live on three-pence a day."

There was a round of applause. Fluff whispered to Mr. Bott:

"Straight from the shoulder, that. Nothing like a good hard punch!"

"One hundred million men behind it, my lord. The big battalions are irresistible."

"How about England's increasing prosperity? Anything wrong there, Mr. Verney?" asked a man close to the platform.

"It is remarkable till we compare it with the progress made by Germany and the United States. In exports, imports, consumption of coal, and Savings Bank deposits, our percentage of increase is nearly doubled by our rivals. We own one fifth of the earth, and the King's subjects number four hundred millions. Why should we take second place? And yet, at the present rate, unless you develop and perfect the Empire, England will become a negligible Power within fifty years."

"Protection means political corruption," shouted a man at the back. "We don't want bloated millionaires and Trusts and a Tammany Hall in this country. That's what Protection has done for Uncle Sam."

The audience burst into cheers. Mr. Bott looked uneasy. Fluff nudged him, and whispered: "How will he answer that?"

"No, we don't," said John, in a ringing voice. "But by Heaven, gentlemen, you will have political corruption and a Tammany Hall here in London, unless you exercise more discretion in the selection of your representatives. Corruption ravages American politics because the politicians are corrupt, because the best men keep out of politics, and the baser sort have been

allowed a free hand. For an American without resources there is no easier and better paid profession
than that of politics. It doesn't need brains, or
courage, or physical strength. The one thing necessary is plenty of cheek and an elastic conscience.
Gentlemen, I am speaking irrespective of party when
I tell you that the problem before you is that of progress and pace. It's all a question of pace. Mr.
Scaife affirms that the Duke whom I am proud to
serve goes too slow. I retort that Mr. Scaife goes too
fast. He is exceeding the speed limit and courting
catastrophe. Mr. Kitteredge, also, is forcing the pace
even more than Mr. Scaife. I have no faith whatever in Mr. Kitteredge as a political economist, and I
distrust him profoundly as a statesman, because he
is widening the gulf between the rich and the poor,
instead of bridging it; but I do respect Mr. Kitteredge
as a worker, and if he accomplishes nothing more than
to make us think out plans better than his own, he
will not have lived in vain. I ask for your votes to-
morrow, even if I do move too slowly. Back the tortoise rather than the hare! Mr. Scaife is rushing
sixty miles an hour at his conclusions, leaving behind
his too highly powered chariot the mangled body of
common sense and common experience. According to him the State should own everything and control everybody. The People's Friend proposes to
manage every detail of your lives. He possesses
rare executive ability. Give him the chance, and he
will do more than wash you. He wants to marry you,

work you, scrap you, and bury you. Don't forget that
the scrapping is part of the scheme. If you doubt me,
visit Samarkand! Well, gentlemen, all this seems to
me another word for Protection of the most offensive
kind running amuck! If Mr. Scaife is going to be allowed to carry his Socialistic schemes to their logical
conclusion, you will have ceased to be freemen, and the
greatest — and dullest — tyranny which the world
has yet seen will regard you indifferently as slaves."

"Never, never, NEVER!" shouted a huge docker.

Somebody began to sing "Rule, Britannia," and
the audience joined in with enthusiasm. The National
Anthem followed, and the meeting dispersed. John
received many congratulations.

"Didn't know you had it in you, Jonathan," said
Fluff admiringly. "By Jove, you binged 'em up, and
no mistake!"

Bott alone remained slightly pessimistic.

"We had no cry," he remarked to Fluff, "and as a
Tariff Reformer Mr. Verney is too lukewarm. He is
not quite sure of himself; Mr. Scaife is cock-sure.
However, if you can persuade Mr. Verney to let me
use the leaflet, I predict victory. I shall be at the
Conservative Club till midnight."

"Right," said Fluff.

With some skill he managed to get John out of the
hall without offending any garrulous supporters. As
soon as they were alone in the motor, he said without
beating of bushes:

"I've heard all about that proof. Bott-told me.

Jonathan, father, and you are wrong. Scaife ought to be pilloried."

"For Sheila to look at."

"By Jove!   I had clean forgotten that little darling."

"Just so."

Fluff whistled softly, and said no more.   When they reached Trent House, he sent a telephone message to the expectant Bott.

"Trump card cannot be played."

CHAPTER XX

POLLING day dawned bright and clear. Partly on this account interested spectators from other constituencies began to arrive early in the morning, and in certain places crowds collected, more or less good-tempered, but determined to cheer or jeer the ubiquitous voter if he flaunted the colours of his candidate too audaciously. The polling booths where a large majority of votes was assured to one or other of the candidates attracted no attention. The visitors gathered about the doubtful districts near the docks and slums, fully understanding that something nearly as exciting as a League football-match was in progress.

The papers controlled by Scaife and his different syndicates had eclipsed all previous records. They were hawked about by shrill-voiced urchins carefully culled from the ranks of the unemployed. In such matters Scaife's agent was superior to the great Bott.

Up and down the congested thoroughfares rushed the innumerable motor-cars sent by both parties to carry voters to the poll. Certainly, John had a slight "pull" on the possibilities of locomotion. Powerful Dukes and lovely Duchesses have many friends very "anxious to oblige." Enormous cars owned by plutocrats who had never crossed the threshold of Trent House were placed at John's disposition. The Duchess accepted the loan of these superb, highly powered vehicles in the spirit with which they were offered. Mr. Bott smiled blandly.

"Other things being equal," he remarked, "victory smiles upon the man of many motors."

"Scaife is a man of many voters," said Fluff, grinning.

"Can he bring them to the poll, my lord?"

"I hope there will be no accidents," the Duchess murmured.

"All our men have been instructed to drive very carefully."

By an odd coincidence the words were hardly out of Bott's mouth when John rushed into the Committee-Room, pale and excited.

"I've run over a child," he gasped.

"Killed it?" asked the Duchess.

"Badly hurt, I fear. I took it to the nearest hospital."

"Damn!" exclaimed Mr. Bott. John had never heard him swear before. He added details:

"Little fellow ran bang into us. We were crawling along — simply crawling! He seemed to dive under the wheels."

"Most unfortunate," groaned Mr. Bott. "If you will excuse me, I will see what can be done."

John said impatiently:

"Everything humanly possible is being done."

"Mr. Scaife will make use of this, Mr. Verney."

"What?"

Mr. Bott smiled compassionately.

"It will be an — asset."

Shaking his massive head, he went out of the room. Fluff said, excitedly: "What does he mean? How can Scaife 'use' this? John, I suppose you were crawling — eh?"

"Of course.   I shall go back to the hospital."

"Take me with you," said the Duchess.

"But your speech?" exclaimed Fluff.

John had promised to deliver a few final words from a platform erected on one of the large wharves.   It was to be the last shot — grape and shrapnel at close quarters.

"Hang the speech!"

"But if you disappoint them?"

"Come on!   Don't jaw!"

Fluff glanced at his watch.

"We can just do it," he remarked, in a relieved tone.

But they didn't do it. Afterward the mighty Bott, commenting upon John's failure to keep his word to an expectant and doubtful crowd, remarked that such breaking of pledges might be magnificent, but was not politics.   For John went back to the hospital to find the child in the hands of the surgeons, and he refused to leave till he heard that the injuries were less severe than had been at first supposed.   Presently the greatest surgeon in London assured him that all would be well. An arm and three ribs were broken, but seemingly there were no internal complications.

John returned to his Committee-Room, where Bott met him. The great man was slightly flustered.

"A blunder in elementary tactics," he growled out. "You ought to have addressed your meeting, and told them quite simply exactly what had occurred. With your voice and manner you might have satisfied them. At this moment you couldn't get a hearing, and you might be half killed. As I predicted, Scaife has made the most of it. Sharp work — very!"

It was now midday, and a leaflet, briefly entitled "*Butchered!*" was being distributed in thousands. ·

"Scaife is capable of having arranged the whole thing," added Bott.

"What! Arrange to have a child killed?"

Bott withdrew to repel this unforeseen attack. John and Fluff went on together to meet some supporters. Passing through the streets John was recognized. Some of the hooligans yelled out, "Murderer!"

"Well," said Fluff, between his teeth, "how are you feeling now, Jonathan? Perhaps, after this, father and you will fight the devil with his own weapons."

John, however, remained obstinately silent. Fluff, who had promised to fetch his mother from the hospital, dropped John amongst his own friends and sped northwest again. When he told the Duchess what had passed, she became nearly as indignant as her son. ,

"If I could see Mr. Scaife — !" she exclaimed.

"You'll see him. He's everywhere — and Sheila with him."

"If she knew —— ?"

By this time it was nearly one. The Duchess's car passed one of the principal taverns, gaily decked with red flags and streamers.

"Scaife's headquarters," said the Duchess. "And there's his big Napier. Stop!"

The chauffeur pulled up.

Fluff stared at his mother.

"Stop?" he repeated blankly. "Not here, not in the middle of his own crowd."

"Stop farther on," amended the Duchess.

"What are you up to now, mother?"

"I mean to ask Mr. Scaife before Sheila if he authorized the publication of this leaflet."

"You are going to push your way in there?"

"Yes, but I must have a leaflet."

"You're a wonder. Well, they won't recognize you through that veil."

The Duchess had her own way, triumphing where a woman of less resolution must have been defeated. She learned that Scaife and Kitteredge and Grandcourt were lunching together in Room 14, but unapproachable.

Finally, Fluff and she reached the first floor of the tavern, but a big fellow in the doorway of No. 14 refused to allow any strangers to pass.

"Strict orders," he said emphatically.

The Duchess raised her thick motoring veil, and the stout doorkeeper saw one of the loveliest faces in Europe.

"I am the Duchess of Trent," she said simply. "And I must see Mr. Scaife — on important business."

The man opened the door.

The room was full of smoke, and reeked with the odours of beef, tobacco, and beer. Scaife jumped up with an exclamation. The Duchess advanced slowly, seeing men only. She divined that Sheila must have been sent home before the leaflet was distributed. Grandcourt and Kitteredge rose also. Lord Samarkand, who had the appearance of a Boer farmer after an enormous meal, remained seated. The Duchess confronted Scaife.

"I beg your pardon," she said, in her silvery voice, "but I pushed my way in to tell you that I have just left the injured child. An arm and three ribs were broken, but there are no other injuries, and Sir Thomas Ryder, who examined him, tells me that the boy will be running about my garden in less than three weeks."

"I am delighted to hear it," said Scaife.

"Thanks," replied the Duchess. She glanced at Kitteredge, who displayed his smile. "As a chauffeur of mine was the cause of this accident," she continued, turning again to Scaife, "and as you know that I am incapable of misrepresenting the truth, I wished to ask you in the presence of these gentlemen, to affirm that personally you are not responsible for the publication and distribution of — this."

She held out the leaflet. Scaife smiled, and his voice was under perfect control, as he said:

"What is — this?"

"It won't take long to read."

Scaife glanced at it.

"I'm sure Mr. Kitteredge would like to hear it," suggested the Duchess.

"It's outrageous," said Scaife. "And likely to do infinite harm —— "

"To — us," said the Duchess.

"It shall be suppressed and contradicted at once, Duchess. I am obliged to you for bringing me good news of the child, and calling my attention to this absurd —— "

He paused for an instant, and the Duchess happened to catch the roving eye of Arnold Grandcourt.

"Inexactitude," she suggested.

"Quite. Can I offer you anything, Duchess?"

"Nothing, thanks. I suppose Miss Desmond has gone home?"

"Yes."

Five minutes later they had regained the car. Fluff said savagely: "He was lying."

"Yes. That dreadful father of his looked as if he were about to have a fit."

By five o'clock John knew that Scaife was sure to win. The tide might have been turned by the right word at the right moment spoken to a thousand doubtful dockers, who were willing to give to John a more or less patient hearing. His absence at the hospital turned many of these into Scaifites; the leaflet fell upon fertile soil.

At five the Duchess went home, but Fluff, who was to accompany her, suddenly remembered that the Duffer was somewhere within a mile or two of John's Committee-Rooms, and the need of exploding became so imperative that he immediately jumped into a hansom and was driven to the Mission House which held his old friend and half a dozen other strenuous parsons.

When the Duffer greeted him warmly, he said irritably:

"John has been slaughtered. I'm simply wild. I had to come to you to explode."

"You won't hurt anything here, but have a cup of tea first."

The Duffer's room at the Mission reminded Fluff of the single rooms at the Manor. Also, he beheld upon a nail the identical cap which the Duffer had worn at Lord's, when he distinguished himself by driving four consecutive balls to the boundary. Also, there was an old coloured print of The Hill, and several groups in which Fluff figured.

Fluff exploded.

The Duffer listened, smoking an ancient briar pipe. His expression changed as the spots upon the leopard became more and more visible. Then Fluff produced the facsimile of the rough proof which had defeated John in Hampshire.

The Duffer groaned.

"I thought he was all right," he muttered. "**There** must be a lot of good in him, anyway."

"It's part of your creed," said Fluff savagely, "to believe that the wicked man does turn away from his wickedness, but that's not our experience at the Embassy. John is knocked out. Scaife wins all round, to the sound of marriage-bells."

"John won't let that dear, sweet girl marry a wrong 'un?"

Fluff answered despondently:

"John won't talk very freely to me, or to anybody else. I suppose he can't. When I tried to argue with him last night, he half hinted that he did intend to open Sheila's eyes. But if he does the job properly, will she ever be able to forget that he did do it?"

"Dirty work!" sighed the Duffer.

"I believe you, that's what brought me here. Why shouldn't I do it, eh? Then she'll think of me, instead of Jonathan, as the man who cut her to bits."

"You cared for her, old chap — once?"

"Proposed five times," said Fluff gloomily. "That's over and done with. I never had a chance. In my little soul I knew it. And, mind you, I'm sure John will speak, but he'll pick his time and place, and what I want is this." He bent forward, his blue eyes blazing with excitement. "I should like to blow this devil sky-high to-night, now, when he's inflated with triumph. Think of it! He's simply rolling in success. Every blessed thing has gone his way. And to-night, when the poll is declared, he'll go to Sheila. And when he holds out his arms to her it will be the greatest moment of his life."

The Duffer nodded, staring at Fluff, and letting his pipe go out.

"But suppose I tell Sheila everything this very afternoon. How about his triumph then? Now, speak out, as pal and parson, am I justified in doing this? My mind is whirling; yours is clear. Sheila may loathe me for ever and ever. But Scaife will be ground to powder."

The Duffer said helplessly:

"I can't forget what Scaife has done for me. It's natural enough that you want to grind him to powder, but he's been my benefactor."

Fluff seized the Duffer's hand.

"You're a good old chap," he said affectionately. "And it's hardly fair lugging you in. I suppose this means that I must go it on my own, and — by George! — I shall."

He refused such refreshment as the Duffer pressed upon him, and went his way.

CHAPTER XXI

WHEN Fluff got back to the Committee-Rooms, he found John undergoing soothing verbal massage, a preparation for defeat, to which John was submitting with absent-minded indifference.

"Isn't it rather premature to talk of defeat before the last votes are polled?" Fluff asked of Mr. Bott.

"In ordinary cases, my lord — yes. But here we have had our forces equally divided. From the first the turn of the election depended upon the dockers. These have been carefully watched, and of these, in spite of the fact that our means of transportation are superior to the enemy's, we have taken to the booths about one voter to Mr. Scaife's three. I am reckoned a sanguine man, but I generally know when I'm beaten."

"That settles it," said Fluff.

"Settles what?" John asked with languid interest.

Fluff perceived that he was worn out, hardly able to stand. He led John aside and whispered:

"I am off to Sheila. That devil will triumph here, but he won't find a sweet creature waiting to throw herself into his arms in Eaton Square."

"You are going to tell her?"

"Everything. It's beastly work, but it shall be done thoroughly I promise you. The motor is downstairs. Scaife is dining with the Desmonds to-night, and he will come back to hear the result. I shall come back to report to you. If Bott says Scaife's in, there can be no doubt of it."

John looked at him, recognizing in the boy the same tenacity of purpose which distinguished the Duke. As he gazed at Fluff's face, ordinarily so fair but now darkly flushed with rage and excitement, he felt that his own strength was returning, and with it the power to think lucidly and quickly. What had crushed him was the determination to tell Sheila upon the following morning. He perceived that he had to act instantly, and that he must use a certain amount of guile, otherwise Fluff would insist upon coming with him.

"You have made up your mind?"

"Nothing you can say will prevent me."

"So be it."

"Dash it! You take it more coolly than I expected."

"I realize what you are about to do. And how you must loathe doing it! You are a good friend, Esmé. As for me, I am dead beat. You can take me to Trent House and I'll lie down for a bit. I must face the music to-night."

"I think you are very wise. Come on."

"My coat is in another room somewhere. While I fetch it, will you kindly explain to the excellent Bott that I shall be back within two hours?"

"Certainly. Hurry up, there's not much time to lose."

John disappeared. Outside the room, he scribbled upon a sheet out of his note-book: "I am off to Eaton Square. Meet me at Trent House in an hour's time — John."

Twisting this up, he handed it to a constable, instructing him to deliver it at once. Then he pushed his way through the crowd to the Trent motor. As the chauffeur touched his cap, John said quietly:

"Please drive me to Mr. Desmond's house in Eaton Square."

A moment later he was rushing westward.

Upon arrival he was informed by Trinder that Miss Desmond was lying down, and had left orders with her maid that she was not to be disturbed.

"I must see her. Please tell her so."

"Very good, Mr. Verney."

Alone in the big double drawing-room, John remembered that this lying down before any big event was an established habit. He could hear Sheila saying: "When something grand is coming to me, I like to gloat." Upon the wall opposite hung her portrait, by the greatest of modern French pastellists. Gazing at Sheila's eyes and lips, he felt sick with misery and disgust. To hit such a creature instead of attacking Scaife was dirty work indeed. And when that dirty work was done, something would have been taken from her face, the expression of innocence, so admirably portrayed by the artist, which could never return.

"In the good old days," thought John, "I should have shot the scoundrel."

Then he reflected that the scoundrel would probably have shot him.

A minute later, Sheila was advancing, a puzzled smile upon her face. She had slipped on a tea-gown, a white affair of chiffon and lace, which seemed to accentuate her girlishness. Her hair, also, in slight disorder, reminded him of the pretty hoyden of seventeen, who had bewitched him so completely.

"You caught me napping, Jonathan."

"I had to see you."

"I guess the reason. You have come to tell me the child is not badly hurt, but I know that already. Reginald sent me a wire about an hour ago. I'm so glad and relieved."

"I didn't come about that, Sheila."

"Gracious! How solemn you look!" Her voice quavered oddly. "There hasn't been another accident?"

"No."

"The mere thought of it gave me a pang. You know it's only quite, quite lately I've realized that things happen, dreadful things, when one least expects them. I hardly dare to gloat now."

"I've come here to hurt you," said John, desperately. "I wish I could hurt somebody else instead, but ——"

She interrupted impulsively, confounded by surprise,
distress, and curiosity.

"You have come to hurt — me?"

"Yes. You were always plucky, Sheila. Once
you told me you'd sooner have a bad tooth out than
stopped."

She nodded, as the colour ebbed from her cheeks.
She had sat down, and, as he spoke, unconsciously
she gripped the arms of the chair, and set her chin at
a higher angle.

"Do you remember that Free-Trade leaflet about
groceries which just turned the scale against me in
the New Forest?"

"Of course. I was furious about it."

"Perhaps," said John gently, "you have come to
believe that all is fair in politics?"

"I shall never, never believe that."

"That makes it easier for me." He took from his
pocket the rough sheet of paper; then, without daring
to look at her, he placed it in her hand, saying: "This
is the original proof of that leaflet, which, as you see,
was inspired and corrected by the man who called
himself my friend."

As she took it, he stared at the pattern of the carpet.
Sheila said nothing. When John did permit himself
a furtive glance, he saw that her features were rigid,
and it struck him that she was not so much surprised
as tremendously distressed, and making a supreme
effort to hide that distress. She had the look of one
confronted by some concrete horror heretofore dimly

visualized in mirage or dream, but her courage amazed
him. In a dull voice she asked:

"What have you done with this beside bringing
it to me?"

"Nothing," John replied. A note of gladness
vibrated in his tone.

"You have not 'used' it?"

The verb was often in Scaife's mouth. John.
tried to determine whether she spoke ironically.

"No."

"If you had ——"

Seeing that she was about to swoop upon the truth,
he interrupted hastily:

"Of course, I couldn't."

"Why not?" She began to speak with more ani-
mation. The faintest tinge of colour flowed into her
cheeks, as she repeated: "Why not?"

"Because of the public humiliation to you."

"Thank God! You have not changed. And yet
— it might have won this election. Let us hope you
will win without it."

"I am hopelessly beaten," said John. "I meant
to give you this after luncheon yesterday, but I
couldn't. Sheila, the man you have promised to
marry is now on his way here."

Then he saw fear in her eyes.

"Yes," she faltered.

He bent over her, controlling his emotion, and
speaking with a certain austerity and conviction:

"He nearly ruined Cæsar. Is he going to ruin you?"

She did not answer, and her silence puzzled him. He continued vehemently:

"He lied about this, denied all knowledge of it, as you know, and he lied about his father's peerage. Then he ratted, and the Radicals were enriched by £30,000 and the Scaife influence. He lied about resigning his Samarkand seat. That was arranged——"

"Stop!" exclaimed Sheila.

She rose slowly and stiffly, as if assuming with painful effort the burden of womanhood.

"Spare me, please," she faltered. "I am sore enough."

"God knows how it has hurt me to hurt you."

At this she melted, dissolving slowly into tears, which trickled down her cheeks.

"I could howl with the pain of it," muttered John.

He saw that she was too proud and too plucky to hide her tears. Erect and rigid she whispered nervously:

"I am frightened. Father is out, and Aunt Pen is at Dullingham." She added desperately: "I have always been afraid of him, always, always, ever since he first looked at me. John, will you stay?"

"If you wish it."

She rang the bell, and, when it was answered, said in a firm voice:

"As soon as Mr. Scaife comes, show him in here. When my father returns ask him to join us."

As the man left the room, she whispered:

"Do you think me a coward?"

"A coward! Your courage astounds me."

"I feel a coward inside. Don't talk to me! Let me think! I am dazed."

She walked unsteadily to a writing-table and sat down. John went to the window and opened it. He also felt dazed, unable to understand Sheila's manner or to weigh words which had revealed a pathetic and appealing weakness. He had expected anger, the impulsive, indignant refusal to believe, and then, when belief was forced upon her, the inevitable shrinking from the hand that had inflicted, however unwillingly, so cruel a blow. She had not so shrunk from him, and the thought filled him with gladness.

She wanted him!

But only because she was afraid of Scaife. John knew that Scaife defeated and humiliated could be violent. Had she seen him in one of his rare paroxysms of passion? These thoughts rushed into his mind, exacting answers. Her courage in bearing the tremendous blow contrasted itself with her pitiful fear of meeting the man who had lied to her. He crossed the room. She sat with her head sunk upon her arms, bowed beneath her misery. When he touched her softly, she didn't move.

"Sheila dear," he whispered, "won't you go to your room? Let your father and me deal with this man? It's not work for you."

Her answer was hardly audible ——

"I must stay."

His hand lingered for a moment upon her head,

before he went back to the window. It came to him
swiftly that she still loved Scaife, and might forgive
him. When he realized this an appalling weakness
possessed him also, the weakness of the flesh. Vitality
seemed to be oozing from an overtired body.

He walked out upon a small balcony, gripping the
wrought-iron rail, for he was tottering.

Presently the fresh air revived him, and his strength
began to return. He must prepare for the fight of
his life with a powerful and cunning enemy whom he
had driven to the wall. More, it was likely that Desmond would be on Scaife's side; and very surely this
became a sickening conviction.

Silently he prayed that Sheila might see Scaife
plainly. Prayer to him was no conventional importunity, no repetition of stereotyped phrases. He
believed profoundly that the only prayers which were
answered adequately must be compounded of intense
resolution and aspiration, a draft, so to speak, upon
the Divine Energy which permeates the universe.

Inside, Sheila had lifted her head, and was sitting
upright with a strange expression upon her face.
Upon the writing-table were framed photographs of
three men — her father, Scaife, and John. In a green
leather case, lined with white silk, was a miniature of
Cæsar. She gazed at Cæsar's portrait, then at her
father's, and lastly at Scaife's.

She had been so sure of John, but never absolutely
sure of Scaife. This smote her. And part of Scaife's

fascination, the part she was able to measure, lay in the fact that this uncertainty had excited and beguiled her.

Her thoughts flew back to her father. Had he ever suspected that Scaife was unscrupulous? His words spoken long ago, just after she had returned from France, echoed in her memory: "I am a party man, Sheila." And as a party man he had admitted the necessity of compromise, and of allowing others to do work from which he turned aside. But a wave of revulsion swept such thoughts from her mind. He was her darling father, incapable of baseness however disguised. She hated herself for daring to entertain one suspicion affecting his honour.

Outside, on the balcony, John could hear a big motor approaching. It whirled round the corner of St. Peter's Church, and drew up at Desmond's door. John entered the drawing-room. Sheila was staring at the photograph of her father.

"Sheila, he is here."

She rose at once, turning to him a face very pale but composed.

"Go back to the balcony," she commanded. As John hesitated, she added: "I will call you, when I want you."

He obeyed. From the hall below, Scaife's clear voice was audible. A moment later John's ears tingled with the triumphant declaration:

"John Verney is beaten. The dockers voted for

me. We shan't know the figures till nearly midnight, but I've won, Sheila, I've won, my darling."

He advanced, holding out his arms. With a delicate gesture which made him stop when he was within a few feet of her, she asked quietly:

"How does it feel to be always, always triumphant?"

He laughed gaily.

"By Jove! It feels very jolly."

"What captured the dockers? Another leaflet?"

"Odd that you should ask that! Another leaflet did have something to do with it. My agent, acting I need hardly say without my authority, made use of the accident to the kid. They say it helped. Perhaps it did. One can't say."

"You had nothing to do with its circulation?"

"What a question from you, to me!"

She persisted, looking at him with a smile which he was puzzled to interpret.

"You had no more to do with making capital out of that child's accident, than you had with the publication of the Free-Trade leaflet about groceries?"

"Of course I had nothing to do with either, dearest. You look positively brilliant to-night."

"I have something to say which concerns us and John."

"Bother John! Really, I am rather fed up with John."

He eyed her keenly, perceiving something amiss. When she spoke again her voice was gentler. Did she wish to offer to him one more chance? Or was she luring him on to still deeper disaster?

"People have said things, unpleasant things, about you."

"Naturally. I have enemies."

"A man called upon me just now. He brought a monstrous charge against you."

"Only one?"

"He said —— "

Scaife interrupted rather scornfully.

"So you listened to what he said?"

"I had to. Please let me finish. This man maintains that the Free-Trade leaflet which cost John the New Forest election was inspired by you; that you, John's friend and partner, arranged for its publication and distribution."

This silenced him, but his eyes remained upon hers. It came to him swiftly that here was an opportunity to confess, to throw himself upon her mercy and generosity. He could make the point that he had played a dirty trick not to injure a friend but to win a wife. And he knew himself to be possessed of a fiery eloquence which few could resist. Then he reflected that she could never discover the truth which he had hidden so carefully. Similar charges were brought against all active politicians, and, as a rule, ignored by them.

"My dear child," he murmured, in an amused voice, "do you want me to deny this ridiculous charge?"

"If you can."

"But not surely to you. Tell me the name of my accuser. Give me a chance to deal with him."

"The charge, then, is false?"

"Absolutely. A malicious lie. I'll ram it down the throat of the liar. Tell me his name."

"John Verney," said Sheila, slightly raising her voice.

John came in.

Scaife winced, recovering himself quickly. His eyes sparkled with defiance.

"You?" he exclaimed contemptuously. "I should have thought that you were about as sick of me as I am of you."

"I am sick of you," said John.

"You'll be sicker still in a few minutes, my good man. But you don't propose to have this out before her, do you?"

"I propose that," said Sheila.

"Once before," said John, "I had reason to bring a charge against you. I wanted then to spare her. You insisted upon her being present, because you had planned to humiliate me — and you succeeded."

"I may succeed again." His voice shook with rage, because Sheila's face told him nothing. Was it possible that her trust in him had failed? He turned to her.

"Sheila, I could have staked my life and everything I possess upon your loyalty. Is it possible that you take his word against mine? He's picked a lie out of the dust in which I've rolled him."

"Out of the unconsidered dust — yes," said John.

With admirably assumed dignity, Scaife again addressed Sheila, but this time a note of special pleading informed his words.

"I beg your pardon. I am ashamed of asking such a question. This man's insolent intrusion at such a moment threw me off my balance. I know in my soul that you will take my unsupported word against John Verney's."

She made no answer, gazing curiously into his masterful eyes. He repeated the question with agitation:

"You will, won't you?"

As he bent forward trembling with excitement, the door opened and Desmond came in. His handsome face was twisted by perplexity, for he had just learned that John and Scaife were alone with Sheila. Before he had time to greet his visitors, Scaife said derisively: "This man has brought another lie to your house, an unsupported lie, which I cannot refute so easily as the first."

"You have chosen rather an unseasonable time, Verney?"

Desmond eyed his former secretary and protégé with reproach, for he knew — none better — that Scaife's record was not immaculate, and he feared that John, driven mad by another failure, might have been tempted to spoil the triumph of a rival. It was quite likely, for instance, that he had heard something which, from Sheila's girlish point of view, might be regarded as compromising. John, in short, was telling tales out of school.

"I had to come, sir," John replied firmly. "Another man was coming in my place, to deal with an affair which is entirely mine."

"You are two hot-tempered young men," said Desmond, with ill-assumed geniality. "I am prepared to make allowances, but, frankly, my house is too small to hold the pair of you. I ask you as a favour to me, John, to withdraw."

"I ask him to stay," said Sheila. "He has accused Reginald of being a liar and a false friend; and he has brought proof of it."

"Proof?" exclaimed Scaife loudly. "Let him produce his proof."

"I have it," said Sheila. She took from behind her back the slip of paper. In a dull voice she continued; "John Verney's agent brought this to him."

Desmond glanced at it, puzzled at first, and then with increasing perception of what it meant. In silence he handed it to Scaife, who perceived instantly that Desmond's manner had changed. He recognized the proof as swiftly, and then was conscious of nothing except a rush of blood to his head, and the sense that a knock-out blow had been delivered. As if from an immeasurable distance, Sheila's voice seemed to float to him.

"Have you anything to say?"

With tremendous effort he lifted his head, throwing off the intolerable physical oppression.

"I did it," he declared.

She used the exact words which had slipped from her indignant lips before: "A stab in the back of a friend!"

"Friend? He hated me as I hated him. He stood between you and me. I wanted him out of the way. I'd have stuck at nothing to win you. And from the first I read you, and saw clearly the chords which would thrill beneath my touch. I loved your weakness, which is my weakness, as much as I loved your strength, which is my strength."

"My weakness?"

"You are ambitious. It's in your blood. I admit that I did a damnable action, and would do it again, for love of you. And this man, who had interfered before, was in my way. I saw him clearly for the first time upon the eve of that election, a serious rival. He was fighting me with my own weapons, making a bid for the triumph which I had made possible, which he hoped that you would share. Well"— he laughed derisively —"opportunity gave me a chance to wipe John Verney out."

"The same opportunity gave him the chance to wipe you out, but he held his hand."

"The greater fool he!"

Suddenly, the fierceness vanished from his voice. Passionately he entreated her to forgive him.

"Sheila, can't you make allowance for me? At this moment you condemn me as a coward and a liar; you think me all bad. But there is good in me —

I swear it — which you can develop. Give me another chance! For God's sake, don't throw me over! I'll make any sacrifice you ask. I'll chuck politics at a nod from your sweet head, because I want you, you, you, more than I want anything else in the world."

His tremendous strength and passion swept cver her. She half closed her eyes.

"You know that you love me," he exclaimed, and in his voice there was the familiar note of triumph. The man's extraordinary confidence revealed itself as something inhuman, a dynamic quality either god-like or demoniac.

"Father," she entreated, "tell him to go."

Desmond crossed hurriedly to his daughter, took her in his arms, and kissed her. Releasing her, he looked first at Scaife and then at John.

"Leave us," he said decisively.

"She has not answered my question," said Scaife. "Let her deny, if she can, that she loves me."

John was moving toward the door, when Sheila made a sign to him, and he stood still, as Scaife continued in a softer voice: "I will not press the point. Her silence is eloquent enough."

"I don't love you," said Sheila, but she trembled as she spoke.

"Because I have besmirched myself to you." The cruelty so long suppressed began to blaze in his eyes. He appealed to Desmond.

"Tell her that politics is a game which we play to win."

Desmond said slowly:

"Sheila dear, you are too young and inexperienced to pass judgment on this."

"Make it plainer to her," said Scaife. Then, perceiving Desmond's frowning face, he continued eagerly, addressing Sheila:

"It *is* a game. And outsiders never learn the rules."

She interrupted scornfully: "But there are rules — principles?" She looked at her father.

"Yes, yes," said Desmond hastily.

"Are you for me or against me?" Scaife asked boldly. As Desmond remained silent, he added vehemently: "She has found me out. I tried to spare her. I wanted to keep her blind, but I suppose this moment had to come. For God's sake, explain that I'm no worse than many Right Honourable gentlemen."

"You had better go," Desmond replied.

"So, you leave me in the lurch, do you?"

John saw that he had lost control of himself. Then, to his amazement, Sheila exclaimed passionately:

"I never loved him, John — never! I loved the man I believed him to be. Thousands of women have made my mistake. Thank God! I found him out in time." Then, without flinching, she turned to Scaife: "If I had loved you, I could have forgiven you."

"You never loved me?" he repeated violently.

Again the incredulity in his tone, his refusal, so humiliating to a proud woman, to believe that he was not irresistible, aroused in her a fierce antagonism.

There are moments when weakness, the humble acceptance of human infirmity, the recognition of failure and disaster, the pathetic surrender, constitute a greater claim for pardon than the most tremendous display of strength.   From a boy, Scaife had been a bad loser, unable to endure defeat.

Sheila delivered the last thrust:

"You force me to say that I — hate — you!"

The conviction that it was indeed so struck him with overpowering suddenness. His face flushed crimson, and those watching him beheld the likeness to his father, the coarse, brutal Butcher of Badavarchy. Hoarse with passion, he raised his hand, and Sheila shrank back, thinking he was about to strike her. And he did so mercilessly after a fashion she was least prepared to meet.   A finger was pointed at Desmond.

"His hands are no cleaner than mine."

"You unspeakable cad!" exclaimed John.

If he thought that he might divert Scaife's rage to himself, he was mistaken. Scaife concentrated his energies upon Sheila.

"We have bargained together. Ask him — ask him!"

Sheila uttered an exclamation of distress.

"Father, that is not true?"

Desmond's florid colour faded, his lips twitched.

"He has been a party to my schemes. He knows nothing about the leaflet, but there are other things. Tell her of this new appointment! Admit, as you must, that you owe it to me — that I did the dirty work, the haggling with Grandcourt and Kitteredge."

"Appointment?" repeated Sheila faintly, hardly daring to decipher the expression upon her father's face, wondering why he remained silent, wondering also why John had turned aside.

"He wanted a great position abroad. I asked for it, and he has accepted it. It will be announced to-morrow. He has earned it, make no mistake there, because he put his spoke into the ramshackle wheels of Tariff Reform. He has ratted, and three men know it. When he comes back, to England, he has pledged his word to join us."

"It is — impossible," gasped Sheila.

He turned to John.

"I'll square matters with you elsewhere. Part of the score will be settled when the poll is declared."

"I shall be there," John replied.

Scaife strode to the door. Upon the threshold he addressed a last word to Sheila:

"I wanted you more than anything else in the world, even more desperately than your father wants — office."

The door slammed and he was gone. John heard Sheila whisper:

"Did you bargain? Was it that? Say it was not that?"

"I'm a poor man," Desmond answered brokenly.

"Oh! I can't bear it. I can't bear it."

She stumbled to the sofa and fell upon it. John saw Desmond kneel down beside her. Sheila's sobs penetrated to the inmost fibres of his being, as he slipped silently from the room.

CHAPTER XXII

JOHN returned to Trent House, and when Fluff looked anxiously into his gray eyes and felt the grasp of his hand he knew that one ambition budding at Harrow had come to full fruition. Henceforward he would be to John what John had always been to him.

"How did she take it?" he asked.

John answered the question. When he had finished, Fluff said firmly: "I believe she cares for you. Leave her alone for a bit. And now, Jonathan, no more jaw; we must get you fit for to-night."

"I'm all right. I feel a different man."

"You look a different man," said Fluff slowly.

After dinner, the Duke went back with them to John's Committee-Rooms, where the great Bott displayed a resigned but not uncheerful countenance. He waved a pink evening paper which had fought hard upon Scaife's side.

"Have you seen this?" he asked, indicating a long paragraph.

"No."

"Must have been inspired by Scaife," said Mr. Bott judicially. "Very clever, very clever indeed!"

The paragraph set forth with accuracy every detail
connected with the accident to the child, exonerating
the chauffeur and praising John's humanity in remaining at the hospital when he might have gained
votes by keeping an engagement elsewhere.

"Shuts our mouths," murmured Mr. Bott.

"It won't shut mine," said Fluff.

"There has been a reaction already," continued the
agent. "I should not be surprised if Mr. Verney
found himself quite popular."

"As the defeated candidate," said John. "That
happened in the New Forest."

"You have won a moral victory." Bott appealed
to the Duke. "Your Grace is of my opinion?"

The Duke nodded, watching John, who was reading
the paragraph carefully.

"When did this go to press?" he asked.

"Before five, I should say."

Presently, word came that the result would be announced about half-past ten, earlier than was expected.
John and his friends motored to the big public building
from which the final declaration would be made, and
as the motor crawled at snail's pace through the
crowded streets John was recognized and cheered, even
by the men who carried pink papers.

"They can afford to be generous," growled Bott.

From the appearance of the streets, it was evident
that John's defeat had been accepted as inevitable.
Scaife's colours were omnipresent, and the women
stared at John with compassion softening their hard

eyes. Some of them had wanted to stone him that morning. A group of factory-girls threw kisses and salted words of encouragement. One young woman jumped on to the step of the motor.

"Fair scrapper you are," she shouted. "But you took on too big a feller."

"Thank you," said John politely.

"'It below the belt, wasn't yer?"

"Yes," shouted Fluff.

The girl dropped back into the crowd, as the Duke murmured to Mr. Bott: "Now how on earth did she find that out?"

Mr. Bott replied sententiously: "People who have to earn a living before they are twelve are extra sharp, your Grace."

They approached the vast building in front of which Scaife's supporters had gathered in solid phalanx. With difficulty the police forced a passage for John and his friends to a room next to that in which the votes were being counted. Through an open window, which looked upon the street below, penetrated the hoarse shouts of the crowd. Mr. Bott disappeared for a few minutes. When he returned, his large face bore an odd expression of surprise.

"Those in the know," he declared, "say that the majority will be less than was expected. It seems that Mr. Scaife is in a black temper about it. Indeed, he has offended some of his supporters. He behaves, I hear, as if he were beaten. It's very strange."

"Conscience?" suggested Fluff.

Mr. Bott replied with solemnity: "Mr. Scaife has been endowed with great and brilliant attributes, but a conscience, my lord, is certainly the least conspicuous of them." Then he whispered: "Mr. Verney is taking this amazingly well."

"You see, he fired the shot."

"Bless my soul!"

"He asked me to tell you in strict confidence. Mr. Verney has won a victory greater than that which he has lost."

"We must find another seat for him. He can't be spared."

"He hasn't been in this fight," said Fluff grimly.

Very slowly the minutes passed, till the dramatic movement when the rival candidates met after the votes had been counted and just before they were made known. Scaife, standing beside his father and Kitteredge, glared at the beaten candidate with such malevolence that Kitteredge touched him and whispered something.

"Shocking loser!" said Fluff to John. "Do you remember the second innings at Lord's, when he was clean bowled first ball?"

"Yes."

Immediately, the result was announced to the candidates. Scaife had won by a majority of four hundred and thirteen. His friends began to congratulate him, and the Duke whispered to John:

"You must say something."

John moved a few steps toward Scaife and paused. Scaife said in a hoarse whisper:

"Don't congratulate me, John Verney!"

Kitteredge shrugged his shoulders, tried to smile and failed. Some of the other men showed disgust more plainly. Lord Samarkand stroked his huge jaw, the only man in the room who seemed to be absolutely impassive.

John bowed and returned to his friends. A minute later, Scaife and he were facing the crowd with the Mayor of the borough between them. As soon as the announcement was made, the crowd began to cheer, and for five minutes the uproar was terrific. In answer to cries of "Speech — speech," Scaife held up his hand. Then his voice roared out, imposing silence so savagely that the shouts of the crowd droned slowly away. Scaife leaned forward.

"Thank you," he said. "I won't keep you long. In the House of Commons, not here, I shall endeavour to justify your verdict. I like a fight, and I fight to a finish. This has not been my first fight with Mr. John Verney, and I don't think it will be my last. This contest has been described as being between a Duke's man and the people's man. I am not ashamed of belonging to the people. I mean to stick to them, and I believe they will stick to me. If a man treats me manfully, I endeavour to treat him manfully. If he treats me like a dog, I don't cringe and wag my tail. I bite."

"Quite right, too!" yelled a raucous voice.

The crowd began to cheer again, but there were many shouts for "Verney."

"Try to speak," whispered Mr. Bott. "Smile if they boo."

But, to John's surprise, he was allowed to speak, and his calm, clear voice penetrated as far as Scaife's.

"I am beaten," he said, "badly beaten, but I've enjoyed the fight. If you see me 'bloody beneath my bludgeonings,' I can assure you that I am not 'bowed.'" He drew himself up as the crowd applauded. Then, looking at Scaife, he added ironically: "Mr. Scaife has said many things during this campaign to which I have had to take exception, and I make no apology to you or to him for criticizing his latest utterance upon the interesting theme of behaviour. Speaking as a Duke's man, with some experience of a Duke's methods, I would suggest to Mr. Scaife that it may be better from every point of view to behave like a man always, quite regardless of how others with animal propensities may behave to you. From the bottom of my heart I thank those who voted for me, and I wish you all Good-night."

Upon the following day, Desmond's appointment to a great colonial governorship was announced in the papers. Tories, like Sir Giles Mottisfont and Admiral Pundle, nearly choked over their eggs and bacon when they opened the newspapers. Unionists within a reasonable radius of the House of Commons, shrugged their shoulders and laughed. The *Thunderer*, in a long leader, congratulated the Government upon their choice of a tried public servant, who, without any question of party politics, was absolutely the right man. The Tadpoles and Tapers rushed about whispering that in the event of a Coalition coming into power, Charles Desmond would be offered the most exalted seat in the Cabinet.

The evening papers contained a short paragraph setting forth the breaking of the engagement between Scaife and Sheila. When John called at the house in Eaton Square, he found the blinds down. Mr. Desmond and his daughter, he was informed, had left London for Surrey.

John wrote to Sheila, and she answered his letter, signing it "yours affectionately," but the letter might have been read aloud in Trafalgar Square. He heard from Mrs. Starkey that Penelope Bargus would go out to Australia as an elegant and indispensable adjunct of His Excellency's establishment.

John resumed his secretarial duties. And then, some ten days later, was offered a certain seat for a small constituency.

To his astonishment, the Leader of the Opposition sent for him, and advised him to wait.

"What for?" John asked.

"We should like to see you triumph where you were defeated."

"In the New Forest Division?"

"Dear me — no." After a moment's hesitation, he

added slowly: "Lord Samarkand's health is causing his son anxiety. Therefore I repeat — wait."

Next day, curiously enough, John heard the same story from the Caterpillar, who shook his hand with quite unnecessary violence.

"The Demon is hoist with his own petard. He thought his father would live for ever. The old man has never been sick or sorry — and Heaven knows he's had reason to be both — but he's had a stroke, and the House is going to lose Scaife. You'll have a walk-over this time, my dear old chap."

Later, this was found to be the well-matured opinion of Mr. Bott.

"The facts have leaked out," affirmed that great man.

"What facts?"

"The facts about the Free-Trade leaflet. I have held my tongue, Mr. Verney, but our silence and for-bearance infuriated the man who wanted to satisfy a personal grudge."

John, however, made no pledges. When the Duke said to him: "Are you tired of politics?" he replied:

"I shall never be a very strong party man, but if I'm really wanted ——"

"You are wanted," said the Duke with emphasis. "I sometimes hear a phrase familiar enough in France and America: 'Gentlemen must keep out of politics.' If they do keep out, if the 'machine' triumphs, God help England! You, Jonathan, must stand shoulder to shoulder with the men who work as against the men who talk. There have always been plenty of such men in England. It is the explanation of our greatness as an Empire. The many wish to be ruled by the select few, and to those few — irrespective of party — it should be a labour of love and enthusiasm. Some talkers on our side are as windy and fatuous as certain talkers on the other. The workers may be found everywhere."

The Duke drew a breath. "That's about the longest speech I have ever made."

"You have worked, though," said John.

Shortly afterward it became generally known that Lord Samarkand was lying helpless in his huge house in Kensington Palace Gardens. The devotion of an only son was also chronicled, but John learned from the Caterpillar that Scaife was foaming with suppressed rage. None knew better than he that his remarkable powers would be smothered in the House of Lords. The leading Liberal paper remarked significantly that it was all-important Lord Samarkand's valuable life should be spared.

Next day, as John happened to be leaving his club late in the afternoon the hall porter said abruptly: "Beg pardon, sir, but do you know that Lord Samarkand is dead?"

"Dead?"

"The news has just come over the 'ticker.'"

John went out, pale and distressed. He passed down St. James's Street, and into the Green Park.

He was approaching Trent House, when he saw a familiar figure hurrying toward him. It was Scaife, striding on with head down. Probably he had been to the House of Commons, and had there received the news. John hoped that Scaife would not see him, but as they passed the bigger man raised his head, and to John's astonishment called him by name. John stood still.

"Well met!" said Scaife derisively. "I've been waiting for this. I meant to tell you something upon the night the poll was declared, but Kitteredge burked that opportunity. I hear that you have refused a sure seat in Hampshire because you think that you will step into my shoes. By God! you won't. My father isn't going to die, whatever those damned fools of doctors may say. He's going to live, told me so only yesterday. We Scaifes are tough!" He laughed scornfully, misled, possibly, by the expression upon John's face. Scaife continued, with even less self-control: "When you come into the House, I shall be waiting for you, and sooner or later we'll square accounts. I shan't spare you, John Verney. I'll roll you in the dust, as you rolled me. I wouldn't be balked of that for a million pounds."

John stared in pity at a face deeply flushed with rage and excitement. He decided that it was impossible for him to tell Scaife the truth. Awkwardly, he stammered out:

"Can't you put that from you?"

As Scaife burst into mocking laughter, John heard

the voice of an approaching news-boy, and at the end
of a rising inflection of sound the word "Samarkand."
Instantly he realized that he, the last man surely in
all the world for such a task, had been chosen by the
fates to break this appalling news to his enemy.

"Where have you been?" he asked nervously,
seizing the first words which came into his head.
Scaife seemed astonished. But he answered curtly,
with a deliberate intention to remind John of a former
humiliation:

"I have spent the afternoon with my sister, Miss
Lamb."

"But your father —— ?"

"He was so much better this morning that I had
to tell her. Hullo!"

His keen ear had caught a familiar name. The cry
was repeated, coming to both men with unmistakable
distinctness:

"*Death of Lord Samarkand!*"

"What does he say?" Scaife gasped out.

"Your father died at half-past three this afternoon."

"It's a lie."

The boy's voice floated nearer, stronger, and more
insistent.

"*Death of Lord Samarkand, famous contractor!*"

"O my God!" said Scaife.

His expression of rage and surprise froze the words of
sympathy about to leave John's lips. In silence he
clutched Scaife's arm, but the stronger man tore himself loose.

"Do you think I want your pity?" he asked savagely. He strode away, and the voice of the boy seemed to pursue him relentlessly:

"*Speshul! Extra Speshul! Millionaire contractor dead! Death of Lord Samarkand!*"

Within a fortnight the papers announced that Charles Desmond was about to sail for Australia. John stared at the paragraph, and then went to his Chief's room. His eyes were brighter than usual, as he asked for leave of absence.

"I should like to run down to The Corner, if you can spare me?"

"By all means." He paused, then he gripped John's hand. "My benison go with you, Jonathan."

During the short railway journey, John wondered what Sheila would say to him. He could think of little else, except his own emotions so long restrained and now overmasteringly ebullient. In a vivid description of Desmond's life in the Antipodes, the writer had spoken of the heat. Sheila was a daughter of cool mists. Did she think of sultry tropical nights, contrasting them with dewy mornings in Surrey and the cool woods and fields of England?

An hour later he was being greeted by Trinder, who informed him that Mr. Desmond was engaged for the moment.

"Tell Miss Desmond I am here."

As soon as she came in, he marked an immense change. The child had altogether vanished. He was conscious of a pang, the sense of bereavement which we feel when we have lost something which we have known could not be preserved.

As he held Sheila's hand, he tried to see what had taken the place of that tender radiance of youth so captivating to men who have confronted much sorrow and disappointment. Perhaps at that moment he became sure that he could give what hitherto she had not needed, the sympathy and understanding which alone can heal certain wounds. Because he had found life hard and difficult, always a struggle to be faced without compromise, he was able to apprehend how deeply Sheila, to whom life had been sweet and fragrant and easy, must have suffered when the primrose path became a steep rocky road.

Her first words struck a note of defiance.

"You look wonderfully well, John."

He imagined her thinking: "He's indifferent and cold," and for the moment he was whimsically conscious of his inability to twist his features into the expression she would have deemed appropriate, or to turn upon a reluctant tongue the kindly, ingratiating phrases which flowed so easily from looser lips.

They sat down after the first greeting, and Sheila began to speak of the future. Her voice betrayed weariness, as if she had envisaged too many pomps and vanities. While she was speaking, John tried to find some breach in the outer crust through which he might pass to her heart. He told himself that the woman had become more elusive than the laughing girl. Then he remembered Charles Desmond's word so descriptive

of Scaife's methods — "captured." If Sheila were
to be won, she must be taken by storm. He must
lead his own forlorn hope, dash at triumph or disaster.
Just then, she showed a sign of weakness.

"I am sure I shall be bored out there."

John jumped up; so suddenly that Sheila was startled.
But, in her turn, she beheld the real man unmasked
after many years. He was trembling with passion.
His voice, when he spoke, thrilled upon her ear. Diffi-
dence and hesitation vanished like dew beneath a
tropical sun. The quiet man blazed.

"Don't go then!"

She was too honest to play with him. Very gravely
she replied:

"I must."

He moved closer to her.

"Let me keep you at — home."

His voice trembled at the dear word, and the greatest
orator could have found none more beguiling.

"That is what you are made for," he continued
softly, "that is your sanctuary — home."

Her voice faltered. "We shall have five years,
five long years!"

"Are you going to waste them masquerading as a
sham princess, when I can make you queen of a real
kingdom? Are you?"

"I don't — know."

"We have both been in the dust. Do you mean to
stay there?"

She met his gaze unflinchingly. At once she

began to speak with a force and passion equal to his:
"Is it true you have promised the Duke of Trent
to contest that hateful place again?"

"It is true."

"To think that you, you, John Verney, are not sick
to death of politics, of the truckling, and lies, and
hypocrisy. If you are incapable of dirty work, as
you are, you must look on in silence while others do
what you are ashamed of doing. You will have to
destroy, if you can, good work done by the opposite
side, and uphold bad work which your own party has
substituted. And you will learn to justify such conduct, to plead expediency, and toleration, and the
virtue of fighting the devil with his own weapons."

He smiled, as she paused, panting.

"I could strike you for smiling," she said fiercely.
"Why did you not leave me alone? Why do you
try to tempt me? Why do you talk of home? An
ambitious man has no home. Your home will be the
House of Commons, as it was father's."

John said nothing. Suddenly her mood changed;
her voice grew tender.

"My poor Jonathan, I have always thought of you
as absolutely honest."

"Poor but honest. Thank you, Sheila."

"I was a fool not to place a higher value on your
honesty."

"Honesty cuts a dull figure.

"I was blind."

"You were adorably young."

She made an impatient gesture.

"I have believed in your honesty. When my bitter humiliation opened my eyes, I saw you standing above me. I have thought of you on pinnacles."

John groaned.

"I stand below you, Sheila."

"So it seems," she replied, "because I have climbed above my mean ambitions. Why do they drag you down, why?"

She paused, and he saw the colour rise in her cheeks.

John waited.

"I thought, I believed that you were driven by me to seek my ambitions, not your own."

"That is partly true."

"Would that you could have denied it! Well, because in my ignorance I did so drive you, and because now I recognize my folly and presumption I beseech you to leave pitch alone. Pitch it is, pitch it must be!"

"I do not deny that."

"Leave it alone and then — perhaps —— "

"Yes?"

"Isn't there work at Boscobel for you?"

"Undoubtedly."

"I see you doing that work finely, making all dependent on you better and happier. I might join in that work."

She looked away from him, blushing and confused. This feminine weakness became so alluring, something to snatch at and accept, that John grew pale. His voice was harsh, as he answered:

"I have promised."

"Oh!" ·

The exclamation was eloquent of an immense surprise. John perceived that he had challenged her interest in him superlatively, that perhaps for the first time he had really "captured" it.

"I have promised to do work which must be done; that the work may be distasteful is nothing."

Sheila stared at him, struggling with the unmistakable fact that he had placed his work before her, that he would let her go rather than break a promise. It flashed into her mind that Scaife would have promised anything. Since her bitter humiliation she had wondered whether John would come back to her. But she had never pictured him as a conqueror imposing terms. Again and again she had evoked the thin, slightly bent figure, the kind friend, whom she could cajole and tease so easily. Yes, she had nourished the hope that Jonathan would remain faithful, and, in due time, they might find peace and happiness in Arcadia.

Impetuously she laid her hand upon his arm.

"Do you understand that I have asked you to do this thing for my sake, and that — in return —— "

She paused, blushing.

"I understand," said John.

Her voice faltered, as she exclaimed: "What fools women are!"

"You think my ambitions rank higher than my love."

"It looks like it."

"You have always been first, and so you will remain to the end."

"Words — words!"

The invitation to act was imperative. But dared he risk a decisive move? A year ago he might have hesitated; he was stronger now, with a deeper knowledge of himself and of her.

"Shall I go or stay?"

Once more her eyes met his in a slightly bewildered glance.

"Of course, now that you are are here you will stay to luncheon."

"Not unless I am wanted."

His voice was serious, but she caught the note of tenderness. With a light laugh she attempted to save a situation which was beginning to frighten her.

"You can't leave without breaking bread with us."

"I shall leave now, unless you ask me to stay."

He saw her lips close obstinately, and he remembered how often her will had triumphed over his, and that she too was remembering such triumphs.

"Father will be vexed."

John made no reply. He looked at her with lips as firm as hers, without the flicker of a smile.

"And affronted."

He held out his hand.

"But this is absurd."

"Good-bye."

"Very well, if you choose to behave churlishly, I can't help it. I hardly recognize you."

"I told you that I had changed."

Her hand lay in his, and her lovely eyes challenged him to resist her, if he dared. Greatly daring, he walked to the door, and as he walked he told himself that he must not look back. He reached the door, opened it, passed through, and closed it. He crossed the hall slowly, feeling his limbs grow heavier at every stride. As he touched the handle of the front-door, he heard a soft voice behind him:

"Jonathan! Please — stay!"

Lightning Source UK Ltd.
Milton Keynes UK
UKHW022015310822
408147UK00003B/250